Hermann Klein

Musical Notes

An annual critical record of important musical events. Fourth Edition (Jan. - Dec. 1889)

Hermann Klein

Musical Notes

An annual critical record of important musical events. Fourth Edition (Jan. - Dec. 1889)

ISBN/EAN: 9783337084585

Printed in Europe, USA, Canada, Australia, Japan

Cover: Foto ©Thomas Meinert / pixelio.de

More available books at **www.hansebooks.com**

Musical Notes

An Annual Critical Record

OF

IMPORTANT MUSICAL EVENTS

BY

Hermann Klein.

Fourth Year, Jan.—Dec., 1889.

LONDON & NEW YORK
NOVELLO, EWER AND CO.
1890.

PREFACE.

HITHERTO the scope of MUSICAL NOTES has been confined to a record of the year's Music in London, together with an account of the various leading Festivals as they occur.

In the present issue a new departure is essayed. The ordinary contents are supplemented by a series of articles, embodying in concise form the history of the past year in all the important musical centres of the kingdom. This fresh material, as the signatures will in most cases testify, has been furnished by writers of recognised ability, possessing a perfect knowledge of the proceedings in their respective districts. It is, therefore, to be relied upon as being accurate and, so far as is possible, complete.

My object is primarily to increase the value of this Year-book by making it a more comprehensive work of reference. I hope, at the same time, that I am widening its sphere of usefulness by imparting to its contents a national as distinguished from a metropolitan interest. To keep pace with the ever-active growth of musical life and labour in this country may be no light task; but I feel that these NOTES—still the sole "brief or abstract chronicle" of our musical year—ought no longer to exclude from their pages some regular record of the work that is accomplished among the great music-loving population of provincial England.

HERMANN KLEIN.

INDEX.

	PAGE
ALBENIZ, Señor. *Début*	69
,, at Crystal Palace	104
ALBERT HALL CONCERTS. Miscellaneous—	
Carter, William	6
Patti Concerts	6, 107, 119
State Concert in the Shah's honour	78
AMES, J. C. Pianoforte Concerto in C minor (Op. 8)	35
ARIOSTI. Third " Lesson " for Viola d'amore	114
BACH CHOIR	20, 46
BACH, Emil. Pianoforte Concerto in C minor	71
BACH, J. Sebastian. Church Cantata, " Wachet auf! "	20
,, ,, " Halt' im Gedächtniss "	20
Prelude and Fugue, arranged for orchestra	105
BACKER-GRÖNDAHL, Madame. *Début*	23
Suite for Pianoforte	84
BARNETT, J. F. Sonata for Pianoforte, in A minor	127
BARRETT, Dr. W. A. Madrigal, " On a Mossy Bank," at Bristol	138
BEETHOVEN. Allegretto in C minor, for Pianoforte	53
" Bagatellen " ,, ,,	53
" Unfinished " Pianoforte Concerto in D	81
BELLINCIONI, Mdlle. *Début*	60
BENOIT, Peter. Oratorio, " Lucifer "	31
BERLIOZ. Marche Funèbre, for " Hamlet "	23
" L'Enfance du Christ " revived	126
BIZET. " Pêcheurs de Perles " revived	42
BLAUWAERT, M. *Début*	33
BONAWITZ, J. H. " Requiem "	34
Introduction and Scherzo for Pianoforte and Orchestra	127
BRAHMS. Variations, with Fugue, on a Theme by Handel	17
Four Trios for Female Voices (Op. 17)	51
" German Requiem," revived	33
,, ,, at Leeds	100
Symphony (No 4) at Crystal Palace	24
Sonata for Pianoforte and Violin in D minor (No. 3, Op. 108)	48

INDEX.

	PAGE
BRAUN, Charles. Cantata, "Ritter Olaf," at Liverpool	167
BRERETON, W. H. *Début* at Philharmonic	35
BRIDGE, Dr. J. F. Overture, "Morte d'Arthur," at Crystal Palace ...	24
BRISTOL ORPHEUS GLEE SOCIETY. At St. James's Hall...	52
BUCK, Dudley. Cantata, "The Light of Asia"	19
CARMICHAEL, Miss Mary. "Four Songs of the Stuarts"...	49
CARPENTER, Miss Nettie. *Début* at Crystal Palace	112
CATANEO, Signora. *Début*	77
CHAMBER CONCERTS.	
Bauer, Ethel and Harold	29, 41
Carrodus, J. T.	29
Cusins, W. G.	70
Eissler, Mdlles. Marianne and Clara	50
Gardner, Charles...	70
Hallé, Sir Charles	47, 68
Hann, Messrs.	118
Heckmann, Robert	119
Kiver, Ernest	49
Löhr, Harvey	39
Ludwig and Whitehouse	50, 69
Meyer, Waldemar	51
Musical Artists' Society	119
Musical Guild	52, 69, 117
Nicholl, William	49
Ralph, Mrs. Francis	128
Robinson, Miss Winifred	51
Sarasate, Señor	47, 68, 104
Sergison, W. de Manby	6, 29, 71
Shinner Quartet	53
Thomas, John	71
Thorne, E. H.	71
Tua, Signorina Teresina	70
Wurm, Miss Mathilde	118
CHERUBINI. Posthumous Quartet in E	47
" " in F	48
" " in A minor	68
CLIFFE, Frederic. Symphony in C minor (Op. 1), at Crystal Palace ...	35
" " " Philharmonic ...	65
COBB, Gerard F. Pianoforte Quintet in C	118
COCKLE, George. Comic Opera, "The Castle of Como," produced ...	108
CORDER, Frederic. Cantata, "The Sword of Argantyr," produced ...	95
COWEN, Frederic H. Re-appearance in England	22
Old English Idyll, "St. John's Eve"...	122
CRESER, Dr. William. Cantata, "The Sacrifice of Freia," produced ...	96
CROTTY, Leslie. *Début* in Italian Opera	59
CRYSTAL PALACE CONCERTS	10, 23, 35, 64, 103, 111, 122

INDEX.

	PAGE
D'ANDRADE, Antonio. *Début*	43
DUNCAN, Mdlle. Hélène de. *Début*	85
DUNKLEY, Ferdinand. Prize Orchestral Suite	87
DVOŘÁK, Antonin. String Quartet in E (Op. 80)	39
"Silhouettes" for Pianoforte (Op. 8)	40
DYER, W. Fear. Cantata, "Second Advent of the Redeemer," at Bristol	143

ELLICOTT, Miss Rosalind. Cantata, "Elysium," produced	89
Pianoforte Trio in G, at Bristol	144
Rêverie for Violoncello and Pianoforte, at Bristol	143
Romance and Polonaise for Violin, at Bristol	141
EWAN, Miss Minnie. *Début*	60

FACCIO, Signor. *Début*	77
FERGUSON A. F. *Début* at Oxford	176
FESTIVALS.	
Easter Oratorios at Mile End	34
Gloucester	88
Leeds	93
Lincoln and Peterborough	72
"Reid" (Edinburgh)	151
FILLUNGER, Fräulein Marie. *Début*	15

GARGANO, Madame. *Début*	59
GEISLER-SCHUBERT, Fräulein. *Début*	16
„ at Philharmonic	21
GOLDBECK, Robert. Comic Opera, "Newport," recited	55
GOLDMARK. Overture to "Sákuntalà"	122
GOUNOD. "Roméo et Juliette" at Covent Garden, in French	58
GRIEG, Edvard. Re-appearance at Popular Concerts	15
"Landkjending" (Op. 31)	123
GRIEG, Madame. *Début* at Philharmonic	22
GUILDHALL SCHOOL OF MUSIC 39, 72, 84,	127

HACKNEY CHORAL ASSOCIATION 2, 33,	110
HALL, Charles J., Mus. Doc. Cantata, "Dante's Vision," produced ...	18
HALLÉ CONCERTS. Manchester Band in London 113,	124
HALL, Miss Marguerite. Philharmonic *Début*	35
HAMPSTEAD CONSERVATOIRE OF MUSIC. Inaugural Concert	2
HANDEL. Music to Smollett's "Alceste"	52
Oratorio, "Theodora," revived, at Manchester	173
HANDEL SOCIETY	52
HATTERSLEY, F. Kilvington. Pianoforte Sonata in G minor, at Leeds	183

INDEX.

	PAGE
HAYDN. Oratorio, "The Seasons," revived...	2
Symphony in B flat	44
HEAP, Dr. C. S. Cantata, "The Maid of Astolat," at Birmingham	136
HEGNER, Otto. Début at Crystal Palace	10
Orchestral Concerts at St. James's Hall	102
Suite for Pianoforte, in G	103
HERKOMER, Hubert. Music-Play, "An Idyl"	60
HESS, Willy. Début in London	2
HIGHBURY PHILHARMONIC SOCIETY	21, 52
HOFFMANN, Heinrich. Serenade for Flute and Strings (Op. 65), at Birmingham	136
HOPKINS, Jerome. Dialogue-Oratorio, "Samuel"	6
HUDSON, J. W. Pianoforte Trio in D, at Bristol	141
HUMMEL. Sonata in F sharp minor (Op. 81), at Popular Concerts	15
HUNTINGTON, Miss Agnes. Début	7
HYDE PARK ACADEMY OF MUSIC	84, 128
ISNARDON, M. Début	80
JOACHIM, Dr. Re-appearance at Popular Concerts	25
Presentation of Testimonial	38
KINSEY, Haigh. Pianoforte Trio, at Liverpool	170
KREUZ, Emil. "Liebesbilder," for Viola and Pianoforte, at Cambridge	148
KRUSE, Johann. Début	15
LALO, Edouard. Overture, "Le Roi d'Ys"...	10
Rhapsody for Orchestra...	111
LAMOND, Frederick. Two "Clavierstücke" (Op. 1)	40
Pianoforte Trio in B minor (Op. 2)	40
Sonata for Pianoforte and Violoncello, in D major...	40
Symphony in A, at Glasgow	164
LANGER, F. Concerto for Flute and Orchestra	127
LEEDS CHORUS. Appearance in London	14
LEMMENS-SHERRINGTON, Madame. Re-appearance	33
LESTELLIER, M. Re-appearance	57
LITA, Mdlle. Début	57
LIVERPOOL PHILHARMONIC SOCIETY. Jubilee	165
LÖHR, Harvey. Pianoforte Quartet in E minor (Op. 15)...	39
LONDON BALLAD CONCERTS	6, 118
LONDON SYMPHONY CONCERTS...	2, 13, 112
LONDON SUNDAY SCHOOL CHOIR	28

INDEX.

	PAGE
MACBETH, Allan. Cantata, "The Land of Glory," produced at Glasgow	162
MACCUNN, Hamish. Cantata, "The Lay of the Last Minstrel," at the Crystal Palace	10
MACFARREN, G. A. Opera, "Robin Hood," revived	87
MACKENZIE, Dr. A. C. " Dream of Jubal" in London	8
,, ,, at Gloucester	88
,, ,, at Liverpool	166
Cantata, "Cotter's Saturday Night," produced at Edinburgh	152
"Pibroch" for Violin and Orchestra at Leeds	97
,, in London	105
MACPHERSON, C. S. Symphony in C	27
MANCINELLI, Luigi. Sacred Cantata, "Isaias," in London	8
Orchestral Suite, "Cleopatra"	21
MARTUCCI, Giuseppe. Pianoforte Trio in E flat (Op. 62)	48
MARX, Madame Berthe. Début	47
MASSENET. Interlude from "Esclarmonde"	103
MASSIMI, Massimo. Début	43
MATTEI, Tito. Comic Opera, "The Prima Donna," produced	108
McGUCKIN, Barton. Début in Italian Opera	58
MENDELSSOHN. "Elijah," on the Handel Orchestra	64
Fugue intended for "Athalie"	72
"St. Paul" at the Crystal Palace	111
MONTARIOL, M. Début	42
MONTEITH, Miss Zippora. Début	9
MORGAN, R. Orlando. Cantata, "Zitella," produced	39
MOZART. "Notturno-Serenade" for four Orchestras	124
MUSICAL GUILD. Formation	52
NEAL, Miss Lizzie. Début in Oratorio	2
NEVILLE, Oscar. Comic Opera, "Faddimir," produced	41
NOVELLO'S ORATORIO CONCERTS	1, 8, 19, 33
OBITUARY.	
Atkins, Robert A.	87
Bottesini, Giovanni	86
Bridgeman, John V.	92
Clay, Frederic	121
Colborne, Dr. Langdon	92
Cooke, Grattan	92
Farnie, H. B.	92
Formes, Carl	130
Gungl, Josef	18
Henselt, Adolph von	109
Hueffer, Francis	7
Marriott, Charles H.	130
Mason, T. Monck	92

OBITUARY.—*continued.*
 Métra, O. ... 109
 Monk, Dr. W. H. ... 30
 Moscheles, Madame ... 130
 Murska, Ilma di ... 7
 Ouseley, Sir Frederick A. Gore ... 41
 Patti, Carlotta ... 73
 Puzzi, Giacinta ... 87
 Romer, Francis ... 86
 Rosa, Carl ... 41
 Smith, Sydney ... 30
 Steinway, Charles F. T. ... 30
 Tamberlik, Enrico ... 30
 Tamplin, Augustus L. ... 55
 Varesi, Felice ... 30
 Vaughan-Edwardes ... 30
 Watson W. Michael ... 109
 Winterbottom, William ... 92
 Zoeller, Carli ... 86

OPERA.
 Comic ... 7, 41, 54, 85, 108, 120
 English, at Olympic Theatre ... 6
  „ at Princess's Theatre ... 87
 Italian, at Her Majesty's ... 59
  „ at the Lyceum ... 74
 Royal College of Music ... 82
 Royal Italian, at Covent Garden ... 42, 56, 78
 State performance in the Shah's honour ... 78

OSBORN, Miss Marian. *Début* at Crystal Palace ... 122

PACHMANN, Madame de. Re-appearance at Popular Concerts ... 25
PACINI, Mdlle. Regina. *Début* ... 60
PALERMINI, Signor. *Début* ... 60
PARKER, Henry. Comic Opera, "Mignonette," produced ... 54
PARRY, Dr. Hubert. Symphony in E ("English") ... 44
 Symphony in E minor ... 81
 "Ode on St. Cecilia's Day," produced at Leeds ... 98
  „   „   „ in London ... 110
PEARCE, Dr. C. W. Choral Scena, "Enceladus," at Bristol ... 143
PHILHARMONIC SOCIETY ... 21, 34, 44, 65
PIANOFORTE RECITALS.
 Albeniz, Señor ... 69, 85
 Backer-Gröndahl, Madame ... 84
 Barnett, Miss Emma ... 127
 Bartlett, Miss Agnes ... 119
 Bonawitz, J. H. ... 69
 Bradley, Orton ... 41
 Bright. Miss Dora ... 5, 29
 Douste, Mdlle. Jeanne ... 17, 54
 Frickenhaus, Madame ... 53

PIANOFORTE RECITALS.—*continued.*
    Friedheim, Arthur, and Tivadar Nachèz 85
    Geisler-Schubert, Fräulein 16
    Goldbeck, Robert... 28
    Grieg, Edvard 28
    Hegner, Otto 5, 16, 103
    Janotha, Mdlle. 54
    Lamond, Frederick 40
    Pachmann, Vladimir de 54, 69, 85
    Pauer, Max 28
    Schirmacher, Miss Dora 53
    Schönberger, Herr 53
    Schubert, Johannes 85
    Stavenhagen, Herr 29
    Wild, Miss Margaret 28
    Wurm, Miss Mathilde 41
    Yates, Mrs. Charles 29
    Zimmermann, Miss Agnes 40
PIANOFORTE AND VOCAL RECITALS.
    Armbruster, Carl. " Tristan und Isolde " 6
    Max Heinrich and Emanuel Moor 6, 17
        „   „   and Schönberger 119
PIATTI, Alfredo. Sonata in F, for Violoncello and Pianoforte (No. 3) ... 5
PLANQUETTE, Robert. Comic Opera, " Paul Jones," produced 7
POPULAR CONCERTS 3, 14, 25, 37, 106, 114, 125
POPULAR MUSICAL UNION 33, 119
PROMENADE CONCERTS 87
PROUT, Ebenezer. Overture, " Rokeby " 24
    Cantata, " Damon and Phintias," produced at Oxford 178

RAFF. Pianoforte Quartet in C minor (Op. 202) 68
REEVES, Sims. Morning Concert 84
RICHTER CONCERTS 45, 66, 81
ROGER-MICLOS, Madame. *Début* 87
    „   at Crystal Palace... 103
ROSA, Carl. Death 41
ROYAL ACADEMY OF MUSIC 39, 83, 117, 126
ROYAL AMATEUR ORCHESTRAL SOCIETY 51
ROYAL CHORAL SOCIETY 1, 8, 20, 31, 34, 106, 110, 122
ROYAL COLLEGE OF MUSIC 38, 82, 107, 126
ROYAL SOCIETY OF MUSICIANS 110

SACRED CONCERTS 20, 34
SAINT-SAËNS, Camille. Poème Symphonique, " Phaéton," at Crystal
    Palace 24
SAPELLNIKOFF, M. *Début* 34

	PAGE
SARASATE CONCERTS 46, 68,	104
SARASATE, Señor. Duet, " Navarra," for two Violins	68
SCHLÄGER, Mdlle Toni. *Début*	59
SCHLESINGER, Seb. " Reed Songs "	18
SCHOLZ, Dr. Bernhard. Symphony in B flat (Op. 60)	104
SCHUBERT, Johannes. *Début*	85
SCHÜTT, Eduard. Pianoforte Trio in C minor (Op. 27)	39
SCOTCH CONCERTS 6,	119
SEGUIN, M. *Début*	57
SEMBRICH, Madame. Re-appearance...	71
SHEDLOCK, J. S. Pianoforte Quartet in A minor	29
SIMPSON, F. J. Overture, " Robert Bruce "	111
SINDONA, Signor. *Début*	60
SITT, Hans. Violin Concerto at Gloucester...	89
SLAUGHTER, Walter. Comic Opera, " Marjorie," produced	85
SOLOMON, Edward. Musical Version of " Area Belle "	54
Comic Opera, " The Red Hussar," produced	120
SOUTH LONDON CHORAL ASSOCIATION	126
SPARK, Dr. Oratorio, " Immanuel," at Leeds	183
SPIES, Fräulein Hermine. *Début*	66
SPOHR. Sonata for Harp and Violin (MS.)	50
" Fall of Babylon," revived	110
STAINER, Sir John. Elected Professor of Music at Oxford ... 73,	180
STANFORD, Professor C. Villiers. Symphony in F (No. 4, Op. 31) ...	12
Choral Ballad, " The Voyage of Maeldune," produced at Leeds...	99
" " " in London	110
Pianoforte Trio in E flat, at Oxford	177
Sonata for Pianoforte and Violoncello, in D minor (Op. 39) ...	115
Suite in D, for Violin and Orchestra (Op. 32), at Manchester ...	23
" " " " in London	23
STEPANOFF, Madame. *Début*	82
STOCK EXCHANGE ORCHESTRAL SOCIETY 51,	128
STRAUSS, Richard. Two Movements from Symphonic Fantasia, " Aus Italien "	113
STROLLING PLAYERS' ORCHESTRAL SOCIETY	52
SULLIVAN, Sir Arthur. Oratorio, " The Prodigal Son," revived... ...	91
Comic Opera, " The Gondoliers," produced	128
" Macbeth " Music at Leeds	101
" " Crystal Palace...	112
SYMPSON, Christopher. Thirteen " Divisions " for Division Viol ...	116
TALAZAC, M. *Début* in Italian Opera	42
TAMAGNO, Signor. *Début*	76

INDEX.

	PAGE
THOMAS, A. Goring. Contralto air for " Nadeshda "	71
TONIC SOL-FA CHOIRS, Association of. At Crystal Palace	72
TOULMIN, Miss Mary. " Christmas Carol " for Solo, Chorus, and Orchestra	126
TSCHAIKOWSKY. Solemn Overture, " 1812 "	2
Orchestral Suite in D (Op. 43)	34
Pianoforte Concerto in B flat minor at Philharmonic	34
Re-appearance at Philharmonic	34
VERDI. " Otello " produced at the Lyceum	74
VICINI, Signor. Début	59
VIGNE, Mdlle Jane de. Début	56
VINCENT, Dr. Charles. Cantata, " The Mermaid," produced	51
VOCAL RECITALS.	
Heinrich, Max	41
Henschel, Mr. and Mrs.	17, 127
Kellie, Lawrence	54
Lara, Isidore de	29, 41, 85
Spies, Fräulein Hermine	70, 85
WADDINGTON, Sidney P. Pianoforte Concerto in G minor	38
WAGNER. Overture to " Die Feen "	13
Album-Sonata in C flat	48
Closing Scene, Act I., " Die Walküre "	67
Closing Scene, Act I., " Siegfried "	67
" Die Meistersinger " produced in Italian	78
Duet from " Die Feen "	17
Excerpts from " Parsifal," with chorus	67
WARMUTH, Signor. Début	60
WEBER. Entr'acte from " The Three Pintos "	3
Hymn, " In constant order " (Op. 36)	83
WESTMINSTER ORCHESTRAL SOCIETY	27, 52, 127
WILLIAMS, C. Lee. Cantata, " Bethany," produced	90
WIND INSTRUMENT CHAMBER MUSIC SOCIETY	27, 50, 117
WINGHAM, Thomas. Andante from E flat Serenade, at Crystal Palace	35
String Quartet in G minor	49
WONSOWSKA, Mdlle. Début	70
WOOD, Charles. String Quartet, at Cambridge	145
WOOLNOTH, C. Hall. Choral Ballad, " The Skeleton in Armour," at Glasgow	160
YSAŸE, M. Début at Philharmonic	44
ZANDT, Miss Marie Van. Re-appearance	56
ZAVERTHAL, L. Symphony in C minor	50

MUSICAL NOTES.

1889.

JANUARY.

ONE musical year in London starts very much like another, and these Notes must perforce open once again with the record of a "Messiah" performance at the Royal Albert Hall on New Year's Day. On the present occasion Madame Albani, Madame Patey, Mr. Charles Banks, and Mr. Watkin Mills were the soloists.

At the next Concert of the Royal Choral Society, on the 16th, M. Peter Benoit's Oratorio "Lucifer" was to have been given, but that event being postponed, Berlioz's "Faust" was substituted, the performance deriving a special interest from the first appearance under this Society's auspices of Miss Marguerite Macintyre. The young Scottish vocalist, who was destined in course of the year to considerably advance her reputation as an Oratorio and Concert singer, gave the music of *Margaret* a highly satisfactory rendering. Her clear, sympathetic tones fairly filled the vast building, while her phrasing was marked by singular purity and charm. The audience honoured Miss Macintyre with a hearty greeting, and bestowed upon her liberal applause. Mr. Iver McKay was the *Faust* and Mr. Watkin Mills the *Mephistopheles*. The choruses were, as usual, magnificently sung under Mr. Barnby's guidance.

The performance of "Elijah" at the Novello Oratorio Concerts on the 23rd was the first of the season heard in central London. It was an exceedingly good performance, the choir being in superb form. Madame Nordica, Madame Patey, Mr. Edward Lloyd, and Mr. Henschel were the principal singers, while a new contralto, Miss Lizzie Neal, created a decidedly favourable impression by her rendering of "Woe unto them." Dr. Mackenzie conducted.

On the 14th Haydn's charming but neglected Oratorio "The Seasons" was revived by the Borough of Hackney Choral Association, under the able direction of Mr. Ebenezer Prout. It had not been given in its entirety in the metropolis since 1877, when it was performed by the Sacred Harmonic Society. The Hackney choristers sang as well as usual, and the solos were safely entrusted to Mrs. Hutchinson, Mr. Henry Piercy, and Mr. Robert Hilton.

A series of Concerts in the newly-erected Hall of the Hampstead Conservatoire of Music was inaugurated on the 28th by a performance of "The Golden Legend," given in a Concert-room capable of accommodating an audience of 700, and band and chorus of nearly 300. Mr. G. F. Geaussent, the Principal of the Conservatoire, conducted, and Mr. Carrodus led the orchestra. The solos were sustained by Miss Annie Marriott, Madame Marian Mackenzie, Mr. Lloyd, Mr. Henschel, and Mr. J. T. Hutchinson. On the 26th Dr. J. F. Bridge's Cantata "Callirhoë" was given at the Bow and Bromley Institute, Mr. McNaught conducting.

At the London Symphony Concerts, on the 15th, Mr. Henschel introduced at the end of a not very interesting programme a Solemn Overture, entitled "1812," by Tschaikowsky, who has herein endeavoured to illustrate the events of that memorable year —so fatal to Napoleon, so glorious for the Russians. But it seemed a noisy, bombastic composition, and sadly needed an explanatory analysis. Far preferable items of the Concert were the performance of Wagner's "Siegfried Idyll" and the violin playing of Mr. Willy Hess, Sir Charles Hallé's Manchester *chef d'attaque*. On the 22nd there were included in the scheme an

Entr'acte from Weber's posthumous Opera "The Three Pintos," and Mendelssohn's "Hear my prayer," the solo in the latter being sung by Mrs. Henschel and the choruses by Mr. McNaught's Bow and Bromley Choir. The *Entr'acte*, heard for the first time, proved to be a graceful, delicately-scored piece. Weber left this comic opera in an unfinished state, and the work of completing it was carried out, at the request of the composer's descendants, by Herr Mahler. "The Three Pintos" was only produced in course of the year 1888 at Munich. At the Symphony Concert of the 29th Mr. Hamish MacCunn conducted his Overture "'The Land o' the Mountain and the Flood," which was finely played and rapturously applauded. Herr Hans Wessely gave a finished rendering of a Ballad in F sharp minor (Op. 39), for violin, composed by Mr. Henschel, who also conducted a first-rate performance of Brahms's Symphony in D (No. 2) and Glinka's "Komarinskaja," a Fantasia on two Russian national songs.

The resumption of the Popular Concerts on Monday, the 7th, after the customary Christmas recess, was marked by no features of particular interest. Beethoven's Quartet in E flat (Op. 74), executed by Madame Néruda, Messrs. Ries, Straus, and Piatti, opened the Concert; Rubinstein's Sonata in D (Op. 18), performed by Mdlle. Janotha and Signor Piatti, brought it to a termination. The solo works were of unusually trifling dimensions. Mdlle. Janotha was down only for Chopin's Barcarolle, but added his Berceuse as an encore, playing both beautifully. Madame Néruda gave pieces by Spohr and Leclair, and, in spite of four recalls, declined to play again. Mr. Santley sang a couple of *Lieder* by Brahms and Gounod's "Nom de Marie," accompanied by Mr. Sidney Naylor. On the Saturday following a large crowd went to hear Beethoven's "Kreutzer" Sonata, played by Madame Néruda and Sir Charles Hallé. The "Kreutzer" came last in the scheme, first place being worthily assigned to Mozart's glorious Quintet in G minor (No. 6), which was executed by Madame Néruda, Messrs. L. Ries, Hollander, Gibson, and Piatti. Sir Charles Hallé was heard alone in Schubert's Fantasia Sonata in G (Op. 78), and merited, by an admirable performance, the loud applause he received. Mrs. Henschel sang Purcell's "Nymphs and Shepherds," Goring Thomas's "Midi au Village," and Massenet's "Sérénade de Janette." All three were given to perfection, Mr. Henschel being at the piano. Madame Haas was the pianist on Monday, the 14th. She gave a conscientious and refined interpretation of Chopin's Impromptu in F sharp major, and sustained the pianoforte part in Brahms's A major Quartet. Beethoven's first "Rasoumouski" Quartet opened the Concert. The vocalist was Miss Florence Hoskins, a student at the Royal College. In marked contrast to the small attendance at this Concert was the crush on Saturday, the 19th, when Beethoven's Septet was played by Madame Néruda, Messrs. Hollander, Lazarus, Paersch, Wotton, Reynolds, and Piatti. The scheme opened with Haydn's famous Quartet in C (Op. 76, No. 3), which contains the variations on "God preserve the Emperor." Madame Haas added to the favourable impression already created by her rendering of Beethoven's Sonata in A flat (Op. 110). Mr. Santley sang. On the succeeding Monday Madame Haas joined Signor Piatti in Mendelssohn's duet Sonata in B flat (Op. 45), and performed Bach's Organ Prelude and Fugue in A minor, as arranged for piano by Liszt. The *pièce de résistance* of this programme was Schubert's Octet (Op. 166), gloriously given by Madame Néruda, Messrs. Ries, Straus, Lazarus, Paersch, Wotton, Reynolds, and Piatti. Contrary to latter-day custom, the Octet was put last in the programme, and given without break. Miss Helen d'Alton was heard to advantage in Maud Valérie White's charming song, "Come to me in my dreams." The audience at the afternoon Popular Concert of the 26th was large but not crowded. Beethoven's Quintet in C (Op. 29) was magnificently rendered by Madame Néruda, Messrs. Ries, Hollander, Gibson, and Piatti. Mdlle. Janotha played Schumann's "Carnival"; and, as an encore, the same composer's "Arabeske"; being also heard with Madame Néruda in Beethoven's Sonata in G major, for pianoforte and violin (Op. 30,

No. 3). Mr. Brereton was the vocalist. An interesting Concert was that of the 28th, when Miss Fanny Davies made her *rentrée*, and executed Schumann's "Fantasiestücke" (Op. 111), of which three strikingly original pieces only the third had hitherto been heard at the "Pops." They were beautifully played; and, an encore being insisted upon, Miss Davies gave Mendelssohn's Capriccio in E minor. On the same evening a new Sonata for violoncello and pianoforte, in F (No. 3), by Signor Piatti, was performed for the first time. As in his previous Sonatas, the composer here shows a strict adherence to orthodox form, and lays out his materials with the skill of an accomplished musician. The themes are melodious and effective, notably in the slow movement, a Romanza full of feeling and passion. The Sonata met with emphatic favour, the composer and his talented coadjutor, Miss Fanny Davies, being recalled amid loud applause. Miss Marguerite Hall, who had only just returned to England, appeared and sang, with entire acceptance, songs by Schubert and Goring Thomas.

On the 28th little Otto Hegner gave the first of a series of Recitals at St. James's Hall. He played with neatness and decison the first of Bach's six Partitas (in B flat), and also attempted Beethoven's "Waldstein" Sonata in C (Op. 53). There were passages in the Sonata which, owing to the size of his hands, he could not grasp, but it was altogether a phenomenal performance for a boy of twelve. In the opening movement he was somewhat excited; but, by the time he arrived at the *Finale*, he had fully recovered his self-possession. He was heard besides in Schumann's "Vogel als Prophet" and in a Nocturne and Waltz by Chopin; and concluded the Recital with one of the well-known Rhapsodies by Liszt. There was a large but not very enthusiastic audience.

Miss Dora Bright, a pupil of the Royal Academy of Music, gave the first of three Recitals at Princes' Hall on the 30th. Among other works she was heard in Schumann's Fantasia in C (Op. 17). She made, however, the best impression in some new

Studies by Mr. Walter Macfarren, and in two effective little pieces from her own pen.

A series of three Recitals, given by Mr. Max Heinrich and Mr. Emanuel Moor, began at Steinway Hall on the 16th. On the following day Mr. W. de Manby Sergison gave the first of ten winter Concerts at 62, Warwick Square.

Madame Patti appeared at the Royal Albert Hall before crowded audiences on January 8th and 22nd, and February 28th, these being the last Concerts in which she took part in London previous to her leaving for a tour in South America.

At the London Ballad Concert, on the 16th, new songs by Miss Hope Temple, Mr. Molloy, and Mr. Stephen Adams were introduced. The birthday of Burns was commemorated as usual, on the 25th, by Concerts at the Albert Hall and St. James's Hall.

A "dialogue-oratorio," "Samuel," composed by Mr. Jerome Hopkins, was performed for the first time at Princes' Hall, on the 28th, under the composer's direction. The characteristic feature of this work is that it requires "a singing and a speaking troupe" for its interpretation, declamation in the speaking voice entering largely into its scheme.

Mr. Carl Armbruster commenced, on the 28th, a series of three Afternoon Recitals at the Portman Rooms, in course of which Wagner's "Tristan und Isolde" was sung, with a pianoforte accompaniment, one act being given at each Recital. As a "set-off" against the disadvantage of there being no orchestra, the "friends of Wagner's musical dramas," to whom Mr. Armbruster specially appealed, were vouchsafed a rendering without a single cut. The chief solo parts were sustained by Miss Pauline Cramer (*Isolde*), Miss Margaret Hoare (*Brangäne*), Mr. William Nicholl (*Tristan*), Mr. W. Cunliffe (*Kurwenal*), Mr. B. H. Grove (*Marke*), and Mr. Henry Phillips in the three minor characters.

A short season of English Opera began at the Olympic Theatre, on the 26th, under the direction of Mr. Valentine Smith. "Maritana," "The Bohemian Girl," and other favourite operas were given, and low prices of admission were charged. Mr. Valentine

Smith was supported by a tolerably capable troupe, including Miss Clara Perry, Miss Susetta Fenn, Mr. C. H. Victor, and Mr. Henry Pope, with a good band and excellent conductor in Mr. Isidore de Solla. The chorus and *mise en scène* were not all that could be desired, and, on the whole, the venture failed to prosper.

" Paul Jones," which successful comic opera ran throughout the year, was brought out by the Carl Rosa Light Opera Company, on the 12th, at the Prince of Wales's Theatre, under the management of Mr. Horace Sedger. "Paul Jones" was an English adaptation of M. Robert Planquette's "Surcœuf," produced on October 6, 1887, at the Folies Dramatiques Theatre, Paris. The French libretto of Messrs. Chivot and Duru, freely adapted by the late Mr. H. B. Farnie, embodied a picturesque story; and the music, if not equal to the composer's "Cloches de Corneville" or "Rip van Winkle," proved sufficiently bright and pleasing to satisfy the general ear. It may, however, be asserted, without fear of contradiction, that the attraction chiefly accounting for the long run of the piece was furnished by the representative of the hero, Miss Agnes Huntington, an American contralto new to the English stage. Miss Huntington's beauty and commanding presence, her fine voice and sympathetic artistic style, won for her an immediate triumph. The other chief characters were impersonated by Miss Wadman, Miss Phyllis Broughton, Mr. H. Ashley, Mr. H. Monkhouse, and Mr. Frank Wyatt.

OBITUARY.—Ilma di Murska (operatic singer), Munich, 14th; Francis Hueffer (musical critic of *The Times*), London, 19th.

FEBRUARY.

THE Sacred Cantata "Isaias," written by Signor Luigi Mancinelli and produced under his direction at the Norwich Festival of 1887, was performed for the first time in London by the Royal Choral Society on the 20th. Comparatively slight interest was evinced in this event, and the Albert Hall was by no means well filled. Yet this ought not to have been the case, remembering the curiosity which the work excited at Norwich, and the enthusiastic reception accorded it there. The music of "Isaias" is of that bold, unconventional character which must ever make it interesting to musicians, and, despite certain inequalities, it is a composition of undoubted merit. The beautiful numbers that come early in the Cantata once more made a deep impression. A finer rendering of the choruses could not have been wished for; and the solos were, on the whole, satisfactorily given by Madame Nordica, Miss Lena Little, Mr. Barton McGuckin, Mr. Alec Marsh, and Mr. Lucas Williams. The Cantata was conducted by Mr. Joseph Barnby, whose Psalm, "The Lord is King," opened the Concert. At the performance of "Elijah," given by this Society on the 2nd, Madame Nordica, Madame Belle Cole, Mr. Charles Banks, and Mr. Henschel constituted the leading solo quartet; and the contralto solo, "Woe unto them," was expressively rendered by Miss Julia Neilson.

The "Dream of Jubal," a "poem with music," written by Mr. Joseph Bennett and composed by Dr. A. C. Mackenzie for the Jubilee of the Liverpool Philharmonic Society, was heard in London, for the first time, on the 26th, at Novello's Oratorio Concerts, and received with every sign of favour, the Lancashire verdict being endorsed with emphasis by a large and representative audience. In this very original work the author depicts Jubal, "the father of all such as handle the harp and pipe," as being discontented with his powers and thrown into a deep sleep, wherein an angel appears and reveals to him in a series of visions the varied possibilities that attend the after-development of his art. Amid appropriate scenes, he hears in turn a chorus of praise in Divine worship, a song of comfort in bereavement, a patriotic march and chorus of victory, a song of a labourer in the harvest field, a funeral march and chorus in honour of a hero, and a duet of lovers. At the conclusion of all this he awakes, and, bearing his "chorded shell" to the altar, dedicates the wondrous gift to God, a chorus of invocation ending the work. The peculiarity of this composition is that the story is recited in spoken verse, the reciter being accompanied throughout by the orchestra, while the choruses and solos are restricted to the events of the dream, as above set forth, and the final invocation. The effect is striking, and to some extent new. Mr. Bennett's "poem" is worthy to be so called. His verse is elegant, his diction refined, and his language in all cases poetic and expressive. The music may be described in a word as in Dr. Mackenzie's best vein. Always original, forcible, and appropriate, it is full of melodic charm and technical resource, while more than one climax rises to a height of veritable grandeur. Thanks to a magnificent performance, the beauty and dramatic power of the work made an unmistakably deep impression on all who heard it. The choruses were superbly sung; the soprano and tenor solos were rendered to perfection by Miss Macintyre and Mr. Edward Lloyd; and the difficult task allotted to the reciter was fulfilled with conspicuous ability by Mr. Charles Fry. The composer, who conducted, was awarded a hearty ovation at the close. The new work was preceded by Saint-Saëns's Psalm "The Heavens declare," in which Miss Liza Lehmann sang with fervent feeling the soprano solo; Miss Zippora Monteith, an American soprano, made her *début;* and Miss Lizzie Neal, Messrs. Lloyd, Andrew Black,

Lucas Williams, D. Hughes, and L. Huxtable assisted in the concerted music.

The first Saturday Concert (eleventh of the series) at the Crystal Palace, after the customary recess, took place on the 9th. Mr. Manns was warmly greeted by a crowded audience—attracted chiefly by the announcement that Otto Hegner would play. This veritable "wonder-child" was heard in Beethoven's C minor Pianoforte Concerto (No. 3), the same work that Josef Hofmann played here at the opening Concert of the winter season, October 8th, 1887. Otto's performance, however, was as far superior to his rival's as was his rendering of the C major Concerto (No. 1) last April, when compared with that given by Josef at the Philharmonic Concert of June, 1887, even allowing in each instance for the respective differences of age. Hegner was perfectly at ease from the moment he sat down. From a technical standpoint the Concerto was "child's-play" to him; by far the most difficult thing in it was the elaborate though ill-fitted cadenza written for him by his harmony master, Herr Glaus, of Bâle. His exquisite phrasing of the slow movement, and the crisp, pearly delicacy of his touch in the Rondo, sent the audience fairly into raptures, and he was recalled with enthusiasm. Hegner afterwards played some solo *morceaux*, and added an encore without evincing the slightest fatigue. The programme opened with a novelty—the Overture to Lalo's Opera "Le Roi d'Ys," which clever though unequal work had been very frequently given at the Paris Opéra Comique since its production there in May, 1888. Lalo stands high among modern French composers; he is a man of original ideas and distinct creative power. Unfortunately he was already sixty-one, and "Le Roi d'Ys" was his first real success. The Overture, which is in irregular form, is based on themes heard in course of the Opera, and is a picturesque, cleverly-scored piece. Miss Emily Spada was the vocalist. At the Concert of the 16th was produced for the first time in England Mr. Hamish MacCunn's Cantata "The Lay of the Last Minstrel," written expressly for the Glasgow Choral Union, and performed by that

Society in December, 1888. This work is Gaelic to the core, as well befits a composition founded on one of Scott's poetic masterpieces, and written by a young Scotch musician who has from the very outset betrayed a marked predilection for the use of themes inspired by the national melodies of his country. The libretto, written by Mr. MacCunn's father, is somewhat disjointed, but the shortcoming could scarcely have been avoided without adding considerably to the length of the Cantata, which, from a dramatic standpoint, has at least the merit of being concise. The central figure of the story is the gallant *Sir William of Deloraine*. He rides from Branksome Hall, at the bidding of *Lady Buccleuch*, to Melrose Abbey, and there, with the aid of the Monk of St. Mary's Aisle, obtains from the tomb of the Wizard, Michael Scott, the "Mighty Book" that shall prove a charm and defence against the English invaders. On his way back *Sir William* interrupts a clandestine meeting between *Lady Margaret of Branksome* and *Lord Cranston*, whose family is at feud with the Buccleuchs; and in the combat that follows between the Knights, *Deloraine* is wounded. Later on, when the English Borderers appear at Branksome and are met with defiance at the hands of its noble mistress, it is agreed that their dispute shall be settled by single combat, *Sir Richard Musgrave* representing the English and *Sir William of Deloraine* the Scottish sides. The wounded *Deloraine* is unfit to fight, but, through the influence of the Mighty Book, *Lord Cranston* is enabled to personate him and overcome the English champion, whereupon there is a reconciliation, and *Cranston* is accepted by *Lady Buccleuch* as her daughter's affianced husband. In his setting Mr. Hamish MacCunn once more makes manifest the marked peculiarities of style and powerful grasp of his subject that characterised his previous works. His distinctive melodies serve here a double purpose. They emphasise the Scotch surroundings and they supply a chain of *Leitmotives* that enhance in a notable degree the dramatic interest of the story. The orchestra plays a highly important part, and the masterly skill with which it is written for throughout again excites mingled admiration and wonder at the command of orchestral resource possessed by this young musician. The narrative is carried on by the chorus, and number after number surprises by the extraordinary variety and intensity of its descriptive power, the finest of all being that which depicts the midnight visit of the monk and the knight to the wizard's tomb—a grandly-impressive scene. The "storm and stress" pervading most of the music are agreeably relieved by the duet between the River and the Mountain Spirits, who foretell that the feud will not end "Till pride be quelled and love be free"; and also by the charming number describing the stolen meeting of the lovers. The solos, however, are comparatively few and unimportant, while the treatment of the final chorus, "O Caledonia! stern and wild," scarcely rises in dignity or power to the general level of the work. Mr. MacCunn was enthusiastically applauded when he came upon the platform at the conclusion of the performance. Mr. Manns conducted, and the solos were sung by Madame Nordica, Miss Marie Curran, Mr. Iver McKay, and Mr. Andrew Black, the last-named artist particularly distinguishing himself in the baritone solos. The band did its work splendidly, but the choir sang out of tune and with very little spirit. Another important novelty, brought forward at the Concert of the 23rd, was the Symphony in F major (No. 4, Op. 31), composed by Professor Villiers Stanford, and first produced under his direction at Berlin, on January 14. It was now conducted with characteristic energy and skill by Mr. August Manns, who secured an exceedingly fine performance. Dr. Stanford has prefaced this Symphony with the motto, "Thro' Youth to Strife, Thro' Death to Life." It is an extremely interesting work, revealing rare breadth of conception, elaboration of detail, and musicianly resource; but the listener must not expect to find in its four movements a clearly-defined illustration of the various conditions which the motto indicates. It was, indeed, expressly declared that the composer's aim had been "only to reflect the general sensations of the motto." He has at least been successful in the opening *Allegro*, which plainly suggests the joyous animation and bright aspirations of youth. The *Intermezzo* and *Trio*, in which Dr. Stanford has embodied some phrases from his music to " Ædipus Rex," form a graceful and interesting section, but, beyond a slightly agitated character, the music has in it little that conveys the idea of " Strife." Thenceforward it is as well to ignore the purport of the motto and appreciate for their own beauties alone the singularly beautiful slow movement and the remarkably elaborate, powerfully-wrought *Finale*. These two divisions comprise by far the finest portion of the Symphony. Mr. Manns took unsparing pains to secure a good performance, and fully accomplished that object. The new Symphony was loudly applauded by a large audience. Other noteworthy items of the Concert were Miss Fanny Davies's rendering of Carl Reinecke's Pianoforte Concerto in F sharp minor (Op. 72), and a splendid delivery of Beethoven's Air, "Ah perfido," by Fräulein Marie Fillunger.

Mr. Max Pauer appeared at the London Symphony Concert on the 5th, and gave a capital reading of Beethoven's " Emperor " Concerto. Tschaikowsky's ugly Solemn Overture, " 1812," was repeated, and the remainder of the programme was familiar. At the Concert of the following week one of the largest audiences of the season attended to hear Beethoven's " Eroica " Symphony and a Wagner selection performed in commemoration of the latter composer's death-day, the 13th. The Bayreuth master was again represented at the Concert of the 19th by the Overture to his Opera " Die Feen," written in 1833, when he was a young man of twenty. This piece, now heard in England for the first time, betrays a curious diversity of styles. In the slow introduction appear a stately martial theme and a chorale-like passage, both gems of the Spontini-Meyerbeer influence that was to be developed at its fullest six years later in " Rienzi." The opening subject of the *Allegro* is distinctly suggestive of Weber alike in its romantic character and symphonic style of treatment; but the graceful second subject given out by the flute brings to mind " Tannhäuser" and "Lohengrin"—showing that amid the contending influences now at work the composer's individuality had already a place. The "working-out," again, is suggestive of Beethoven, and it is marked by strong dramatic colouring, though lacking in clearness. The *Coda* so distinctly foreshadows that of the "Flying Dutchman" Overture that one can scarcely help thinking Wagner had it in his mind when he wrote the later work. Both, anyhow, belong to the romantic style of Weber. From the above remarks it may be gathered that the Overture proved interesting to Wagnerian students, and Mr. Henschel earned deserved thanks for bringing it to a hearing in this country. On the same evening Beethoven's Violin Concerto was performed by Mr. Johann Kruse, a young Australian artist, whose *début* at the "Pops" this month is referred to below. The regular series of the London Symphony Concerts now terminated, but an extra Concert was given on the afternoon of the 27th, the feature of the occasion being the London *début* of a portion of the Leeds Festival Chorus, under the direction of their able conductor, Mr. Alfred Broughton. A large crowd attended and did not go away disappointed. The singing of the famous Yorkshire choristers in Mendelssohn's "Walpurgis Night" and the *Finale* of Beethoven's Choral Symphony was a thing to be remembered. The bright, penetrating tone and rich quality of the voices (numbering in all 160), their clean, simultaneous attack, and the marvellous vigour and precision with which they followed the beat, constituted quite a revelation for London amateurs. Altogether, the visit was an immense success, and it crowned in worthy fashion the long series of artistic endeavours that marked Mr. Henschel's undertaking.

The programme of the Saturday Popular Concert on the 2nd contained nothing calling for mention, beyond Emmanuel Bach's Sonata in C minor, for piano and violin, executed by Sir Charles and Lady Hallé. Mr. Max Pauer re-appeared on the following Monday, and gave a masculine, but not, as regards poetic sentiment, a wholly satisfactory rendering of Schumann's

"Etudes Symphoniques." The same evening the new German soprano, Fräulein Marie Fillunger, made a favourable *début* in London, displaying a powerful, well-cultivated organ and exceptional dramatic feeling and intelligence. Mr. Johann Kruse, who made his first appearance at the Popular Concerts on the 9th, is a native of Australia and a pupil of Dr. Joachim. He had visited London the previous season, when his playing in private circles was greatly admired, and led to his present engagement. Mr. Kruse is a thoughtful and capable interpreter of Chamber music, his method and style being distinctly redolent of the Berlin "Hochschule." His intonation was at times faulty, but this was thought to be due to nervousness. Mr. Kruse was leading violinist in Schubert's D minor Quartet, and here, as in Beethoven's String Trio in C minor (Op. 9, No. 3), played with Mr. Straus and Signor Piatti, he infused considerable vigour and feeling into his performance. Mr. Max Pauer brought forward for the first time at the "Pops" Hummel's Sonata in F sharp minor (Op. 81), a work distinguished by exacting mechanical difficulties and constant succession of *bravura* passages rather than musicianly interest of a deeper kind. Miss Marguerite Hall sang, Miss Mary Carmichael accompanying. On Monday, the 11th, the same violinist and pianist again appeared. Mr. Kruse "led" Beethoven's Quartet in E flat (Op. 74), and introduced a Sonata in G minor by Tartini; and also took part with Mr. Max Pauer and Signor Piatti in Brahms's Trio in C minor (Op. 101). Miss Liza Lehmann was the vocalist. The programmes of the 16th and 18th consisted wholly of well-worn materials, save that at the latter Concert Signor Piatti's new Sonata in F was repeated, and at the former Mrs. Henschel introduced a charming setting, by Mr. F. Corder, of Tennyson's lines, "O sun that wakenest." On the 23rd the re-appearance of Edvard Grieg and his accomplished wife caused an enormous attendance. An apology was made for Madame Grieg on account of sore throat, but her artistic singing of her husband's songs proved nevertheless delightful. The Norwegian composer played two of his "Scenes from National Life" (adding another piece as an encore), and joined Signor Piatti in his Sonata in A minor, for piano and cello (Op. 36). These distinguished artists also took part in the Concert of the 25th. Grieg's solos consisted of the "Improvisata," from his Op. 29, the "Albumblatt," from Op. 28, and the "Stabbe-Lat," from the set of twenty-three Norwegian Dances (Op. 17); while with Madame Néruda he played his well-known Pianoforte and Violin Sonata in F major (Op. 8). How all these things were given it is needless to say. Grieg has been aptly described as the "Scandinavian Chopin," and he deserves the name, not only in virtue of the tender poetic sentiment and ineffable grace of his compositions, but the exquisite charm and perfection of touch and *technique* that he brings to bear upon their interpretation.

For Recital-givers and their patrons this was a busy month. The average attendance at Otto Hegner's Recitals grew larger as they went on. On the 18th he played Beethoven's Sonata in E flat (Op. 31, No. 3). The Minuet was a trifle hurried, but, taken for all in all, it was an amazing exposition of precocious musical intelligence. Among Otto's other achievements were a brilliant performance of Weber's Rondo in E, a neat and delicate reading of Chopin's Nocturne in D flat, and a delightful display of sure, even fingering in one of Bach's English Suites. The third Recital of the series took place on the 25th.

Fräulein Geisler-Schubert, a grand-niece of the famous composer, gave a Pianoforte Recital at Princes' Hall on the 13th, and proved herself worthy of the great name she bears. She is a pianist of a very high order, and interprets Schubert's music to perfection. Her reading of his romantic Fantasia Sonata in G (Op. 78) was technically all that could be wished. But, in addition to digital skill, Fräulein Geisler possesses a charming touch, and she plays with feeling and intelligence. Moreover, without any trace of exaggeration, she gives a vivid and sympathetic rendering of the work in hand. Among other things she took part with those excellent artists, Messrs. Straus and E. Howell, in the master's Pianoforte Trio in B flat (Op. 99).

Mr. and Mrs. Henschel gave two of their enjoyable Vocal Recitals on the 15th and 22nd. The selection at the first included a duet from Wagner's youthful opera "Die Feen," an interesting novelty, listened to with curiosity by an audience that crowded Princes' Hall. Like the overture referred to above, the duet recalls the style of the composer of "Der Freischütz" in a singularly marked degree. It deals with a sufficiently trite dramatic situation—an unexpected reunion of two lovers, who tease each other about their doings since they parted, a pretended quarrel ending up with a happy reconciliation. It is just one of those bright, joyous duets, interspersed with neat and effective dramatic touches, such as Weber himself might have penned. The voice parts and the accompaniment are brimful of tripping melody, and a spirit of gaiety and humour pervades the whole. Needless to add that the piece was delightfully sung by Mr. and Mrs. Henschel, Mr. Frantzen being at the piano. The programme of the second Recital consisted wholly of compositions by Mr. Henschel, including his "Serbisches Liederspiel," the Trio from his 80th Psalm, and several new songs. Mr. and Mrs. Henschel were assisted by Miss Marguerite Hall, Miss Lena Little, Mr. Shakespeare, and Mr. Max Heinrich.

The scheme of Mdlle. Jeanne Douste's Recital at Princes' Hall, on the 14th, was made up of compositions by Schumann and Brahms. The former master's Sonata for pianoforte in G minor (Op. 22) received an especially good rendering. Included in the Brahms selection was a set of twenty-five Variations with Fugue on a theme by Handel, marked in the programme "first time." Whether an absolute novelty or not, this composition proved full of interest as well as scholarly resource, and was admirably executed by Mdlle. Douste. The vocalist was Herr Oscar Niemann.

At his third and last Recital at Steinway Hall on the 13th, Mr. Max Heinrich sang a selection of songs by Brahms, and was associated with Miss Lena Little in duets by Dvorák, Cornelius, and Schumann. He also introduced a cleverly-written and interesting set of "Reed Songs" by Mr. Seb. Schlesinger, a talented amateur composer well known in New York, and now residing in London.

In the theatre of the University of London, on the 23rd, was performed a Cantata, entitled "Dante's Vision," composed by Mr. Charles John Hall as his exercise for the degree of Doctor of Music. The event was of more than ordinary interest, inasmuch as it was the first occasion of a work being performed with full orchestra at the London University. The solos were sustained by Miss Kathleen Grant, Mr. Percy Palmer, and Mr. C. Ackerman, and the choruses were sung by the choir (men and boys) of St. John's, Waterloo Road.

OBITUARY.—Josef Gungl (dance-music composer), Weimar, 1st.

MARCH.

At the Novello Oratorio Concerts on the 19th was performed a Cantata, entitled "The Light of Asia," the composition of an American musician, Mr. Dudley Buck, the words being taken from Sir Edward Arnold's richly imaginative poem of the same name. This work attracted considerable attention, not merely on account of its subject, but because it was the first choral composition of important dimensions by a leading American composer yet heard in this country. "The Light of Asia" is not cast in the mould calculated to win for it popularity with general audiences. One great defect, to begin with, is that an acquaintance with the original poem is requisite in order to thoroughly understand the motive of the story, and to realise the nature of such beings as the divinely-sprung *Siddârtha* and the pure, noble, womanly *Yasôdhara*. Another difficulty is the total absence of dramatic incident and contrast; the entire work is in narrative form, and this engenders a sense of monotony before the end is reached. The solos, which should afford the necessary relief, are inferior in interest to the choruses and concerted numbers. Oratorio lovers found plenty to admire in the scholarly counterpoint and fugue of Mr. Buck's choruses; they enjoyed his massive, flowing harmonies and graceful, expressive melodies; they admired his refined instrumentation, and marked many a delicate touch of fancy in his *ensemble* writing. On the other hand, for individuality, power of characterisation, and dramatic effect (save in the use of representative themes) they looked in vain. The numbers that made most effect at St. James's Hall were the picturesque scene of *Siddârtha's* temptation, the Spring-song, and the Wedding hymn, the dreamy chorus, " Softly the Indian night sank o'er the plain," and the two really charming duets for *Yasôdhara* and *Siddârtha*. These duets lost nothing in the hands of Madame Nordica and Mr. Edward Lloyd, who threw all possible fervour and expression into their music. The bass solos had an admirable exponent in Mr. Andrew Black. The band and chorus did their work in a manner that earned the highest praise ; while Dr. Mackenzie conducted with infinite care and zeal, making the most of his opportunities, and altogether securing a highly poetic reading of the work.

On Ash Wednesday, the 6th, there was a performance of Gounod's " Redemption " at the Albert Hall, with Miss Robertson, Madame Patey, Mr. Charles Banks, Mr. Robert Hilton, and Mr. Watkin Mills as soloists. Sacred Concerts took place on the same day at the Crystal Palace and St. James's Hall, and the crowd that attended the latter was agreeably surprised to find Mr. Sims Reeves able to fulfil his engagement. This was the first time the veteran tenor had been well enough to sing in public for several weeks.

The Bach Choir gave a most interesting Concert at St. James's Hall on the 5th, the scheme including two Church Cantatas by the Leipsic Cantor, now introduced for the first time. They proved to be worthy examples of a numerous family, particularly the Cantata framed upon the hymn " Wachet auf!" The choruses in this are after Bach's best manner. The two duets for soprano and baritone (sung by Miss Liza Lehmann and Mr. Plunket Greene) were also interesting. In the second Cantata, " Halt' im Gedächtniss "—the opening chorus set to these words is singularly fine—the solos were sung by Miss Emily Himing and Mr. Charles Wade. The best piece of choral singing heard during the evening was in the splendid eight-part Motet, " Singet dem Herrn." At this Concert Dr. Joachim (who had made his *rentrée* at the "Pops" on the previous evening) gave a magnificent performance of Sebastian Bach's fine Concerto in A minor, and the equally fine, though more familiar Sonata in G minor. Both works were given from memory, and with an energy and feeling and a mastery of detail characteristic in the highest degree of the performer's individuality. After each effort he was recalled again and again amid spontaneous and hearty plaudits. Professor Stanford conducted the Concert with judgment and tact, and Mr. Frederic Cliffe presided with ability at the organ.

At the fourth Concert of the Highbury Philharmonic Society, on the 25th, the chief feature in the programme was Frederic Clay's Cantata " Lalla Rookh." This graceful work was well given under Mr. G. H. Betjemann, the chorus singing well, and the orchestra showing a very creditable degree of efficiency. Following the Cantata came three movements from " Cleopatra," an Orchestral Suite written by Signor Luigi Mancinelli—a Funeral March, Barcarolle, and Triumphal March—performed for the first time in London.

The Philharmonic Society inaugurated its seventy-seventh season on Thursday evening, the 25th, with more than usual éclat. The large and brilliant crowd that attended was attracted in a great measure by the co-operation of the distinguished Scandinavian musician, Edvard Grieg, whose popularity was just now extraordinary. The Prince and Princess of Wales, with Prince Albert Victor and Princess Victoria, arrived just after the commencement of Sterndale Bennett's " Parisina " Overture, wherein the magnificent Philharmonic orchestra was not heard to the best advantage; nor did its real form stand revealed in the Schumann Pianoforte Concerto, which came next. Indeed, the entire rendering of this most fascinating of pianoforte works was distinctly unsatisfactory. The soloist, Fräulein Geisler-Schubert, was either indisposed or paralysed by nervousness. She played innumerable false notes, and, save in the *Intermezzo*, never seemed to have a firm grasp of her theme. Yet had Schubert's grand-niece proved herself an artist of such undeniable capacity that it was impossible to visit her present shortcomings with severe criticism. The *pièce de résistance* of the Concert, however, was the performance of Grieg's " Peer Gynt " Suite (Op. 46). It was subsequently stated on authority that Grieg was amazed by the playing of the Philharmonic band. Never had he heard before such a *pianissimo*, such *nuances*, such transitions from light to shade! His astonishment was fully shared by the audience, who enjoyed the additional pleasure of realising for the first time (thanks to Mr. Joseph Bennett's admirable analysis) the true significance of these poetic, exquisitely - scored movements. Ibsen's hero, *Peer Gynt*, was now understood to be a peasant lad with fantastic ideas and great ambitions, who travels far, has many loves, goes home to find his mother on her death-bed, wanders forth again, and ultimately returns old and grey to settle down with his faithful betrothed *Solveig*, who has waited for him since his youth. To know the exact source of Grieg's inspiration was to enjoy his music the more; certainly the delicious "Anitra's Dance" and the wondrously tender passage illustrating the "Death of Aase"—dying as her wayward son sits by her bedside and relates his adventures—impressed as they necessarily failed to impress in a mere abstract sense when Mr. Henschel introduced the Suite at the London Symphony Concerts. The final "Dance of the Imps"—chasing and tormenting *Peer Gynt* in the subterranean halls of the King of the Dovre Mountains— made a tremendous effect, and after three recalls Grieg returned to the Conductor's desk and repeated it. The Concert was an unqualified triumph for the Norwegian composer and his wife, who made her Philharmonic *début*, and sang in her usual quaint, impulsive, and expressive manner. Dr. A. C. Mackenzie, who conducted the Concert in Mr. Frederic Cowen's absence, secured excellent performances of his "Burns" Rhapsody and Beethoven's Fourth Symphony.

At the second Philharmonic Concert, on the 28th, Mr. Cowen resumed his duties as Conductor of the Society, and was very heartily welcomed on his return from Australia, where he had directed the whole of the musical performances given in connection with the Melbourne Centennial Exhibition. The only works he now had to conduct were Schubert's "Unfinished" Symphony, Mendelssohn's "Midsummer Night's Dream" music—each admirably given—and the vocal pieces sung by Mdlle. Antoinette Trebelli. The novelty of the evening, Professor Villiers Stanford's Violin Suite in D (Op. 32), enjoyed (as at Berlin last January, and still more recently at Manchester) the advantage of an interpretation at the hands of Dr. Joachim, to whom it is dedicated. This work impressed by merits of a technical kind rather than the charm of spontaneous grace or attractive melody. In it Dr. Stanford has employed the titles, and to a certain extent the form and rhythms, of the old Suite movements, but his themes, save in one or two instances, are not striking, while the task set the leading instrument cannot be said to possess interest in a degree commensurate with its difficulties. The dulness of the Overture, the Allemande, and the Ballade is only partially relieved by the livelier Tambourin and the final Gigue in *Rondo* form. Dr. Joachim played the Suite with marvellous skill, and was recalled, together with Dr. Stanford, who conducted. A distinct success was won by a Norwegian artist, Madame Backer-Gröndahl, in Grieg's A minor Pianoforte Concerto, which the composer now came forward to conduct. Madame Backer-Gröndahl, who finished her studies under Von Bülow and Liszt, possesses a superb *technique*, and adds to rare brilliancy of style the charm of a full, rich tone and singularly delicate, sensitive touch. The beauty of the performance, materially enhanced as it was by the exquisite refinement with which the accompaniments were executed under the master's guidance, made such an impression that both composer and interpreter met with an ovation, and had to return thrice to the platform. Mdlle. Antoinette Trebelli greatly pleased in her two operatic airs, one the "Non mi dir" from "Don Giovanni," the other "Sombres forêts," from "Guillaume Tell," her efforts being loudly applauded by the large audience that filled the hall.

The only fresh items at the Crystal Palace Concert, of the 2nd, was a short but impressive "Marche Funèbre," written by Berlioz for the last scene of "Hamlet." It is the third of three pieces for orchestra and chorus, published during the lifetime of the composer as "Tristia" (Op. 18). The choral element in it is of a simple kind: it consists of the repetition of an "Ah" on a note passing from *forte* to *piano*. The March has, as superscription, the last nine lines in the play, beginning "Let four captains bear Hamlet like a soldier to the stage." The piece was admirably executed and warmly received. Fräulein Marie Fillunger sang "With verdure clad," to the German words. The Concert concluded with Beethoven's Choral Symphony, with Fräulein Fillunger, Madame Belle Cole, and Messrs. Chilley and Watkin Mills as solo vocalists. On the following Saturday Brahms's Fourth Symphony was played for the first time before a Sydenham audience, as was also Dr. Bridge's Overture "Morte d'Arthur"; and Madame Néruda was heard in the Beethoven Violin Concerto. Mr. Plunket Greene sang. At the Concert of the 16th M. Ernest Gillet played Raff's Violoncello Concerto in D and a couple of solos. The orchestral selection embraced Beethoven's Pastoral Symphony, and the Overtures to "Oberon" and "Die Meistersinger." Mr. Edward Lloyd sang an air from Gluck's "Iphigenia" and some songs by Dvorák. The scheme of the 23rd was of a less familiar order. Included in it was a new Overture to Sir Walter Scott's "Rokeby," written expressly for these Concerts by Mr. Ebenezer Prout. It is a clear, straightforward, musicianly work, full of graceful ideas, and orchestrated with the skill of a master. Splendidly played, the Overture was received with emphatic applause, in response to which the composer bowed his acknowledgments from the gallery. Raff's "Lenore" Symphony, not played here since 1881, afforded the audience a more or less interesting forty minutes; and Liszt's Pianoforte Concerto in A received an attentive hearing, for the sake of Herr Stavenhagen's extraordinary manipulation of the solo part. This artist, who is deemed the greatest of all Liszt's pupils, treated every *tour de force* as though it were a trifle. Saint-Saëns's Poème Symphonique "Phaéton," new to this repertory, closed the Concert. It is a striking bit of "tone-painting," and as closely suggestive of the fate that befel the son of Apollo as anything in music could very well be. This, like everything else in which the orchestra was concerned during the afternoon, received a splendid rendering, and Mr. Manns put down his *bâton* covered with laurels. On the 30th Dr. Joachim went down to Sydenham and delighted a large audience with a masterly performance of his " Hungarian " Concerto and some Bach solos. Miss Lena Little appropriately sang a contralto *scena* from the great violinist's opera " Marfa." Schumann's D minor Symphony, Mendelssohn's " Hebrides " Overture, and Beethoven's " Leonora " Overture (No. 3) completed a strong programme.

At the Saturday Popular Concert, on the 2nd, Madame de Pachmann was the pianist, now making her first appearance here since the days when she was Miss Maggie Okey. Her delicate touch and irreproachable mechanism were delightfully manifested in some short pieces by Raff, Rubinstein, and Weber, after which she was thrice recalled. Madame Néruda led Brahms's fine Septet in G, and Miss Liza Lehmann sang, among other things, Dessauer's pretty *bolero* " Le Retour du Promis." Dr. Joachim's re-appearance on Monday was as usual the occasion of a gala evening. A larger crowd may have been associated with this annual event, but never a heartier display of warmth. The great violinist and his companions, Messrs. Ries, Straus, and Piatti, were recalled twice after a magnificent interpretation of Beethoven's E minor Quartet (Op. 59), and they wound up the Concert with an equally fine rendering of Haydn's Quartet in B flat (Op. 64, No. 5). Dr. Joachim's glorious playing in the *Adagio* from Spohr's Sixth Concerto roused a perfect storm of applause, and he added for an encore the Scherzo (Op. 135), by the same composer. Miss Agnes Zimmermann was the pianist, and Miss Lehmann again sang. At the succeeding afternoon Concert the combined appearance of Grieg and Joachim drew one of the largest crowds ever seen at a Popular Concert. It was the first occasion on which these eminent musicians had been heard together in a London Concert-room. Dr. Joachim led off with Mozart's String Quintet in D (No. 8), with Messrs. Ries,

Hollander, Gibson, and Piatti for his coadjutors. Next came Madame Grieg, accompanied, of course, by her husband, whose songs, "A lovely evening" and "Hope," she sang charmingly. Then the composer returned alone and played his deliciously quaint Suite "in the old style" ("Aus Holbergs Zeit"), which, as arranged for string orchestra, was given at the last Birmingham Festival. His lovely touch and refined phrasing found ample scope for display in this clever imitation of harpsichord music. The succeeding item was that which brought the two heroes of the afternoon together—viz., a Sonata by Grieg in G minor, for pianoforte and violin (Op. 13), not previously given at these Concerts. Although not less characteristic of its composer's style than the familiar work in F (Op. 8), it scarcely conveys the same impression of spontaneity and freshness; it is more elaborate in treatment and development, and presents greater executive difficulties. Nevertheless, the Sonata is piquant and interesting, while the rendering it now received was only to be expressed by the word perfection. The composer and his gifted associate vied with each other in the brilliancy and charm of their playing, and roused their auditors to a display of unrestrained enthusiasm. Afterwards Madame Grieg sang more songs, and this memorable Concert concluded with a fine performance of the Fragments from an unfinished Quartet (*Andante* and *Scherzo*) by Mendelssohn. Another attractive constellation was provided at the evening Concert of the 11th, when Madame Néruda and Dr. Joachim performed in their own incomparable manner Bach's D minor Concerto for two violins. The programme further included Beethoven's Quartet in F minor (Op. 95), Schumann's "Faschingsschwank aus Wien," played by Miss Fanny Davies, and some songs artistically interpreted by Miss Marguerite Hall. On Saturday, the 16th, Beethoven's Quartet in C minor (Op. 18, No. 4) received an ideal interpretation at the hands of Messrs. Joachim, Ries, Straus, and Piatti; and the same master's "Sonata Pastorale" was given by Mdlle. Janotha in her best manner. Dr. Joachim was heard with Mr.

Straus in Spohr's Duo Concertante for two violins in A minor
(Op. 67), and with Mdlle. Janotha and Signor Piatti in Schumann's F major Pianoforte Trio (Op. 80). Fräulein Fillunger
sang songs by Schubert and Brahms. On the Monday following Dr. Joachim gave Tartini's "Trillo del Diavolo," while
Madame de Pachmann played three Chopin Studies. Mr. Santley
was the vocalist both at this and at the afternoon Concert of the
same week, the programmes of which were wholly familiar. On
Monday, the 25th, Miss Davies and Dr. Joachim played the
" Kreutzer" Sonata ; and on the 30th Herr and Madame Grieg
appeared for the last time. The Norwegian musician introduced
his characteristic " Lyric Pieces " (Op. 43), and with Madame
Néruda he played his duet Sonata in C minor (Op. 45), already
heard more than once, but a fresh addition to the Popular repertory. It has never, perhaps, been so splendidly performed. The
" Queen of Violinists " also led Dvorák's String Quartet in E flat
(Op. 51) and Schubert's *Allegro assai* in C minor.

   The Wind Instrument Chamber Music Society, an institution
newly formed under the Presidency of Lord Chelmsford, for the
purpose of performing works written for wind and stringed
instruments, started operations this month. The Society, in
addition to giving Concerts, aimed also at promoting the publication of works and offered prizes for new compositions. Thus
twenty guineas were now offered for a Quintet for flute, oboe,
clarinet, bassoon, and horn. Three Concerts were given during
the season at the Royal Academy of Music, and the first of these
took place on the 22nd. Three works were then given—
namely, Beethoven's Quintet in E flat (Op. 16), a Quintet in the
same key by Mozart, and a Sonata, bearing the title of " Undine,"
for pianoforte and flute, by Reinecke. The executants were—
flute, Mr. Vivian ; oboe, Mr. Malsch ; clarinet, Mr. G. A. Clinton ;
horn, Mr. Borsdorf ; bassoon, Mr. T. Wotton ; and pianoforte,
Mr. Eugene Dubrucq.

   The Westminster Orchestral Society gave a Concert on the
13th, at which was performed for the first time a Symphony in C,

written by the Society's Conductor, Mr. C. S. Macpherson. It proved to be a work of unequal merit, the two middle movements being the best of the four. At the same Concert Miss Winifred Robinson played Dr. Mackenzie's Violin Concerto, the composer conducting, and Miss Kate Norman and Mr. Ernest Birch sang.

The Annual Festival of the London Sunday School Choir took place at the Royal Albert Hall on the evening of the 23rd. The executive forces occupied the whole of the available space, and, in addition to a body of some 1,500 voices, selected from the various metropolitan districts, there was a band of eighty instrumentalists, whose co-operation furnished a new and valuable feature in the proceedings of the Society. To this was partly attributed the marked advance now shown over the performances of previous years. The Conductor, Mr. Luther Hinton, made manifest a perfect control over his executants. The first part of the programme consisted of sacred music.

Perhaps the most attractive and eventful of the month's Recitals was that given at St. James's Hall, on the 20th, by Herr Grieg, with the assistance of his accomplished wife and M. Johannes Wolff. This excellent violinist joined the composer in the duet Sonata in C minor (Op. 45), while the latter was heard alone in his Suite "Aus Holbergs Zeit," and some short solos—namely, a delicate Berceuse in G, the Humoreske (one of his earliest pianoforte pieces) in G sharp minor, and the "Norwegian Bridal Procession." The clever and genial Norwegian Dances (Op. 35), for four hands, were charmingly rendered by the husband and wife. Madame Grieg sang besides some of the best known of the composer's songs.

Mr. Max Pauer gave a Recital at Princes' Hall on the 7th. Mr. Robert Goldbeck, a pianist from New York, gave a *soirée musicale* at Steinway Hall on the 19th, and exhibited elegance and refinement of style in various pianoforte works, including a Concerto of his own composition. On the 20th Miss Margaret Wild executed a long and exacting programme of pianoforte music at her Recital at Princes' Hall.

Mr. Carrodus gave a series of "Drawing-room" Concerts at the new Hampstead Conservatoire Hall, assisted by his sons and other talented artists. Among the works performed may be mentioned a Quintet in A, by Kuhlau, for flute and strings, wherein the wind instrument was played by Mr. W. O. Carrodus, a young executant of much promise; also a Pianoforte Quartet by Mr. H. R. Rose, who himself presided at the piano. At the Concert of the 18th Mr. Carrodus "led" a Piano Quartet in E flat by his master, Molique; and another of his sons, Mr. E. Carrodus, distinguished himself in a solo for contra-bass.

Herr Stavenhagen, an incomparable interpreter of the music of his late master, Liszt, gave at his Recital at Princes' Hall, on the 27th, magnificent performances of the difficult Sonata in B minor and two of the Paganini-Liszt Studies. Herr Stavenhagen also gave Haydn's Variations in F minor, Schumann's Papillons (Op. 2), and Beethoven's Sonata in A flat; and though at times too demonstrative, his playing showed intelligence and feeling of a high order. The programme concluded with an unprinted version of Liszt's Rhapsody (No. 13). There was a large and enthusiastic audience.

The programme of Miss Dora Bright's third and last Pianoforte Recital, on the 27th, comprised pieces by Sir G. A. Macfarren, Dr. Mackenzie, Mr. G. J. Bennett, and others. Miss Bright played the last four of Mr. Walter Macfarren's twelve new Studies, and gave a satisfactory reading of Beethoven's Sonata in D minor (Op. 31, No. 2).

Miss Ethel and Master Harold Bauer gave a Concert of Chamber Music at Princes' Hall, on the 26th, when, among other items, they performed Sonatas for piano and violin by Brahms (Op. 100) and Grieg (Op. 45)—both difficult works and exceedingly well played. Concerts and Recitals were also given this month by Mr. Isidore de Lara, Mr. de Manby Sergison, and Mrs. Charles Yates.

An interesting Pianoforte Quartet in A minor, by Mr. J. S. Shedlock was played for the first time on Sunday evening, the

10th, at one of the South Place Institute Concerts, given under the direction of that talented musician. The work, which is in the usual four movements, created a highly favourable impression, and was warmly applauded.

OBITUARY.—Dr. W. H. Monk (organist, composer, and teacher), London, 1st; Sydney Smith (pianist and composer), London, 3rd; Enrico Tamberlik (operatic singer), Paris, 13th; Felice Varesi (operatic singer), Milan, 18th; Charles F. T. Steinway (pianoforte manufacturer), Brunswick, Germany, 25th; Vaughan-Edwardes (concert singer), Kingston-on-Thames, 26th.

APRIL.

CONSIDERABLE interest attached to the production, by the Royal Choral Society, on the 3rd, of M. Peter Benoit's Oratorio, " Lucifer." As the first important choral work that emanated from the " leading light " of the new Flemish musical school—a work composed in 1865, produced at Brussels in 1866, and given in Paris in 1883 with marked success—" Lucifer " had special claim to a hearing in a country so peculiarly the home of oratorio as this. It is not, perhaps, the form of oratorio we most like or are most accustomed to. It lacks the relief afforded by regular solo numbers interspersed amid choruses, concerted pieces, and declamatory passages—a shortcoming that must be partly attributed to the Flemish poet, Emanuel Hiel, whose picturesque verse stops short at many a point where descriptive or reflective utterances for a single voice would supply the necessary relief, besides creating links between the various scenes. There is no connected story, and little, if any, dramatic action. *Lucifer* is the only personage who appears, mankind being unrepresented save in a collective sense as the recipient of the blessings and gifts of nature. The three Elements, Earth, Water, and Fire, whose aid *Lucifer* invokes in his attempt to incite man to rebellion against God, are embodied by solo singers —Earth by a bass, Water by a tenor, and Fire by a soprano and a contralto in combination. The supreme climax of the subject, which would be the actual battle between the forces of *Lucifer* and Heaven, is passed over altogether. Perhaps the author did not think music capable of describing it, or perhaps it was the composer who regarded as sufficient the task of illustrating the means employed by the elements, without venturing to depict the struggle itself. Unfortunately the result of this omission is to deprive the work of what coherent dramatic interest it might possess, and to leave it a more or less disconnected series of "tone-pictures." M. Benoit's music possesses the originality which comes of systematic striving after the unconventional rather than a natural and spontaneous inspiration. He splashes his colour upon the canvas with an effect that may sometimes be striking, but is more often crude and coarse. His capacity for developing his themes is extremely limited, and he is thus led to indulge in excessive repetition, with a result that is undeniably monotonous. Benoit makes comparatively sparing use of the lighter materials of his art, preferring to rely upon massive choral effects, elaborate antiphonal treatment, and contrasts and surprises of the most startling kind. The better to carry out this purpose, he has written nearly the whole of the choruses for double choir, a device which enables the composer on occasion to fling his exclamatory phrases, like re-echoing thunderbolts of sound, from side to side of the orchestra. In this manner some remarkable effects are obtained, as, for example, in the number that describes *Lucifer's* defeat, where Death mocks him with a weird "Ha! ha! ha!" Benoit's infelicitous employment of *Leitmotives* serve to recall the fact that "Lucifer" was written a quarter of a century ago, when Benoit knew more of Berlioz than of Wagner. On the other hand, that he then knew how to write graceful, rhythmical melody is clearly manifested by the charming solos for the tenor and bass voices. If "Lucifer" did not satisfy as a work, it at least supplied the medium for an interesting experience, for more striking choral effects have rarely, if ever, been heard in the Albert Hall. The ease with which Mr. Barnby's intelligent singers surmounted every formidable obstacle evoked the warmest admiration. The placid beauty of the opening chorus, the tumultuous agitation of the number that follows, the noble impressiveness of the "Hosanna" in the third part, and the broad, massive grandeur of the final chorus of praise were, indeed, very finely realised. The performance, on the whole, was excellent. Of the Belgian vocalists who came over to take part in it, M. Blauwaert, who sang the part of *Lucifer*, displayed a superb low baritone voice and good declamatory method. M. Constantin de Bom (an amateur) undertook the tenor, and M. Henri Fontaine the bass solos. Madame Lemmens-Sherrington and Madame Patey jointly sustained the music allotted to Fire; the former re-appearing after a lengthened absence—her organ wonderfully well preserved, and her style as artistic as ever. There was a moderate attendance, but no lack of applause, certain numbers being very warmly received. Mr. Barnby conducted in masterly fashion.

A first-rate performance of Handel's " Saul " was heard at the last of the Novello Oratorio Concerts on the 9th. Mr. Lloyd was not well enough to sing, but his place was efficiently filled by Mr. Henry Piercy, who has rarely been heard to such good advantage. The other solos were well sustained by Miss Anna Williams, Madame Patey, Mr. Gawthrop, and Mr. Watkin Mills. The band and chorus were in their best form. During the " Dead March " the audience remained upstanding as a mark of respect to the late Duchess of Cambridge. Dr. A. C. Mackenzie, who conducted with his usual care and spirit, received a hearty ovation at the end of the evening. The subsequent decision not to resume these Concerts occasioned widespread regret. Distinguished throughout by high artistic aim and exceptional completeness of execution, the discontinuance of this undertaking constituted a serious loss, so far as the Metropolis is concerned, to music generally and oratorio in particular.

On the 15th the Borough of Hackney Choral Association revived Brahms's " German Requiem," not heard in London since its performance by the Bach Choir some years before. The solos were sung by Madame Eleanor Farnol and Mr. W. G. Forington, and Mr. Ebenezer Prout conducted. On the 6th the Popular Musical Union gave their first performance of Gounod's " Redemption " at the People's Palace, Mile End, under the leadership of Mr. W. Henry Thomas. A Concert of Sacred Music was given at Princes' Hall on the 17th, at which Mr. J. H. Bonawitz's "Requiem" and a selection of miscellaneous pieces were performed. The solos were undertaken by Miss Alice Steel, Miss Louise Bourne, Mr. Charles Karlyle, and Mr. Max Heinrich, who proved equal to their somewhat exacting task. Mr. Bonawitz conducted. In the miscellaneous part the ladies' choir (trained by Mr. Charles Karlyle) sang a difficult "Ave Maria," by Lachner. Another "Ave Maria," for soprano solo, by Luzzi, was neatly sung by Miss Alice Steel, who joined Messrs. Karlyle and Heinrich in a Trio by Astorga. Mr. Heinrich's rendering of "With joy the impatient husbandman," from the "Creation," was warmly applauded.

The Good Friday musical entertainments in and near London were eagerly patronised. The Royal Choral Society gave its usual "Messiah" performance, the solos being sung by Madame Nordica, Madame Belle Cole, Mr. Banks, and Mr. Mills. This was the Society's last Concert of the season. At the Crystal Palace and the Alexandra Palace there were capital Sacred Concerts, and in the evening an immense crowd assembled in St. James's Hall at the bidding of Mr. Ambrose Austin, to hear Rossini's "Stabat Mater" and a selection of "Gems from the Oratorios." The newly-arranged Easter Musical Festival at the Great Assembly Hall, Mile End Road, started with "The Messiah," Miss Anna Williams, Madame Marian McKenzie, Mr. Harper Kearton, and Mr. Egbert Roberts being the soloists. This highly creditable undertaking continued with performances of "St. Paul," "Elijah," and "Belshazzar."

A large and enthusiastic audience greeted the famous Russian composer, Tschaikowsky, on his re-appearance at the Philharmonic Concerts on the 11th. He was accompanied this time by a *protégé*, M. Sapellnikoff, who played his Pianoforte Concerto in B flat minor (Op. 23), first introduced at the Crystal Palace in 1876, and therein displayed a *technique* of astonishing brilliancy and vigour. Tschaikowsky also conducted his Orchestral Suite in D (Op. 43), a work of considerable charm and rare musicianly resource, now heard by an English audience for the first time. Of its five divisions, the Fugue, the quaint Divertimento, and the characteristic Intermezzo proved most deserving of admiration; but the greatest effect was made with the curiously-scored " Marche Miniature," an apparent attempt to imitate a musical-box, the repetition of which was insisted upon. The final Gavotte movement and its noisy, inappropriate *Coda* are decidedly weak. The work was splendidly given, and at the end the composer was recalled. Mozart's Symphony in E flat and the Overture to "Lurline" respectively opened and closed the Concert, these items being conducted by Mr. Cowen. The vocal element was supplied by Miss Marguerite Hall and Mr. W. H. Brereton, who made their *débuts* at the Philharmonic Concerts, and were both recipients of loud applause.

Berlioz's "Faust" was given at the Crystal Palace Concert on the 6th before a full audience. Mrs. Hutchinson took Madame Valleria's place as *Margaret* at the last moment, Mr. W. H. Brereton was the *Mephistopheles*, and Mr. Edward Lloyd the *Faust*. There was only a moderate attendance at the next Concert—the last of the series. The programme included the *Andante* from Mr. T. Wingham's graceful Serenade in E flat (first time here), and a new Pianoforte Concerto in C minor, by Mr. J. C. Ames, an English pianist and composer, who had studied in Stuttgart and Dresden. The Concerto introduced by that admirable player, Mr. Oscar Beringer, is marked Op. 8 in the list of Mr. Ames's works, which further embraces such ambitious efforts as a String Quartet, a Choral setting of a Psalm, a Pianoforte Trio, and a Violin Concerto. However, the composition now heard did not create a very lively impression. Schubert's Symphony in C and Sterndale Bennett's " Naïades " Overture were also in the scheme. Miss Macintyre sang.

One feature in Mr. Manns's annual benefit Concert at the Crystal Palace, on the 20th, alone sufficed to render it memorable. This was the production of a new Symphony in C minor (Op. 1), composed by Mr. Frederic Cliffe. Mr. Cliffe, a native of Bradford, was one of the students at the National Training School, and is a Professor at the Royal College of Music. He came forward with little, if any, reputation as a composer, and, that he had never written any serious works of importance was sufficiently indicated by the Opus number of his present effort. Surprise that a young musician should offer a Symphony as his Opus 1 deepened into astonishment when the *coup d'essai* proved to be worthy in all respects of the eulogium of the eminent analytical writer who described it to Sydenham amateurs. The latter were genuinely delighted. They scarcely waited for the last chord before calling up the composer, and then, after cheering him heartily, they paid him the rare compliment of bringing him forward a second time. Truth to tell, Mr. Cliffe's Symphony in C minor is a work of surpassing merit, so rich in promise that if the young composer can only go on as he has begun, there must be a brilliant future in store for him. No appreciative listener could fail to be struck with the beauty and originality of Mr. Cliffe's themes, the clearness and power that mark their development, the rare sense of symmetry and contrast pervading each movement, and the fertile command of orchestral resource displayed throughout. Mr. Cliffe is a man with ideas, and he knows, it is evident, how to express them. The musician who can take a simple phrase out of his slow movement, and enlarge and glorify into the wonderfully grandiose *Coda* that forms the ending of this Symphony, must be made of more than common stuff. Not that this is the only device imparting homogeneity to the various sections of the work. Perhaps some day an "analyst" will discover the frequent recurrence all through of the two beats which start the opening *Allegro*, and try to invent a meaning for them, as was done for the "four taps" in Beethoven's Symphony in the same key. Of the four movements, the *Scherzo* is perhaps the least striking, while the slow movement, or *Ballade*, is the most attractive and spontaneous. Madame Nordica, Madame Tremelli, Mr. Brereton, and Herr Stavenhagen took part in the

Concert, and Mr. Manns received a hearty farewell greeting at its close. The famous Conductor had deserved well of his supporters. He had conducted an interesting series of Concerts with indefatigable energy and consummate skill; and he had wound up his labours by bringing to the front a young native composer of exceptional promise.

Madame Néruda and Dr. Joachim repeated at the Monday Popular Concerts of the 1st their matchless performance of Bach's Concerto in D minor, for two violins. Both at this and the following afternoon Concert the work done was of an entirely familiar nature, Miss Fanny Davies playing short compositions by Mendelssohn, while Mr. Max Heinrich and Miss Florence Hoskins were the vocalists. The audiences were now invariably crowded, as they usually are when the last of the " Pops " is drawing near. On the 8th Dr. Joachim played Bach's " Chaconne " and led Beethoven's Posthumous Quartet in B flat—two masterpieces in which he is inimitably grand. Madame Frickenhaus played the Sonata Appassionata. On Saturday, the 13th, the instrumental scheme was all Beethoven—the String Quintet in C, the Violin Romance in F, the " Moonlight " Sonata, and the " Kreutzer " Sonata—a combination that caused the largest crush of the season, and the biggest rush for balcony seats ever experienced at a " Pop." Dr. Joachim's coadjutors were, in the Quintet, Messrs. Ries, Straus, Gibson, and Piatti; and in the Romance and the " Kreutzer," Mdlle. Janotha. Mr. Hirwen Jones sang. At the final Concert of the series, on the Monday following, the most attractive item in an attractive programme was the Schumann Pianoforte Quintet in E flat (Op. 44), performed by Miss Agnes Zimmermann, Messrs. Joachim, Ries, Straus, and Piatti. This was a superb treat, intensely appreciated. Next in order may be placed the Haydn Quartet in B flat (Op. 76, No. 4), executed by the same matchless combination of string players. Signor Piatti's perfect rendering of the *Largo* and *Allegro*, by Veracini, elicited a demonstration of unusual warmth, and so, too, did the performance of some of the

Hungarian Dances, by Dr. Joachim and Mdlle. Janotha. Miss Fanny Davies was entrusted with the only pianoforte solo — a distinction well earned by her services during the season and thoroughly justified by her charming playing in Chopin's Barcarolle. Another English favourite at the "Pops," Miss Liza Lehmann, was the only vocalist of the evening. She sang an old English song, "Oh listen to the voice of Love," Schubert's "Schlummerlied," and "Hark, the lark," and her own pretty song "If thou wilt be the falling dew," winning equal acceptance in all. Mr. Frantzen accompanied. After the Concert a portion of the audience met in another part of the building, for the purpose of witnessing the presentation to Dr. Joachim of a Stradivarius violin, subscribed for by his English friends and admirers in honour of the fiftieth anniversary of his first appearance in public. In presenting the gift on behalf of the subscribers, Sir Frederick Leighton delivered one of his most elegant speeches; and Dr. Joachim, when he had recovered from his emotion, made a reply full of simple modest feeling, genuine gratitude, and kindly allusions to dear friends, some living, some now no more. The wonderful "deep red" Cremona cost £1,200, and the fine Tourte bow accompanying it was obtained as a favour for £50. Dr. Joachim was right, therefore, when he described the gift as a noble one. But more than all was its value great as embodying the unbounded admiration and esteem in which the "king of violinists" is held by English amateurs.

At the Royal College of Music Orchestral Concert, on the 4th, a Pianoforte Concerto in G minor by a student, Mr. Sidney P. Waddington, was played for the first time. It proved to be a clever and elaborate work, and in all respects an achievement full of high promise. The difficult solo part was splendidly played by another student, Miss Polyxena Fletcher. At the close the composer, who had played the drums, was twice called forward. The scheme also included the Overture to "Die Meistersinger," Brahms's double Concerto for violin and cello (Messrs. Jasper Sutcliffe and W. H. Squire), Bizet's Suite "L'Arlésienne," and the Septet from Goetz's "Taming of the Shrew." Professor Stanford conducted.

Some good work was done at the Royal Academy Orchestral Concert on the 20th. Miss Amy Clapshaw displayed a pleasing voice and style in " Bel raggio," and Mr. Edwin Houghton a bright, resonant, tenor voice in an air from Dr. Parry's " Judith." Mr. Gerald Walenn gave evidence of decided progress in his violin solo, and of the pianists chief praise may be awarded to Miss Dora Matthay and Mr. Gilbert R. Betjemann. The only work by a student in the scheme was Mr. Theo. Ward's *Andante* for organ, harps, and stringed orchestra, already performed by the Strolling Players' Orchestral Society. Dr. Mackenzie conducted. The balance of the choir was anything but satisfctory, male voices being still in an absurd minority.

At the Guildhall School Concert on the 3rd was performed a new romantic Cantata for female voices, entitled "Zitella," written by Mr. D. H. Parry, and composed by Mr. R. Orlando Morgan. The work was admirably given under Mr. Weist Hill, and well received.

A String Quartet in E, by Dvorák (Op. 80), was heard for the first time in England, among a group of other more or less interesting novelties, at Mr. Harvey Löhr's eighth annual Concert, given at Princes' Hall on the 5th. The most striking of the four movements contained in this thoroughly characteristic work is the *Andante con moto* in A minor, based upon a beautiful, original melody of the Slavonic type. The *Scherzo* is genial and graceful, while the final section is full of animated spirit and contrapuntal resource. Capitally played, Dvorák's Quartet made an impression that led to its speedy repetition. Also new to London amateurs were a Pianoforte Trio in C minor (Op. 27), by Eduard Schütt, a well-designed, melodious work; and Mr. Harvey Löhr's Pianoforte Quartet in E minor (Op. 15), the latter of which (published by Breitkopf and Härtel) consists of the four usual movements, all remarkably clear in structure and development and characterised by considerable melodic charm. This effective work was very well received. Mr. Löhr played as solos some pieces of his own, and a set of twelve "Silhouettes" (Op. 8), by Dvorák, one of the Bohemian composer's early pianoforte works, now given here for the first time publicly. The string players who assisted were Messrs. Szczepanowski, S. D. Grimson, W. Richardson, and W. E. Whitehouse.

The young Scotch pianist, Mr. Frederick Lamond, evinced a gratifying amount of improvement at his Recital on the 10th. He made his re-appearance in the metropolis after an absence of three years, and the meagre audience that occupied St. James's Hall justly made up for paucity of numbers by unusual warmth of approbation. Mr. Lamond, now came before us not only a brilliant executant, but a refined and finished artist, and he more especially proved himself such by his interpretation of Beethoven's Sonata in A flat (Op. 110). On the 17th he gave a second Recital, which was much better attended. He now appeared in the double capacity of pianist and composer, the programme containing two "Clavierstücke," Nos. 6 and 7, from his Op. 1, a Pianoforte Trio in B minor (Op. 2), and a Sonata for violoncello and piano, in D major. Of these works the Trio is at once the most ambitious and the most imbued with strength and feeling; but it is like its companions in that it betrays a want of restraint fraught with very wearisome results for Mr. Lamond's hearers. The young Scotchman has ideas, but his form is vague, his movements are diffuse, his style is rhapsodical. There is evidence in Mr. Lamond's music of a talent for composition, and he may one day write with less of the headstrong spirit of youth and more regard for the "canons of art." Mr. Straus and Signor Piatti acted as Mr. Lamond's coadjutors, and, like himself, threw all their intelligence and energy into the work in hand. In his solos the Recital-giver once more impressed by the earnest sentiment and charm of his playing.

Miss Agnes Zimmermann's Recital, on the 4th, drew a numerous assemblage to Princes' Hall, and among other things finely played by this talented artist may be mentioned a particularly impassioned and intellectual rendering of Schumann's Pianoforte Sonata in G minor. Recitals were also given in course of the month by Miss Mathilde Wurm, Miss Ethel and Master Harold Bauer, Mr. Max Heinrich, Mr. Isidore de Lara, and Messrs. Ernest Paxon and Orton Bradley.

Little can be said in favour of "Faddimir," a comic opera by Mr. Arthur Reed and Mr. Oscar Neville, produced at the Vaudeville Theatre on the 29th. The music might have passed muster had the book been less extravagant and nonsensical, but as it was the combination was barely tolerable. The plot depended solely for its motive and humour upon the question whether the inhabitants of a Russian town were or were not to be compelled to wash themselves with soap! The chief parts were taken by Mr. Eric Thorne, Mr. Herbert Reeves, Mr. Wilfrid Shine, Miss Lily Linfield, and Miss Florence Perry.

The news of the death of Mr. Carl Rosa, in Paris, on the morning of the 30th, came as a shock to the whole country. By the decease of this popular *impresario* English Opera was deprived of its champion and its chief source of strength. Carl Rosa had during the last few years of his life become associated with various branches of musical and theatrical enterprise, and he had shown that their transfer to a limited company could be attended by advantage to himself and profit to his shareholders. His name will, however, be always associated with the prosperous revival of opera in the vernacular, more especially between the years 1875 and 1885, when, thanks to his courage and enthusiasm, native musicians were brought to the front as opera-writers, the works of Wagner and other modern composers were given for the first time in the English language, and the lyric stage in the provinces was raised to a higher level than it had ever before attained.

OBITUARY.—Sir Frederick Arthur Gore Ouseley (composer; Professor of Music at Oxford University), Hereford, 6th; Carl Rosa (founder of the Carl Rosa Opera Company), Paris, 30th.

MAY.

THE Royal Italian Opera season began at Covent Garden on Saturday, the 18th, under the management of Mr. Augustus Harris, whose operatic interests had shortly before been made identical with those of the Carl Rosa Company. On the opening night Bizet's Opera "Les Pêcheurs de Perles" was given in the presence of a brilliant and crowded assemblage, who, if they were not enchanted with the music of Bizet's early opera, manifestly enjoyed the performance, and did not tire of gazing round the elegant house, radiant in all the glory of fresh decorations and filled from the floor to the first tier with the cream of the British aristocracy, headed by Royalty in the persons of the Princess of Wales, her daughters, and the Duchess of Edinburgh. Miss Ella Russell, as *Leila*, and Signor F. d'Andrade, as *Zurga*, made the chief successes, their duet in the last act kindling the one spark of enthusiasm for which the music afforded a loophole. M. Talazac, formerly leading tenor at the Opéra Comique, was not quite at home in his part or in the new *locale*. The *mise en scène* was a vast improvement on that of 1887, and some alterations made by Signor Mancinelli tended slightly to strengthen the final scene. The orchestra, with Mr. Carrodus as *chef d'attaque*, was again superb at all points; while the chorus was quite equal to that of the previous year. In "Faust," on the 20th, Miss Macintyre proved herself a sympathetic and engaging *Marguerite*, though scarcely strong enough dramatically in the later scenes. M. Montariol, a Belgian tenor, made a successful *début* as *Faust*, displaying an agreeable and tolerably powerful voice. M. Winogradow, the Russian baritone, made a capital *Valentine*. Signor Castelmary was an effective *Mephistopheles*, and Madame Scalchi was the *Siebel*. "Carmen," on the following night, was given under the direction of that capable and experienced *chef d'orchestre*, Signor Arditi, who met with a warm greeting. Madame Marie Roze was the *Carmen*, and her rendering of the character as to all save its vocal requirements was quite perfect. Miss Macintyre's beautiful voice was heard to rare advantage in the music of *Michaela*. Signor Francesco d'Andrade was the *Toreador*, and his brother, Signor Antonio d'Andrade, was received with favour on making his first bow here as *Don José*. The new tenor had a rather small voice of good telling quality, which he used with skill; moreover, he was an actor of some intelligence and power. A performance of "La Traviata," with Miss Ella Russell in the title-part, was followed by one of "Aïda," on the second Saturday of the season, the Prince and Princess of Wales being present. An encouraging amount of success was won by Madame Valda in the part of *Aïda* and by Signor Antonio d'Andrade in that of *Radamès*. The lady sang with artistic feeling, and presented a picturesque, interesting embodiment. The tenor, albeit over-weighted, compensated for physical shortcomings by an abundance of earnest spirit and vigour. His brother made, as usual, a superb *Amonasro;* Madame Scalchi acted better than she sang as *Amneris;* and Signor Abramoff was the *Ramphis*. Signor Mancinelli conducted the performance of "Aïda," and also that of a companion masterpiece of the modern Italian school, to wit, Boïto's "Mefistofele," given before another brilliant audience on the 28th. In the latter work Miss Macintyre now sustained the part of *Marguerite* as well as that of *Helen of Troy*, and did it equal justice. Signor Massimo Massimi, a Russian tenor, with a small voice and most unimpressive style, made an unsuccessful *début* as *Faust*. Signor Novara, who undertook the difficult *rôle* of *Mefistofele* at a moment's notice, fairly earned on his merits the suffrages of the audience. Mr. Barton McGuckin, who was to have made his Italian *début* in "Lohengrin," on the 30th, had the misfortune a day or so before to injure an ankle. His place in this opera was taken by Signor A. d'Andrade. Madame Nordica made her *rentrée* as *Elsa*, a character she had never previously undertaken. She invested it with rare sympathy and charm, and acted throughout with admirable intelligence. The music lay well within her means, and the fresh, bright quality of her voice enhanced the beauty of more than one familiar passage. Madame Fürsch-Madi was an interesting *Ortrud*, Signor F. d'Andrade a splendid *Telramund*, Signor Castelmary an excellent *King*, and Signor Abramoff an efficient *Herald*.

The special attraction at the fourth Philharmonic Concert on the 9th was the *début* of a Belgian violinist, M. Ysaÿe, who gave an intelligent, though somewhat affected, reading of the Beethoven Concerto. He exhibited a fine tone and a superb *mécanisme*, but critical hearers objected to his restless, fussy style, and the lack of breadth and dignity in his phrasing. The fact remains that he made a complete conquest over his audience, and was so enthusiastically received that the Philharmonic directors at once engaged him for their next Concert. Mr. Cowen conducted one of Haydn's Symphonies—an early work in B flat, only recently published, and now given for the first time in London—and his own clever, if unequal, Symphony in F (No. 5), which showed off the splendid orchestra to rare advantage. Mdlle. Tremelli was the vocalist; but neither in a Rossinian air nor the "Voce di donna" from Ponchielli's "Gioconda" was the style of the singer satisfactory. At the fifth Concert of the series (the 23rd) M. Ysaÿe's performance of the Mendelssohn Concerto was a brilliant display of virtuosity, and a decided improvement upon his reading of the Beethoven. He again had an ovation. Mdlle. Janotha played Beethoven's Pianoforte Concerto in G, and Herr Carl Meyer, of Cologne, sang Wolfram's Fantasy ("Tannhäuser") and a Ballad by Loewe with declamatory power and feeling. The most interesting item in a long programme was a new Symphony in C, for small orchestra, composed in 1887 by Dr. Hubert Parry. This was received with the unqualified favour due to a work of singular beauty and merit. The essentially English character of the themes was at once recognised, and the work quickly became known as the " English " Symphony. Elaborate in construction and detail, it yet came out on first hearing as clear and comprehensible as a Suite of Handel's or an Overture of Mozart's. It is brimful of life and spirit, the vigour of the quick movements being at times extraordinary. The *Finale* gives the idea of a succession of lively Old English tunes and dances; actually, it is a set of elaborate variations on a single theme. The slow movement, in grateful contrast, contains a delicious flow of suave melody, and is exquisitely scored. The new Symphony was played by the Philharmonic orchestra (*minus* trombones, tubas, contrafagotti, or the heavier " percussion " instruments) with a refinement and delicacy beyond all praise, the composer conducting.

The Richter Concerts began on Monday, the 6th, with a wholly familiar programme, embracing the Overture to " Die Meistersinger," the Prelude to " Parsifal," Brahms's Variations on a theme by Haydn, Liszt's Second Hungarian Rhapsody, and Beethoven's " Eroica " Symphony. With the orchestra at its highest level of excellence, and the *bâton* in the hands of Dr. Hans Richter, it may be taken for granted that these pieces were magnificently played. Each, too, was applauded with enthusiasm by a crowded and fashionable audience. At the second Concert, on the 13th, the *bonnes bouches* of an unusually varied programme were Beethoven's " Leonora " Overture (No. 3), Mozart's " Prague " Symphony, and Wagner's " Good Friday's Spell " from " Parsifal." Glinka's " Komarinskaja," clever as it is, becomes monotonous ; and Schumann's Symphony in B flat (No. 1) was not faultlessly given. On the other hand, a week later, the execution of a Wagner programme (in honour of the master's birthday) constituted the finest performance of a series of Wagnerian excerpts ever heard under Hans Richter's direction. The great Conductor and his men were heart and soul in their work, and whether realising the poetic beauty of the " Siegfried-Idyll," the sublime grandeur of the " Trauermarsch," the profound passion of the "Tristan" music, or the sonorous energy of the "Walkürenritt," the result in each case approached as near to perfection as could be. In the love duet from "Die Walküre" Miss Anna Williams declaimed the part of Sieglinde, and Mr. Edward Lloyd, as heretofore, that of Siegmund. At the Concert of the 27th the indisposition of Mr. Edward Lloyd prevented the promised introduction of the "Schmiedelieder," from "Siegfried." In the regretted absence of the English tenor an overflowing crowd consoled itself by listening to a repetition of some of the instrumental excerpts played at the previous Concert, in addition to Beethoven's "Pastoral" Symphony and Mendelssohn's "Athalie" Overture.

The Bach Choir gave an afternoon performance of Dr. Parry's Oratorio "Judith," at St. James's Hall, on the 6th, before a crowded assemblage. Miss Anna Williams, Miss Lena Little, Mr. Edward Lloyd, and Mr. Watkin Mills were the soloists, and Professor Stanford conducted. The work was again well received, the composer being called at the end of each part. The choruses were by no means irreproachably given, the balance being imperfect and the attack wanting in vigour. Miss Lena Little sang the music of the Queen-mother for the first time, and proved herself a worthy exponent of the lovely ballad which she sings to the children. The great mistake of the afternoon was giving the Oratorio in its entirety; it merely served to emphasise the advantage gained by the "cuts" introduced in the preceding performances.

Señor Sarasate made his first appearance for the season at St. James's Hall on Saturday, the 11th, inaugurating with his accustomed success a series of six Concerts, four of which were orchestral. The audience was large, and the gifted Spanish *virtuoso* received a hearty and spontaneous welcome. He performed three works—viz., Max Bruch's Second Concerto (D minor, Op. 44), Raff's *morceau caractéristique*, "La Fée d'Amour," and his own Fantasia on Airs from "Carmen," displaying in each the transcendent powers of execution and indescribable charm of style which have won for him a unique position among the popular violinists of our day. Mr. Cusins conducted, and, in addition to an excellent rendering of the accompaniments, secured a creditable performance of Liszt's Symphonic Poem "Tasso" and Mendelssohn's Overture to "Athalie." On the following Saturday Señor Sarasate played the Mendelssohn Concerto and the Violin Concerto in G by Emile Bernard. His first Chamber Concert on the 25th did not draw the same overflowing crowd; but it was a very large audience, and not a whit less demonstrative. The Concert began with Weber's Duo Concertante (Op. 48), a work written for clarinet and pianoforte. The arrangement for violin is ineffective, and it was surprising that Señor Sarasate should have shown so little respect for the intentions of a great master as to bring forward this unwarrantable piece of work. He also took part in Schubert's "Rondeau Brillant," Raff's Sonata in A (Op. 78), and four of Dvorák's "Slavonic Dances." The *virtuoso's* coadjutor in these compositions was Madame Berthe Marx, a new pianist possessing an undoubtedly fine *technique* and crisp, but not very sensitive touch. The lady played as solos Chopin's Barcarolle and a Study by Rubinstein, exhibiting plenty of control over the keyboard, but little command of varied expression.

Sir Charles Hallé began his weekly Chamber Concerts at St. James's Hall on the 10th, the programme containing as a novelty one of the recently-published Quartets of Cherubini. The opening *Allegro maestoso*, in the key of E major, is classic both in form and character. The *Larghetto* is graceful, though somewhat long. The *Scherzo*, written for muted strings, has a good deal of character, but appears patchy. The bright *Finale* is, on the whole, the most satisfactory of the four movements. A point worthy of notice is the humour displayed by the composer in the *Codas* of the *Larghetto* and *Finale*. The quartet was admirably interpreted by Madame Néruda and Messrs. Ries, Straus, and F. Néruda. The programme concluded with Dvorák's fine Pianoforte Quintet in A (Op. 81). Sir Charles Hallé played two of

Schubert's Impromptus, and took part with Madame Néruda in Beethoven's Sonata in G (Op. 96). The only unfamiliar item in the scheme of the following week was a new composition from the pen of Signor Giuseppe Martucci, whose Pianoforte Trio in E flat (Op. 62) revealed a style as advanced as that of his countryman, Signor Sgambati, and lucid and interesting in about the same degree. Forty minutes of this tedious kind of music proved rather trying, despite such talented interpreters as Madame Néruda, Sir Charles Hallé, and Herr F. Néruda. On the 24th was performed, for the first time, an Album-Sonata in C flat, written by Wagner in 1853 for his wife's friend, Frau Wasendonck. The composition consists of a single movement, not in strict form, but very pleasing and effective in character, and decidedly redolent of Beethoven. It was listened to with curiosity and the player was much applauded. Sir Charles also played with Lady Hallé the new Sonata by Brahms in D minor (No. 3, Op. 108), introduced this month by Miss Fanny Davies. A week later another of the posthumous quartets of Cherubini was brought forward—that in F (No. 5)—by many regarded as the finest of the series.

The Sonata by Brahms, for pianoforte and violin (D minor, Op. 108), to which reference has just been made, was performed for the first time in England at a Concert given by Miss Fanny Davies, in Princes' Hall, on the 7th. The new work proved to be nowise inferior in charm and grace to the preceding Sonata for the same instruments (Op. 100). That it is its equal in all other respects may be taken for granted, since Brahms only gives to the world music stamped with the impress of his individuality and power, and replete with evidence of his unlimited technical resource. The *Adagio*, based upon a lovely melody taken from one of his own songs, is the gem of the four movements, but all are models of clearness and symmetry, and the Sonata may be listened to with delight from first to last. Miss Davies and Herr Ludwig Straus played it admirably, and were warmly recalled. The popular young pianist was heard alone in Sterndale Bennett's Toccata and Schumann's Sonata in F sharp major. She also accompanied the latter composer's " Spanisches Liederspiel "— restoring the usually omitted "Spanische Romanze"—the vocalists being Fräulein Fillunger, Miss Hilda Wilson, Mr. W. Shakespeare, and Mr. Ffrangcon Davies.

Mr. Ernest Kiver's annual Concert, given at Princes' Hall on the evening of the same day, was made noteworthy by the first performance in public of a String Quartet in G minor, by Mr. T. Wingham, heard a few weeks previously at the Brompton Oratory. It is a short but interesting work in the usual four movements, each of which reveals the hand of the skilled and earnest musician. The opening *Allegro con fuoco* is bright and energetic and the themes are well contrasted. The second movement is an *Arietta con variazioni*, founded on the melody composed by Samuel Webbe to the hymn " O Roma felix," sung on the Festival of St. Peter and St. Paul. The variations are scarcely such in the strict sense of the term, the theme being repeated in each as a *canto fermo* with varied contrapuntal treatment, while the concluding variation is in the form of a canon with double counterpoint. The *Minuet*, written as a canon on the octave, is another striking example of scholarly resource, while the *Finale* terminates with an effective reference to the melody of the hymn. This clever work was ably played by Messrs. Szczepanowski, George Wilby, Ellis Roberts, and Charles Ould, and so well did it please the audience that the composer had to leave his place in the hall and bow his acknowledgments from the platform.

Mr. William Nicholl gave the last of a pleasant series of Chamber Concerts at Steinway Hall on the 3rd. The programme consisted (with the exception of a couple of violin solos played by Miss Lucy Riley) of sets of songs by various composers, so well contrasted in character as to preclude any sense of monotony. First came Brahms's " Gipsy Songs " (Op. 103), well interpreted by Miss Louise Phillips, Miss Marguerite Hall, Mr. William Nicholl, and Mr. Wilfred Cunliffe. Then Grieg's "Reminiscences of Mountain and Fjord " were alternately rendered by Miss Hall and Mr. Nicholl; and "Four Songs of the Stuarts," composed by

Miss Carmichael (given for the first time), were divided in similar fashion between Miss Phillips and Mr. Cunliffe. Miss Carmichael's new songs won special favour. The Concert ended with "Three Songs of the North," arranged by Mr. Malcolm Lawson, and tastefully sung by Mr. William Nicholl.

Messrs. Ludwig and Whitehouse gave their second Chamber Concert at Princes' Hall on the 14th, when, aided by Messrs. G. Collins, A. Gibson, and H. Heydrich, they did justice to Brahms's Quintet in F (Op. 88) and Beethoven's Quartet in B flat (Op. 18, No. 6). Grieg's duet Sonata in C minor was spiritedly played by Mr. Ludwig and Madame Haas, while Mr. Whitehouse's violoncello solos elicited warm applause. Miss Liza Lehmann sang.

A MS. Sonata for harp and violin, by Spohr, was introduced at Princes' Hall, on the 8th, by Mdlles. Marianne and Clara Eissler, to whom the score was recently presented by the composer's niece. It is a thoroughly characteristic work, rich in melodic charm, and most effectively written for both instruments. It was played with grace and finish by the two sisters, whose programme further included violin and harp solos, and some pianoforte pieces executed by Miss Freda Eissler.

Concerts were given at St. James's Hall, on the 1st and 8th, by the String Band of the Royal Artillery, under the direction of Mr. L. Zaverthal. At the second Concert a new Symphony in C minor, composed by the Conductor, was produced with great success, the *Scherzo* being especially noticeable for the brightness of the subject and the ingenuity of its construction. The clever scoring of the whole work further testified to the musical ability of the composer.

The Wind Instrument Chamber Music Society gave the third and last of its opening series of Concerts at the Royal Academy of Music, on the 3rd. A Concertstück, by Rietz (Op. 41), and Rubinstein's Quintet (Op. 55) for pianoforte and wind instruments were the principal works performed, the executants being Messrs. Vivian, Malsch, Clinton, Borsdorf, T. Wotton, and

Eugène Dubrucq. Four Trios, by Brahms, for female voices, with accompaniment of horns and harps (Op. 17), were also given by a select choir of Academy students.

Herr Waldemar Meyer gave a Chamber Concert at Princes' Hall on Wednesday afternoon, the 22nd, at which he played, among other pieces, Bach's "Chaconne," Handel's Sonata in A, and a Suite for violin and pianoforte by Franz Ries. In the rendering of these compositions Herr Meyer exhibited his usual excellent qualities, and he had an able coadjutor in Herr Gustav Ernest. Some vocal pieces were sung by Frau Schoepffer, a Dresden artist, who displayed a powerful soprano voice and good artistic style.

Miss Winifred Robinson's programme, at her Chamber Concert at Princes' Hall on the 31st, included Dvorák's duet Sonata in F (Op. 57), executed with Miss Fanny Davies; the *Adagio* and *Rondo* from Spohr's Ninth Concerto; and Mendelssohn's Trio in C minor (Op. 66), the violoncello part in this being undertaken by Mr. C. H. Allen Gill.

Dr. Charles Vincent gave a Concert on the 9th, at the Drill Hall, Hampstead, when his Cantata "The Mermaid," for ladies' voices, was performed for the first time. The libretto, founded upon Hans Andersen's fairy tale, is the work of Mr. Lewis Novra. The music is easy, tuneful, and pleasant. The work was given under the composer's direction.

The Amateur Choral and Orchestral bodies of the metropolis were extensively occupied throughout the present month, which, as usual, was one of the busiest of the whole year. Their doings, however, must necessarily be recorded with the utmost possible brevity. The Royal Amateur Orchestral Society, now in its seventeenth season, gave exceedingly attractive Concerts at the St. James's and Princes' Halls, and performed well-chosen programmes with great spirit and care, under Mr. George Mount. The same observation applies to the Stock Exchange Orchestral Society and Male Voice Choir, directed by Mr. George Kitchin, which rising body made a distinct advance, and gained, by its really excellent performances, the unqualified commendation of connoisseurs. The Strolling Players' Orchestral Society also gave a number of agreeable and fashionably-attended Concerts, under the Conductorship of Mr. Norfolk Megone. The Westminster Orchestral Society ended its series of Concerts of works by living English composers on the 29th. Mr. Hamish MacCunn's Ballad "The Ship o' the Fiend," Mr. Goring Thomas's graceful Airs de Ballet, Mr. Cowen's " Welsh " Symphony, and Miss Dora Bright's Pianoforte Concerto (played by the composer) were the principal compositions heard on this occasion. On the 29th, at the Portman Rooms, the Handel Society performed Bach's " Magnificat," Mozart's Symphony in D, and Handel's music in Smollett's " Alceste." Mr. F. A. W. Docker conducted. Among the suburban societies which, at about this time, finished up their season's work in creditable style, may be mentioned the Highbury Philharmonic Society, which, on the 6th, attacked Berlioz's " Faust," and, under Mr. G. H. Betjemann's able guidance, scored a distinct success; the Clapham Choral Society (under Mr. Walter Mackway), the St. Mary's Choral Society (under Mr. Sidney Hann), the Primrose Hill Choral Society (under Mr. George Calkin), the North-East London Choral Society (under Mr. John E. West), the Streatham Choral Society (under Mr. Charles S. Macpherson), the St. James's Choral Society (under Mr. R. Felix Blackbee), and the West Hackney Choral Society (under Mr. F. L. Kett).

The Bristol Orpheus Glee Society paid a visit to London on the 28th and gave a Concert at St. James's Hall, under the direction of its talented Conductor, Mr. George Riseley. The refinement and delicacy with which this well-balanced and well-trained body of voices executed a varied selection of part-songs elicited hearty and unanimous praise. A wish was expressed that the Society might repeat its visit another year.

The Musical Guild, a Concert Society consisting of ex-scholars and ex-students of the Royal College of Music, gave the first of a series of four Concerts of Chamber Music at the Town Hall,

Kensington, on the 22nd. This project received abundant encouragement from the College authorities, many of whom were among the audience that assembled to start the new undertaking. The opening piece of the programme was Schubert's Quintet in C (Op. 163), which received a highly meritorious rendering at the hands of Messrs. Jasper Sutcliffe, Wallace Sutcliffe, Emil Kreuz, W. H. Squire, and J. T. Field. Schumann's Pianoforte Trio in F (Op. 80) was performed by Miss Annie Fry, Miss Winifred Holiday, and Mr. W. H. Squire; and the remaining pieces comprised a pianoforte solo played by Miss Marian Osborn, a viola solo for Mr. Emil Kreuz, and some songs given by Miss Anna Russell and Mr. Daniel Price, Mr. Frederic Sewell accompanying. The vocal pieces included refined compositions by Mr. Charles Wood and Mr. W. E. Duncan, also former pupils at the Royal College. The programme of the second Concert, on the 29th, included Mozart's String Quintet in G minor, Bach's Concerto in D minor for two violins (played by Messrs. Haydn Inwards and Arthur Bent), and Mendelssohn's Octet in E flat (Op. 20).

The Shinner Quartet gave a Concert at Princes' Hall on the 15th, when, under the leadership of that painstaking young violinist, Miss Emily Shinner, an interesting programme was gone through. In Brahms's Quintet in F minor these clever ladies had the assistance of Miss Agnes Zimmermann.

The more important Recitals of the month may be briefly passed in review. Madame Frickenhaus had a numerous audience at Princes' Hall on the 4th. Her rendering of Beethoven's Sonata in E (Op. 109) was marked by especial refinement and intelligence. Miss Dora Schirmacher's Pianoforte Recital on the 15th in the same hall was chiefly interesting for the first performance in England of three short pieces by Beethoven, published in 1888 by Breitkopf and Härtel. The first of these was an Allegretto in C minor—a crisp, characteristic little movement, written about 1796—and the others were "Bagatellen," written in 1797. Herr Schönberger was heard at his best at the

Princes' Hall on the 21st. His choice of works was also irreproachable, excepting perhaps the Liszt transcriptions of Bach's Organ Fugues, which satisfied only as a medium for technical display. Herr Schönberger pleased his hearers by his thoughtful, refined interpretation of Beethoven's early Sonata (Op. 2, No. 3), and another admirable performance was that of Schubert's Sonata in C minor.

M. Vladimir de Pachmann gave the first of two Chopin Recitals at St. James's Hall on the 27th. The meagre attendance was dispiriting, but this admirable artist has never interpreted his favourite master more delightfully. His scheme included the Sonata in B flat minor, the Fantasia in F minor, the Allegro de Concert in A, the Ballade in G minor, and various minor pieces. On the following day Mdlle. Janotha gave an attractive Recital at the same Hall, assisted by Madame Néruda and Madame Antoinette Sterling. On the 30th Miss Jeanne Douste gave a Pianoforte Recital, the programme of which consisted exclusively of works by Chopin. Her selection included the Mazurka in F sharp major, which, as Mr. Ernst Pauer clearly demonstrated some years ago, was never written by Chopin at all, but by Karl Mayer. The Mazurka is included in the Klindworth edition of Chopin's works, but it appears with a note frankly stating its authenticity to be doubtful. As a matter of fact, the publisher, Gotthard, was deceived by a Polish Countess, who came to him in distress, and sold him the manuscript as the autograph of "her illustrious compatriot," whereas it was undeniably Mayer's composition, and copied out after his death in imitation of Chopin's handwriting. Mr. Lawrence Kellie gave Vocal Recitals at Steinway Hall on the 7th and 28th, at which he brought forward numerous songs from his own pen.

A so-called romantic Comic Opera in three acts, entitled "Mignonette," by Messrs. Oswald Brand and Henry Parker, was produced at the Royalty Theatre on the 4th, but met with no success.

A capital musical version of the old farce, "The Area Belle," bearing the title of "Penelope," composed by Mr. Edward Solomon to lyrics written by Mr. George P. Hawtrey, was produced at the Comedy Theatre on the 9th, and most favourably received. On the same afternoon Mr. Robert Goldbeck gave, at Devonshire House, a Concert performance of the music of his "American Opéra Comique," entitled "Newport." The solos were undertaken by Miss Florence Wright, Miss Sybil Grey, Miss Rosina Brandram, Messrs. William Foxon, Wallace Brownlow, and John Thorman. A small chorus and orchestra assisted, while Mr. and Mrs. Goldbeck helped in the accompaniments at a grand pianoforte.

OBITUARY.—Augustus L. Tamplin (organist), London, 8th.

JUNE.

The Italian season at Covent Garden pursued its course in a manner satisfactory to manager and opera-goers alike. On Saturday, the 1st, Madame Albani returned in "La Traviata"; another old favourite, Signor Cotogni, playing *Germont père*. In the following week six performances were given, starting with "La Sonnambula," which was revived for the *rentrées* of Miss Marie Van Zandt and M. Edouard de Reszke. The young *prima donna*, cordially welcomed after a lengthy absence from the London operatic stage, afforded veritable pleasure by an embodiment as fresh and interesting as when it introduced her to us at Her Majesty's some eight years before. Her voice had slightly increased in power, while her vocalisation was characterised by the same delightful neatness and charm as of yore. M. Edouard de Reszke imparted unusual dignity to the part of the *Count*, and sang his music with rare beauty of voice and style. M. Montariol was the *Elvino*, and Mr. Randegger conducted. On the Tuesday M. Jean de Reszke re-appeared in "Aïda," and started for the season with a brilliant triumph. Madame Nordica was a sympathetic *Aïda;* Mdlle. Jane de Vigne, a young mezzo-soprano with a pleasing voice and well-cultivated style, made a successful *début* as *Amneris*, and Signor Cotogni played *Amonasro*. "Le Nozze di Figaro" drew a full house on the Wednesday, the cast being strong at all points. Madame Albani as the *Countess*, Miss Ella Russell as *Susanna*, and Signor Cotogni as *Figaro* repeated familiar impersonations with all the old success; while Miss Marie Van Zandt made a charming *Cherubino*, and Signor F. d'Andrade essayed the part of the *Count* with the best possible results. Altogether it was an exceedingly good performance of Mozart's comic masterpiece that Signor Arditi conducted. On the Thursday "Rigoletto" served to re-introduce Madame Melba, whose performance as *Gilda* revealed a manifest improvement, both from a vocal and histrionic standpoint, in the abilities of this talented artist. M. Lassalle also made his first bow for the season as the *Jester*, a part he had not played here before. He sang in French, presenting an embodiment that was picturesque, interesting, and full of strength. M. Montariol was the *Duke*, Madame Scalchi sang *Maddalena* in her usual style, and Signor Novara made a first-rate *Sparafucile*. On the Friday "Faust" was given with an almost complete change of cast. Madame Nordica was the *Marguerite*, and her rendering of the character once more afforded unalloyed pleasure. M. Talazac was seen to better advantage as *Faust* than in his previous impersonations. M. Lassalle made, as heretofore, a splendid *Valentine*, and another performance *hors ligne* was M. Edouard de Reszke's *Mephistopheles*. The week wound up with a brilliant performance of "Lohengrin," the cast including M. Jean de Reszke as *Lohengrin*, with Madame Albani as *Elsa*, M. Edouard de Reszke as the *King*, and a new Belgian baritone, M. Seguin, as *Telramund*. On Tuesday, the 11th, M. Lassalle was too indisposed to appear in "Guillaume Tell," and the title-part was filled by M. Seguin, who sang it in French, and acquitted himself on the whole remarkably well. He displayed a voice of excellent quality, if somewhat limited range, and sang and acted like a thorough artist. Mdlle. Lita, a Roumanian soprano, made a not very successful *début* as *Mathilde*. M. Lestellier re-appeared after several years' absence in the part of *Arnold;* but his voice sounded worn, and he took his high notes with difficulty, besides not invariably singing them in tune. M. Edouard de Reszke was of immense assistance in the great trio, while the Choral Finale in the Gathering of the Cantons was magnificently rendered. In "Don Giovanni," two days later, Signor F. d'Andrade filled the part of the hero with distinction and grace, but M. Lestellier gave no more satisfaction as *Don Ottavio* than he had as *Arnold*. Signor Ciampi appeared as *Leporello*, Miss Van Zandt making a charming *Zerlina*, Madame Valda a thoroughly competent *Elvira*, and Madame Fürsch-Madi a dramatic *Donna Anna*. The general performance, under the experienced guidance of Signor Arditi, left little to be desired.

On Saturday, the 15th, Gounod's "Roméo et Juliette" was produced at Covent Garden for the first time in French. The representation commanded the favour of a brilliant audience, and remained a regular attraction until the end of the season. The general opinion was that the opera was far more enjoyable when heard in the original tongue than it had ever proved when sung in the Italian version. Moreover, M. Jean de Reszke's *Roméo* approached more nearly to the Shakespearian ideal than that of any singer or actor seen during the last two or three generations. He was, indeed, *Roméo* in all but the boy-lover's years; and even that disparity was forgotten in the admiration aroused by his handsome presence, his refined, noble bearing, and his impassioned style. The great tenor had in Madame Melba a *Juliette* not unworthy to share his success. She looked the part fairly well, she sang with rare vocal grace, employing her beautiful voice with invariable taste and *aplomb;* and, thanks to increased emotional intensity, she was able to do adequate justice to the histrionic requirements of the *rôle*. In the various duets of the opera these two artists won an emphatic triumph. M. Edouard de Reszke was, as in days gone by, an incomparably fine *Frère Laurent;* while M. Montariol as *Tybalt*, M. Winogradoff as *Mercutio*, M. Seguin as *Capulet*, Signor Castelmary as the *Duke*, Mdlle. Jane de Vigne as *Stefano*, and Madame Lablache as *Gertrude* complete an *ensemble* calculated to fill the *habitués* of the Grand Opéra with envy. The opera was mounted in magnificent style, the chorus (which sang in French very creditably) appearing in new costumes. Signor Mancinelli was the Conductor. On Monday, the 17th, Mr. Barton McGuckin made, as *Lohengrin*, his first appearance in Italian Opera. Although somewhat nervous at the outset, he sang his music with his accustomed declamatory vigour and finish. He looked the part well, and acted it intelligently. Mr. McGuckin obviously possessed the sympathies of his audience, and fairly divided honours with Madame Albani. On the following night "Les Huguenots" was given with a powerful cast. M. Jean de Reszke again made a glorious *Raoul*, and Signor F. d'Andrade a capital *Nevers*. The *Marcel* of M. Edouard de Reszke and the *St. Bris* of M. Lassalle were new assumptions here, and both proved remarkably fine in every respect. Miss Ella Russell appeared as the *Queen* and Madame Scalchi as *Urbano*. The part of *Valentine* was entrusted to a well-known Viennese artist, Mdlle. Toni Schläger, who now made her London *début*. She was terribly nervous; but this did not prevent her achieving a considerable success. She exhibited the qualities of dramatic singer and an actress of experience. Her upper notes, however, had lost their freshness, and she did not look the character. The choruses in Meyerbeer's masterpiece were grandly given, but the band was noisy, and at times even rough. After this there succeeded a series of repetitions until the 29th, when "Il Trovatore" was given, with Mdlle. Schläger, Madame Lablache, M. Lestellier, and Mr. Leslie Crotty in the cast, the last-named artist making his first appearance on the Italian stage in this country.

Mr. Mapleson began a season of Italian Opera at Her Majesty's on Saturday, the 1st, with a representation of "Il Barbiere di Siviglia," given under the direction of Signor Bevignani. Only a section of the chorus was available, but in other respects there was little fault to be found with the manner in which Rossini's opera was rendered. Madame Gargano, a light soprano, with a flexible, well-trained voice, and considerable stage experience, made a favourable *début* as *Rosina*; Signor Vicini, a new tenor, acquitted himself creditably as *Almaviva*; and Signor Padilla was the *Figaro*. The house being re-decorated and re-upholstered throughout, presented an unusually bright appearance. On the following Tuesday "La Sonnambula" was performed, with

Mdlle. Regina Pacini, a youthful soprano, also new to the London boards, as *Amina*. Madame Gargano appeared on the Thursday in " Lucia di Lammermoor." Another new tenor, Signor Warmuth, made a fairly acceptable *Edgardo*, and Signor Galassi was, as in byegone days, a good *Enrico*. A week later " Faust " was mounted, with Mdlle. Zélie de Lussan (who appeared as *Carmen* at Covent Garden one night during the 1888 season) as the *Marguerite*. She made a sympathetic and pleasing exponent of the character. Mdlle. Bellincioni made her *début* as *Siebel*, and Signor Palermini, another new-comer, proved himself the possessor of an agreeable baritone voice and artistic method in the part of *Valentino*. Signor Runcio re-appeared as *Faust*, and Signor Darvell was a moderate *Mephistopheles*. Later on " Il Trovatore" was given, with Mdlle. Dotti, Mdlle. Tremelli, Signor Warmuth, and Signor Galassi in the cast ; but it did not draw. In fact, the audiences here were consistently meagre. A new tenor, Signor Sindona, made his first appearance in *Lucia*, and met with little success ; but somewhat better results attended the *début*, on Tuesday, the 25th, in " Rigoletto " of Miss Minnie Ewan, a young American soprano of considerable promise. She sang *Gilda's* music very prettily indeed. Signor Galassi sustained his old part of *Rigoletto*, Signor Warmuth made a passable *Duke*, and Mdlle. Bellincioni was the *Maddalena*. This opera was mounted with new dresses and scenery ; but it proved to be only the final flicker before the candle went out. The house did not open on the Saturday night for the repetition of " Faust," and the first appearance of Madame Sembrich, announced for the following Monday, never took place. Truth to tell, Mr. Mapleson was *au bout de ses ressources ;* for the season had been one of steady loss, and agencies were at work that proved too powerful for the veteran *impresario* to battle against.

Several performances were given this month of Professor Herkomer's new pictorial music-play, entitled " An Idyl," the production of which created a lively curiosity in artistic circles. To say that it represented a distinct advance upon the experiment of the preceding year is to tell but the barest truth. The marvellous realism of the scenes and the effects of light; the quaint simplicity of the story and the personages; the charm and interest of the music, and the unique conditions marking the performance could not fail to imbue the spectator with a profound admiration for the genius of the man from whose brain and fingers the whole thing emanated. The points of difference between Mr. Herkomer's earlier "romantic fragment" and the present piece are that the latter is in three acts instead of one, that it embodies a clear and dramatic story, that it contains some accompanied dialogue, and that the musical setting generally is on a more elaborate scale. A series of graceful lyrics from the pen of Mr. Joseph Bennett supplies the groundwork for solos, recitatives, and choruses, these being connected by a continuous *mélodrame* (music illustrating action *without* words), which the composer has contrived to invest with rare appropriateness, and at times with dramatic power. Added to these features of progress there was now an increase in the size of the stage and a consequent enlargement of the various pictures, which included a beautiful sunlit scene. The rising of the curtain discloses the narrow street of an English village in the fourteenth century, with a blacksmith's forge on one hand, a row of quaint old houses on the other; and in the background, beyond the old cross at the meeting of the roads, a stretch of undulating landscape, growing dim amid the warm grey twilight of harvest-time. John, the smith, and his assistants take from the roaring fire of the forge a lump of red-hot iron, and proceed to beat it upon the anvil, their hammers keeping time with the rhythm of the music. The old people sit on benches and watch the work. They sing a chorus, "Sinks the sun adown the west," peaceful and flowing in character, interrupted by a tripping passage for the boys as they dance round in a ring. Anon a hunting party passes through the village, then the sound of the Angelus is heard, and then a kind of *berceuse* is played by the orchestra as an aged Granny gathers the children round and tells them a story. Meanwhile, the smith has been approaching the end of his day's labour. He has sung his bright old-fashioned song, "Dobbin waits in penthouse here," beating time on the anvil as at first, and his men have taken off their aprons and put up the shutters of the smithy. Now the moon begins to rise—as it only does at Bushey and in nature—and the reapers return singing their animated chorus in 6-8 measure, a cleverly-written number, ending with a quaint ecclesiastical cadence. *Edith*, the smith's pretty daughter, heads the band; she is warmly embraced by her father, and *Dick-o'-the-Dale*, her manly lover, watches her with anxious glance, for she is not so tender and kind as usual. It is now nearly dark, and a dance is called for, but there is no one to play the rebeck *Edith* is holding, until suddenly young *Fitz-Hugh*, the lord of the hall, who has for some time been gazing upon the scene, comes forward and gently takes the instrument from her hand. He mounts the anvil and quickly sets all dancing to an old jig, a brisk, lively tune (9-8 time), at the conclusion of which the villagers disperse and make for home. *Edith* lingers dreamingly at the threshold, and in the soft moonlight the enamoured *Fitz-Hugh* steals up and addresses her in sweet words and suavest melody. His song, musically speaking, may be a trifle rhapsodical, but it is very impassioned, and evidently goes straight to the maiden's heart. Ultimately she tears herself away and rushes indoors, whilst *Fitz-Hugh* departs trolling a serenade. His retreating figure is watched by the old smith, who has come out again and is deeply moved by what he fears will be a dark cloud in the sky of his daughter's happiness. The orchestral *mélodrame* here grows almost tragical in its intense agitation, and so continues until the curtain has fallen upon the scene. A rather lengthy introduction precedes the second act, the scene of which is laid in the interior of the smith's dwelling. The blue moonlight streams in at the window, and on the other side of the room stands the fireplace, aglow with burning logs, above which hangs the steaming pot containing the family supper. The music changes to a gay theme as *Meg*, the servant-maid, and *Jack*, the apprentice, proceed to lay the supper-table. They sing and quarrel and chase each other, the first violin meantime performing sundry realistic skakes and runs. Then the smith and the others enter and take their places. When grace is said all rise and turn towards the crucifix, and there is a little religious bit of music that reminds one of Gounod. As the meal is served we hear a charming passage for orchestra, and then comes the talk at the supper-table, uttered by each in turn to a quaint pastoral theme with varied accompaniment. Allusions are made to the young lord's behaviour; *Edith* protests; the others reply; ultimately the smith, commanding silence, leaves the table. When they are alone he calls his daughter to his side, and, meaning to warn her of her danger, sings her an old ballad, "There lived a maid in Avondale," relating the fate that befel a winsome lass who deserted her true lover for a "gay young lord." *Edith* understands, for when left alone she repeats snatches of the ballad, and then bursts into tears. As she does so the voice of *Fitz-Hugh* is heard singing a serenade full of melodious grace, accompanied by a harp. The girl's agitation is complete when the daring young fellow enters the room; but happily *Dick* is at hand, and he leads her out. Then comes an interview between the two men, embodying at once the best dramatic situation and most dramatic music in the play. The opening recitative, with trombone accompaniment, wherein *Dick* begins to upbraid the youthful lord, contains some rather long and awkward pauses; but the solo is interesting and expressive, and works up to a really admirable climax. *Fitz-Hugh*, moved by *Dick's* appeal, leaves the place. *Edith* re-enters to find her lover weeping, but she quickly throws herself into his arms, and amid another passionate strain of music the act ends. The third scene, showing the village street once more under the rich light of a noonday sun, opens with a delicate passage for the strings and wood-wind, leading to a flowing, subdued melody, during which a couple of strolling mummers enter the lonely scene. In the most comic manner they sing a fragment of an old ballad, and accompany each other, pausing ever and anon as they look up at the houses for the gifts which no one bestows. The reason why the village is deserted soon becomes apparent. A religious chant is heard in the distance, and the sound of an organ. The bells peal, boys enter singing a pretty "flower chorus" as they strew the path with blooms, and soon a bride and bridegroom, no other than *Edith* and *Dick*, are seen heading the procession on its way back from church. Thus all ends amid smiles and happiness, while the young lord himself comes down from the hall to wish the newly-wedded couple every joy, and add his congratulations to those expressed by the villagers in strains of full, rich harmony. To sum up, Professor Herkomer's score revealed a wonderful wealth of ideas, and his mastery of orchestral colour and device excited the surprise of musicians. The performance of this remarkable play was excellent. The Professor himself impersonated with great success the homely smith, Miss Dorothy Dene made a charming representative of *Edith*, and the other parts were all in well-trained hands. The chorus was thoroughly competent, and the band worthy of a conductor such as Dr. Hans Richter, who honoured alike himself and the gifted painter in directing this notable artistic undertaking.

Mendelssohn's "Elijah" was performed on Saturday afternoon, the 22nd, upon the Handel Orchestra of the Crystal Palace, with a chorus of 2,900 and a band of 363 players, Mr. August Manns conducting. Glorious weather favoured the undertaking, and the attendance was, in consequence, enormous. More than 24,000 persons passed the turnstiles, these figures being largely in excess of the previous record for any but Handel Festival Concerts, and then only for certain rare performances of "The Messiah" or "Israel in Egypt." The summer Concerts at which the "Redemption" and "Golden Legend" were given on a Handel Festival scale were not attended by anything near the above numbers; while the sale of reserved seats was also without precedent—all of which goes to show that the popularity of "Elijah" is founded on a solid basis, and that amateurs gladly seized the opportunity to hear it under the unique conditions attained at Sydenham. How grandly the "Baal" choruses, the "Thanks be to God," the "Be not afraid," and other massive choruses would sound might have been imagined beforehand; and the realisation was assuredly on a level with one's highest anticipations. Scarcely once throughout the entire afternoon did the huge choir waver or hesitate in its attack. The quality and volume of tone were magnificent, and some of the effects created in the numbers referred to were supremely fine. Truly, the cheers which rewarded Mr. Manns were well and bravely earned. Madame Albani sang the whole of the soprano solos, and in "Hear ye, Israel," her clear tones rang through the vast space like the ringing notes of a clarion. Mr. Edward Lloyd also made a fine effect in "If with all your hearts," and Madame Patey had an ovation after "Rest in the Lord." In the absence from England of Mr. Santley, Signor Foli was entrusted with the music of the Prophet, and although it was at times too high for him, he acquitted himself, on the whole, exceedingly well. The concerted pieces went capitally, efficient service being here lent by Miss Emily Squire, Miss Jessie King, Mr. Maldwyn Humphreys, Mr. Ffrangcon Davies, and Mr. Plunket Greene. Mr. A. J. Eyre presided at the organ.

The most conspicuous feature in the Philharmonic Concert of the 6th was a terrific thunderstorm. It did its best to upset Madame Backer-Gröndahl during the performance of Beethoven's "Emperor" Concerto, and to destroy some of the most delicate effects in Mr. Frederic Cliffe's new Symphony in C minor. Fortunately the elements outside came off only second best in the struggle. The Scandinavian pianist—an executant and interpreter of the first order—maintained her coolness in a wonderful manner. A more beautiful or successful rendering of this Concerto has not been heard for a long time, and the audience would not be satisfied until Madame Gröndahl had returned three times to the platform. Mr. Cliffe conducted the performance of his Symphony, which was received with a degree of enthusiasm not inferior to that which marked its production at the Crystal Palace a few weeks before. Connoisseurs agreed that it was a most extraordinary work for an Opus 1, and it is certainly replete with rare interest and technical ability from the first bar to the last. The Overtures to "Anacréon" and "Die Zauberflöte," the introduction and closing scene from "Tristan," and some vocal pieces (artistically sung by Fräulein Fillunger), made up the balance of the programme, Mr. Cowen wielding the *bâton* as usual. At the afternoon Concert, on the 22nd, which brought the Philharmonic season to a close, the instrumental works performed under Mr. Cowen's direction were the "Eroica" Symphony, the Overture to the "Flying Dutchman," and Sullivan's Overture "Di Ballo." M. de Pachmann played Chopin's Andante Spianato and Polonaise (Op. 22), and for an encore Henselt's Study "Si oiseau j'étais." Signorina Teresina Tua also appeared, and after executing splendidly Max Bruch's Violin Concerto in G minor, was likewise called upon for a *bis*. The clever Italian artist gave a movement from one of Bach's Sonatas. Fräulein Hermine Spies (a German mezzo-soprano whose *début* at the Richter Concerts is recorded below) was the vocalist, and her courage in attempting the contralto air, "Return, O God of Hosts," from Handel's "Samson," was rewarded by complete success—that is, if rapturous applause may be accounted such. Still, despite her good English accent and broad, artistic delivery, the audience naturally preferred her rendering of a couple of Germn *Lieder*. In these (accompanied by Herr Francesco Berger) Fräulein Spies was simply incomparable. The Philharmonic season of 1889 was both artistically and pecuniarily satisfactory.

At the Richter Concert, on the 3rd, the famous Viennese *chef d'orchestre* conducted fine performances of Weber's "Euryanthe" Overture, Wagner's "Tannhäuser" Overture, an excerpt from the "Nibelungen," and Brahms's Symphony in F, No. 3. The chief attraction of the evening, however, was the singing of Fräulein Hermine Spies, who achieved a distinct success, despite the fact that she began badly with Gluck's "Che farò." Fräulein Spies spoiled the air by her incorrect Italian pronunciation. But in the songs by Schubert, Schumann, and Brahms she fairly surpassed every other *Lieder* singer who had preceded her in English Concert-rooms. The voice is a rich, mellow mezzo-soprano, beautifully produced, and capable of the most delicate modulations of colour—a gift which enables Fräulein Spies to achieve highly effective dramatic contrasts. For example, in " Der Tod und das Mädchen " one might have imagined the utterances of *Death* and the *Maiden* to be delivered by two different singers; so again in the dialogue of Brahms's " Vergebliches Ständchen," despite the speed at which this was taken. The talents of the new artist commanded instant and emphatic recognition. On the following Monday evening there was a crowded room, the scheme including Schubert's glorious Symphony in C, Schumann's " Manfred " Overture, Dvorák's " Symphonic Variations," *Hans Sachs's* Monologue from Act II. of " Die Meistersinger,", and, for the first time, the long closing scene from Act III. of " Die Walküre." Miss Fillunger and Herr Carl Mayer sang splendidly in the last-named excerpt, the only familiar portions of which were *Wotan's* " Abschied " and the " Feuerzauber." There was a brilliant crowd at the Richter Concert given on the 24th in conjunction with the Wagner Society, whose annual gathering in honour of the master's memory was thereby made to assume a form worthy of its object. The Richter Choir assisted, and took part in an extensive selection from Wagner's works, including *Sachs's* " Address to Walther " (sung by Mr. Max Heinrich) and the closing chorus from " Die Meistersinger "; the " Verwandlungsmusik " and " Graal-Feier," from Act I. of " Parsifal "; and the " Kaisermarsch," which was performed as originally written, with chorus. The " Parsifal " excerpt was exceedingly interesting, and, although the voices were not always refined nor the bells quite in tune, the effect of this beautiful music was quite impressive. The closing scene from Act I. of " Siegfried " was also given for the first time at these Concerts. Mr. Edward Lloyd sang the music of *Siegfried*, and Mr. William Nicholl that of *Mime*, and the former's rendering of " Schmiedelieder " (Smithy songs) created quite a *furore*. Mr. Lloyd also sang the "Farewell to the Swan," from the last act of "Lohengrin," declaiming this also with the rarest intelligence and charm of style. The Overture to "Rienzi" and Sachs's Monologue, "Wahn, Wahn!" made up the balance of one of the most attractive Wagner schemes and one of the best executed ever heard in this country. Dr. Hans Richter conducted with consummate ability, and was again and again enthusiastically applauded.

Señor Sarasate at his third Concert, on the 1st, performed the Beethoven Concerto (playing a marvellous cadenza in the first movement), Saint-Saëns's Concerto in B minor (No. 3), and his own "Zigeunerweisen." There was again an enormous attendance. A week later the Spanish artist gave his second Chamber Concert with the co-operation of Madame Berthe Marx. They played together the "Kreutzer" Sonata, Schubert's Fantaisie (Op. 159), and Raff's "Fée d'Amour." Several encores were asked for and granted, one being evoked by Madame Marx's execution of the Liszt Rhapsody (No. 12). The lady certainly exhibited a fine *technique*. St. James's Hall was filled to its utmost capacity at the last Concert of the series, on the 15th, and the demonstrations that marked the final appearance of the famous fiddler were of the heartiest description. He was heard in Mackenzie's Violin Concerto, in Lalo's "Symphonie Espagnole" for violin and orchestra, and in a Duet for two violins, entitled "Navarra," composed by himself and played with Miss Nettie Carpenter. The band, admirably conducted by Mr. Cusins, was also heard in Beethoven's "little" Symphony in F, and the Overture to Lalo's Opera "Le Roi d'Ys."

Raff's effective Pianoforte Quartet in C minor (Op. 202) was introduced for the first time at Sir Charles Hallé's Chamber Concert on the 7th; and on the following Friday Cherubini's Quartet in A minor—the last he ever wrote and the sixth of the posthumous string quartets—was brought forward. On the 21st the scheme included the new Quartet, by Dvorák, in E (Op. 80), produced at Mr. Harvey Löhr's Concert in April, and Brahms's

Trio in E flat (Op. 40) for pianoforte, violin, and horn. The series of these Concerts concluded on the 28th with a wholly familiar programme.

Messrs. Ludwig and Whitehouse gave their last Chamber Concert on the 11th. The principal items were Schubert's Quintet in C and Brahms's new duet Sonata in D minor (Op. 108), Mr. Ludwig having Miss Zimmermann for his companion in the latter work.

Señor J. Albeniz, a new Spanish pianist, gave a Recital at Princes' Hall on the 13th, and fairly astonished his audience by his extraordinary *technique* and characteristic playing. At times he was apt to descend to tricks of virtuosity; but his rendering of pieces by Scarlatti and Liszt, and some light and tasteful movements from a Suite of his own, was extremely effective. Señor Albeniz played the "Moonlight" Sonata, but made a much more favourable impression in the Finale of Chopin's Sonata in B flat minor. The *technique* was perfect, and besides he imparted to Chopin's music a peculiar colour and meaning by clever shading and pedal effects. He was much applauded.

M. Vladimir de Pachmann gave his second Chopin Recital on the 14th, at St. James's Hall, when his various performances were enthusiastically applauded by a large audience. The two most important pieces were the Sonata in B minor (Op. 58) and the Barcarolle (Op. 60).

The members of the Musical Guild gave their last Concert at Kensington Town Hall on the 19th, performing Beethoven's Sonata in F for pianoforte and horn, his String Quintet in C, and Brahms's Pianoforte Quartet in G minor.

The scheme of Mr. J. H. Bonawitz's historical Organ, Harpsichord, and Pianoforte Recital, given at Princes' Hall on the 8th, contained no fewer than forty-five pieces, numbered and placed in chronological order, from the organ "Benedicite" of Conrad Paumann (1410-1473) down to Liszt's Pianoforte Transcription of the "Tannhäuser" March. We have in our midst few musicians so capable as Mr. Bonawitz of doing justice to so varied and comprehensive a programme. His performances on each of the three keyboards were marked by rare facility, clearness, and intelligence, and all were followed with appreciative interest by a numerous audience.

Signorina Teresina Tua gave, on the 6th, a morning Concert at Princes' Hall, assisted by Mdlle. Wonsowska, a pianist of some ability, with whom she was heard in Brahms's Sonata in A (Op. 100). Since she was previously here the young Italian violinist's style had considerably matured and her tone had gained in strength. Among her solos was the Mendelssohn Concerto, which Mr. Ganz accompanied.

Fräulein Hermine Spies gave a Vocal Recital at Princes' Hall on the 12th. The programme contained songs by Haydn, Mozart, Schumann, Brahms, Bizet, and other composers, and all were rendered in an absolutely faultless manner. Fräulein Spies entered thoroughly into the character of each song, drawing from her audience at one moment a tear, at another a smile. She sang for the most part in German, but was also heard in French (Bizet's "Pastorale") and English (Henschel's "O hush thee, my baby"), and seemed quite at home in both languages. Miss Ethel Bauer played two pianoforte solos.

The Annual Concert given by Mr. W. G. Cusins at St. James's Hall, on the 20th, attracted a large and fashionable audience. The instrumental portion of the programme included Mendelssohn's Trio in D minor, in which Mr. Cusins had the assistance of Signorina Teresina Tua and Signor Piatti; also his own pianoforte solos and some pieces for viola d'amore by Milandre, played with much taste by Mr. Van Waefelghem. Vocal pieces were contributed by Madame Valda, Madame Patey, and Mr. Barrington Foote, another and not the least attractive feature being humorous recitations delivered by Mrs. Kendal.

An interesting programme was presented by Mr. Charles Gardner at his annual *Matinée musicale* on the 15th, at Willis's rooms. Mr. Gardner's solos included compositions by Dvorák, Raff, Edward Bache, and himself, which he executed in refined and finished style. He also joined Messrs. Ludwig and Whitehouse in Sterndale Bennett's delightful Chamber Trio in A major. Two or three of Mr. Gardner's pupils took part in the Concert, the vocal portion of which was sustained by Miss Louise Phillips, Miss Louise Collier, and Mr. W. H. Brereton.

Madame Sembrich made her first and only appearance in London, after a long absence, at an evening Concert given by Mr. Emil Bach at St. James's Hall, on the 25th. The distinguished prima donna had been announced to appear at two Concerts, supported on each occasion by an orchestra under the direction of Mr. W. G. Cusins; but owing, presumably, to the very meagre attendance at the first, the other was abandoned. The programme included a Pianoforte Concerto in C minor, by the Concert-giver, heard for the first time—a somewhat laboured work, in which Mr. Bach himself sustained the solo. Naturally, however, the most attractive feature of the evening was the singing of Madame Sembrich, whose voice seemed to possess all its pristine freshness and charm, and whose vocalisation was not less brilliant than heretofore. These qualities were abundantly demonstrated in airs from "Le Nozze" and "Lucia," in addition to *Lieder* by Mozart, Schumann, and Rubinstein, and a Waltz by Arditi, all of which evoked the heartiest manifestations of pleasure. Miss Lena Little also sang, for the first time, the contralto air written by Mr. Goring Thomas for the intended Berlin production of his opera "Nadeshda." Some violoncello solos, played by M. Hollman, and Mr. Cusins's Concert-Overture "Les Travailleurs de la Mer," completed the scheme.

Mr. W. de Manby Sergison gave his annual Concert on the 26th, at Princes' Hall. A highly interesting programme was provided. A capital Chamber Concert was also given by Mr. E. H. Thorne at the Princes' Hall, on the 15th. Among the items in the programme were Bach's Concerto in D minor for two violins, Schumann's Quintet in E flat (Op. 44), and Dr. Hubert Parry's Partita in D minor for violin and pianoforte.

Mr. John Thomas gave his annual Harp Concert on the 29th,

at St. James's Hall. The programme contained pieces for a band of harps, also a charming Trio for harp, violin, and organ, and two harp duets by the Concert-giver. Among the artists who took part in the programme were Madame Valleria, Madame Edith Wynne, Miss Liza Lehmann, Miss Eleanor Rees, Mr. Hirwen Jones, Mr. Daniel Price, and Misses Clara and Marianne Eissler.

The Guildhall School Orchestra of 110 performers was heard to signal advantage at the Concert directed by Mr. Weist Hill on the 15th, in the Hall of the City of London School. The programme opened with a "Marche Joyeuse" by Fanny Archbutt, a pupil at the Guildhall School. This bright, animated piece was cleverly orchestrated, and altogether a very creditable exercise. The opening *Allegro* of Beethoven's "Choral" Symphony, played more than once before by the Guildhall Orchestra, was now given with increased finish and refinement. The chief individual success of the afternoon was Miss Amy Porter's performance of the *Allegro* from Popper's dry but difficult Violoncello Concerto (Op. 24). This was in all respects an admirable piece of playing. The vocal efforts of Miss Magdalena A'Bear, Miss Isabelle Ikin, Mr. John G. Hooker, and Mr. Arthur Bonner met with hearty approval.

The Association of Tonic Sol-fa Choirs gathered at the Crystal Palace on the 29th, and gave a Concert in the Handel Orchestra. The voices taking part numbered about 3,000, Mr. L. C. Venables conducting. Mendelssohn's "Athalie" was performed, and, apart from an admirable rendering, the event derived special interest from the first performance of an unpublished Fugue, originally intended by Mendelssohn to have formed part of the *Finale* of "Athalie." The fugue, an elaborate and well worked-out composition, was capitally sung by the choir to an organ accompaniment.

The combined choirs of Lincoln and Peterborough Cathedrals, aided by contingents from local neighbouring Choral Societies, gave their second Triennial Festival in Lincoln Cathedral on

Wednesday, the 26th. "Elijah" was given in the afternoon, and Handel's "Dettingen" Te Deum, followed by Mendelssohn's "Hymn of Praise," formed the evening programme. The soloists were Miss Anna Williams, Miss Wilson, Mr. Barton McGuckin, and Mr. Watkin Mills. The band and chorus numbered over 550 performers. The attendance was not very large.

Sir John Stainer was, on the 25th, unanimously elected to the post of Professor of Music at Oxford University, in the room of the late Sir Frederick Gore Ouseley. The appointment gave universal satisfaction. A gifted and scholarly musician, a man respected for his high integrity and all-round excellent qualities, and a resident at Oxford, no one could have been chosen who would be so well fitted for the post, or be likely to do so much for the advancement and progress of musical art at the University as Sir John Stainer.

OBITUARY.—Carlotta Patti (vocalist), Paris, 28th.

JULY.

ON Friday, the 5th, Verdi's latest opera, "Otello" (originally produced at La Scala, Milan, in February, 1887), was given for the first time in England, before a crowded and distinguished audience, at the Lyceum Theatre, by a company expressly brought over from Milan by Mr. M. L. Mayer, the well-known director of the French Plays. The opera was mounted here with a very remarkable degree of completeness. Not only was the *mise en scène* a counterpart of that designed for La Scala, but the entire troupe, principals, conductor, band, chorus and all, were the same that had been there engaged in the representation of Verdi's work. Against this tremendous advantage one serious drawback had to reckoned — the inadequate size of the present *locale*. Admirably as Mr. Irving's house may be adapted for his own Shakespearean productions, it is scarcely fitted for lyrical representations on an important scale. Yet this did not prevent a just appreciation of what Verdi has accomplished in "Otello," for with such an interpretation there was little chance of forming wrong conclusions. In his libretto, Signor Boïto has neither mangled our great poet's tragedy out of shape nor emasculated his language. On the contrary, he has preserved with rare skill the construction and the beauty of each. The actual text is largely employed throughout, as a perusal of the late Dr. Hueffer's excellent English version will at once show. The opinion that "Otello" should have been called "Iago" is by no means unreasonable. Until the last act the *Moor's* "ancient" is absolutely the central figure of the story. Verdi likewise has devoted special care to the treatment of this part. He has lavished upon *Iago's* music a wealth and power of characterisation that the other leading personages share in a much lesser degree. It positively teems with diabolical cynicism. The opera is in four acts. The first opens, without prelude or overture, upon a stormy scene on the seashore at Cyprus, where, amid the howlings of the tempest, *Iago, Cassio,* and the others receive upon their arrival the new governor, *Otello,* with his Venetian bride, *Desdemona. Otello* comes ashore as the realistic storm abates and enters the adjacent castle, whilst *Iago* plots with *Roderigo* and sounds *Cassio.* He sings to them a strange, *bizarre* drinking-song, in which the chorus joins. Then come the quarrel and fight, and the re-entry of *Otello,* who after a time is left alone with *Desdemona,* and the two sing a love-duet of marvellous reposeful beauty, bringing the act to an ending full of peace and charm. The second act takes place in a room in the castle. After a brief colloquy between *Iago* and *Cassio,* the former remains alone, and proclaims his belief in a "cruel God who has created him after His own image." To this original and magnificently dramatic monologue succeeds a long scene between *Otello* and *Iago,* amidst which a graceful distant chorus is prominent. *Desdemona* enters and pleads *Cassio's* cause, and there is a charming duet, changing to a quartet, in which *Iago* and *Emilia* join, the growing jealousy of *Otello* and the conflicting emotions of the others being wonderfully depicted. There is now a fine soliloquy for *Otello,* culminating in a tremendous climax of passion as he seizes *Iago* by the throat; and then comes a long duet, lasting, with superb effects of dramatic contrast, until the end of the act. In the next act, in the great hall of the castle, there is a fine scene between *Otello* and *Desdemona;* then another beautiful passage for the former alone. *Otello* overhears and misinterprets the talk between *Iago* and *Cassio* with reference to the handkerchief, this forming a most effective trio. The ambassadors from Venice arrive amid an imposing sound of trumpets, and we then have treated with masterly power the scene in which the *Moor* insults and even strikes his wife before the whole assemblage, this leading to a long, elaborate, and somewhat involved *ensemble*. *Otello* and *Iago* are ultimately left together, and the act ends with a fine dramatic situation, as the villain stands gloating over the inert, outstretched body of his despairing master. A very lovely and original orchestral passage precedes the last act, the scene of which is, of course, laid in *Desdemona's* sleeping chamber. Very beautiful, too, is the whole of the music sung by *Desdemona*, both whilst *Emilia* is completing her toilet and when she is left alone. The exquisite " Willow Song " and the sublime Prayer are simply inspirations of genius. Another masterstroke is the unison phrase for the double basses when *Otello* enters, and, indeed, the beauty of the music is fully sustained throughout the scene wherein the *Moor*, having awakened his sleeping wife by kissing her, proceeds to converse with her ere he kills her. Full of tragic power is Verdi's treatment of the final episode, when *Emilia* discloses *Iago's* villainy and *Otello* kills himself. The ending to the opera is an ending worthy of a noble and singularly satisfying work, the strength and imaginative power revealed throughout being doubly marvellous when one remembers that the composer is far advanced in his "seventies," and has been writing operas for just half a century. " Otello " does not, on the whole, surpass " Aïda " in characteristic beauty and charm, although it may do so in truthfulness of dramatic spirit and depth of tragic expression. In "Otello" Verdi has sought after realism in his style of treatment, and, to a great extent, his effort has been successful, but not invariably, as may be perceived in the intricate *ensemble* of the third act, which cannot compare either for lucidity or grandeur with the finale to the second act of "Aida." The new opera was received with warmth, if not enthusiasm, and drew large houses during the twelve representations that were given, though the receipts unfortunately were not large enough to save the *entrepreneur* from a serious loss. Of the artists who took part in the Lyceum performance, two, Signor Tamagno and M. Victor Maurel, appeared in the *rôles* which they created at Milan. The former artist, who now made his *début* in London, is a robust tenor, possessing a voice of phenomenal range and power. His high notes have an immensity of volume, a penetrating resonance that simply amaze the listener. In a word, it is just the magnificent organ that is needed to emit *Otello's* passionate outbursts of rage and jealousy. At these moments Tamagno is almost terrible in his energy, and, save that he rather over-uses the *voce parlante*, his superb tones convey with tremendous effect the sensations that overwhelm the *Moor*. In the expression of love in the duet of the first act he is less successful, but yet he can sing with tenderness and pathos, as he clearly proves in the wonderful bedchamber scene. A truly great impersonation was the *Iago* of M. Maurel. Never did this accomplished baritone appear before in so favourable a light. In order to look the character he sacrificed his beard, thus giving full opportunity for the study of his marvellous facial expression, through which could be seen the innermost workings of *Iago's* mind. It might be that these changes were somewhat over-elaborate, but they were undeniably interesting, and, together with M. Maurel's finished acting, they helped to make the embodiment one of rare psychological force. *Iago's* music, as has already been said, possesses an individuality of its own, strongly suggesting the cynical, contemptuous nature of the man. This was realised in the fullest degree through the subtle vocalisation of the French baritone, who won a complete and signal triumph. Signora Cataneo, an intelligent dramatic artist, failed to satisfy in the part of *Desdemona*, which she neither looked nor understood. The remaining characters were adequately sustained. The opera was conducted by Signor Faccio, the famous *chef d'orchestre* at La Scala and the greatest man in his "line" that Italy now owns. Quiet and unobtrusive as is his method, he yets holds every one under perfect control. It would be impossible to imagine a more refined rendering of the wonderfully picturesque instrumentation with which Verdi has endowed this work; and yet the orchestra contained seventy players—too many for a theatre like the Lyceum, had it not been for the masterly skill shown in their direction.

The chorus, admirably trained, was more remarkable for its intelligence and ability to sing in tune than for beauty of voice. The mounting and stage management of "Otello" were beyond praise.

A State performance took place at the Royal Italian Opera on Tuesday, the 2nd, in honour of the Shah of Persia, who, accompanied by the Prince and Princess of Wales and other members of the Royal Family, occupied a large improvised box in the centre of the grand tier. The house presented a magnificent sight, bouquets of flowers being given by the management to every lady in the stalls and boxes. The programme, printed on white satin, formed a charming souvenir of the event. The selection comprised the Overture to " Guillaume Tell," the Mad Scene from " Lucia " (sung by Madame Melba), and Beethoven's " Leonora " Overture, these pieces being executed before the Royal party took their places. The fourth act of " Faust" was then given, with Madame Albani, the De Reszkes, and Lassalle. In the so-called " Concert " that followed, Madame Melba sang the waltz-air from " Roméo," Madame Marie Roze was heard in a waltz of Arditi's, Miss Ella Russell gave " Caro nome," and Madame Nordica wound up with " Ah! fors' è lui." Afterwards came the second act of " Mefistofele," Miss Macintyre, Madame Scalchi, Signor Antonio d'Andrade, and Signor Castelmary furnishing the quartet ; while the Brocken Scene supplied an impressive ending to this very brilliant and successful function. On the Friday of the same week the Shah attended a State Concert at the Royal Albert Hall.

The next operatic event of importance was the production at Covent Garden, on the 13th, for the first time in Italian, of Wagner's "Die Meistersinger von Nürnberg." This work was first given in London at Drury Lane in 1882, in course of the famous German season directed by Herren Franke and Pollini. Its beauties commanded instant recognition, brought into relief as they were by a performance of memorable excellence, and Wagner's comic opera drew the largest receipts recorded during that ill-managed undertaking. The only other production here occurred two years later, inaugurating the series of German performances given at Covent Garden by Herren Richter and Franke concurrently with Mr. Gye's regular Italian season. The bold idea of producing "Die Meistersinger" in Italian was only formed in 1888, when "Die Meistersinger" was again brought strongly *en évidence* through being mounted for the first time at Bayreuth. But no Italian version existed, and it was of vital importance that the task of preparing one should be entrusted to a first-rate man. Fortunately that man was found in Signor G. Mazzucato. Taking into consideration the wide difference in the character of the two languages, it would be difficult to conceive a closer rendering of Wagner's libretto, as regards alike metre and diction, poetic spirit and rhythmical vigour, than Signor Mazzucato has written. The colloquialisms of the original have been happily reproduced, thus preserving in an essential degree the homely modes of expression characteristic of Wagner's simple Nuremberg folk. Yet in the adaptation of the more elegant lines there is not a trace of commonplace. Signor Mazzucato thus distinctly enhanced the probabilities of "Die Meistersinger" succeeding in Italian. He was not, however, the only individual secured by Mr. Harris whose services to the same end were of special value. A very warm tribute of praise was due to Herr Saar, the experienced *maestro al piano*, who had conducted the work at Strasburg, and to Signor Lapissida, who had already stage-managed it at Brussels. Mr. Harris naturally found the aid of these able men invaluable; while, in putting the finishing touches to the *mise en scène*, his own hand was by no means idle. Among the critical audience that assembled to witness the initial representation was a large muster of professed Wagnerites, who frankly declared that they came anticipating a failure. The greater, therefore, was their surprise, and perhaps pleasure also, to find the performance carried out from first to last in the spirit of the master's intentions. The rendering of the opera was marked by as much completeness and accuracy of detail and unity of artistic purpose as though it had been the familiar " Lohengrin " or " Tannhäuser." In a word, the representation as a whole would have done credit to any leading German opera house, not excepting even Munich ; and to say this is to pay the *impresario* of Covent Garden the highest possible compliment. The cast was remarkably strong. As *Eva* Madame Albani had only one fault—she was not youthful enough in appearance for the goldsmith's impulsive daughter ; but her impassioned singing and acting sufficed well-nigh to atone for the shortcoming. M. Jean de Reszke made a superb *Walther von Stolzing*, looking the Franconian knight " from top to toe," and singing not only the lovely " Preislied " but the music of the entire part as it had never been sung on the stage before. M. Lassalle was an equally ideal *Hans Sachs;* he gave a most poetic delineation of the character, and declaimed his music as if it had been written for him. M. Isnardon, a Belgian artist new to London, furnished a clever and diverting impersonation of *Beckmesser*, despite certain slight exaggerations; and satisfactory also were the bright, animated *David* of M. Montariol, the imposing *Pogner* of Signor Abramoff, the admirable *Kothner* of M. Winogradoff, and the efficient *Magdalena* of Mdlle. Bauermeister. The chorus did its exacting work wonderfully well, while the orchestra executed the glorious instrumentation with delightful refinement. The audience burst into loud applause on each fall of the curtain, and at the close accorded a special ovation to Signor Mancinelli, the talented Conductor, and Mr. Harris, who both thoroughly merited the honour. In all four representations of " Die Meistersinger " were given before crowded houses, without change of cast, save on the last occasion, when the part of *Eva* was successfully undertaken by Madame Valda.

The remaining performances of the season at Covent Garden consisted of repetitions. Down to the last night (July 27), when " Roméo et Juliette " was given, the attendance was uniformly large, and the season, on the whole, was productive of most satisfactory results, both pecuniary and artistic. Of the old operas, the most successful were "Faust" and "Lohengrin" (given seven and six times respectively); but "Carmen," although coming next with four representations, scarcely maintained its usual popularity. The following table shows the number of performances and operas in which the Covent Garden artists appeared in course of the season:—Mesdames Nordica (4 operas), 9 performances; Fürsch-Madi (2), 9; Melba (3), 10; Albani (4), 11; Marie Roze (1), 4; Macintyre (3), 8; Van Zandt (3), 5; Valda (3), 6; Russell (5), 8; Schläger (2), 4; Lita (2), 2; Scalchi (6), 17; De Vigne (2), 8; Lablache (3), 10; and Bauermeister (10), 30. MM. Jean de Reszke (6), 22; Montariol (6), 17; McGuckin, 1; Talazac (3), 6; A. d'Andrade (6), 7; Massimi (2), 2; Engel (2), 2; Lassalle (5), 14; E. de Reszke (6), 22; Winogradoff (4), 14; F. d'Andrade (9), 18; Crotty, 1; Novara (3), 3; Cotogni (4), 4; Lestellier (3), 4; Seguin (4), 13; De Vaschetti (3), 24; Abramoff (3), 13; Castelmary (3), 11; Miranda (9), 26; Ciampi (2), 5; and Isnardon (1), 4. In all, fifty-three representations of sixteen operas were given during the ten weeks.

At the last Richter Concert but one, on the 1st, was brought forward a new Symphony in E minor, by Dr. Hubert Parry. Unlike the "English" Symphony performed shortly before by the Philharmonic Society, it is a work of large dimensions, and scored for the full modern orchestra. Clear in structure and development, it impressed at once as a strong, clever, and genial work. The *Scherzo* was rightly regarded as the gem of the four movements; it was after this that the composer was called forward, as well as at the end. But the opening *Allegro* is full of breadth and spirit, and the slow movement of deep feeling and melodic charm; whilst the *Finale*, though it seemed a trifle "patchy" on first hearing, is undoubtedly a fine section, and ends the work with a jubilant tone well in keeping with the prevailing sense of masterful energy. Ample justice was done to the beautiful scoring of the Symphony, under the guidance of Dr. Richter, who conducted his friend's composition *con amore*. Another novelty on the same evening was the fragment of an unfinished Pianoforte Concerto in D, attributed to Beethoven. Despite the respectability of Herr Privy Councillor von Bezecny, in whose possession the orchestral parts were found, many musicians have declined to believe in the authenticity of this Mozart-like example of early Beethoven until the original score shall be forthcoming. The fragment, an easy opening *Allegro* such as any skilful lover of Mozart could imitate by the dozen, was neatly played by Madame Stepanoff. The remaining items of the scheme were the closing scene from "Götterdämmerung," and Beethoven's Symphony in F (No. 8). The part of *Brünnhilde* in the former piece was declaimed by Fräulein Fillunger, but not with her customary vigour and purity of intonation. At the concluding Concert of the series, a week later, Berlioz's "Faust" was performed in the presence of a large audience, the soloists being Mrs. Mary Davies, Mr. Lloyd, Mr. Max Heinrich (a first-rate *Mephistopheles*), and Mr. Bantock Pierpoint. The singing of the choir was anything but satisfactory; it began badly, without life or attack, and so went on to the end. On the other hand, the accompaniments were played to simple perfection, Dr. Richter and his orchestra thus winding up an arduous and successful season amid a blaze of triumph.

The annual operatic performance given by the Royal College of Music took place at the Prince of Wales's Theatre, on Wednesday afternoon, the 10th, when Goetz's masterpiece, "The Taming of the Shrew," was rendered in extremely creditable fashion. Considering the difficulties of this work, which fully tested the capacities of the Carl Rosa Company when mounted at Her Majesty's in 1880, the manner in which the Royal College Students acquitted themselves merited and received high praise. In two or three cases individual merit was very conspicuous: for instance, Miss Emily Davies as *Katharine*, Miss Maggie Davies as *Bianca*, Mr. John Sandbrook as *Petruchio*, and Mr. Charles J. Magrath as *Baptista* won admiration by capital acting in addition to first-rate singing. Generally speaking, however, the real value of the performance lay in the spirit and intelligence of the *ensemble*, thus clearly showing that in our leading musical school preparation for the operatic stage is regarded as a serious and earnest study by all concerned. Thanks to able stage management, the traditional "business" of the opera was well carried out, the comic incidents keeping the house in constant laughter. The chorus did excellently, and so, too, did the well-trained College orchestra. Professor Villiers Stanford conducted. An interesting Orchestral Concert was also given on the 24th, by pupils of the Royal College. The programme included Spontini's "Olympia" Overture, Saint-Saëns's Poème Symphonique " Phaéton," the Good Friday Music from " Parsifal," and the " Symphonic Variations " of Dvorák. The band, conducted by Professor Stanford, gave a remarkably good rendering of these works, and also of the accompaniments to Brahms's Pianoforte Concerto in D minor, the solo in which was played with great spirit and an intelligent grasp of her theme by Miss Ethel Sharpe. Vocal pieces were sung by Miss May Richardson and Mr. C. J. Magrath. The balance-sheets of the Royal College of Music, presented on the 18th at the sixth annual meeting, showed the affairs of that Institution to be in a highly flourishing state, the total amount of invested capital being nearly £125,000, and the available balance of revenue account £3,198 19s., or an increase of £533 8s. 7d. over the previous year.

At the Royal Academy Orchestral Concert, on the 26th, at St. James's Hall, interest centred chiefly in the performance (for the first time in England) of Weber's Hymn " In constant order," an early work of the composer's, marked as his Op. 36. The opening Chorus and Quartet at once proclaim the influence of Mozart. After a Recitative, " The gloominess of night," comes a Chorale founded on the tune of an old German Chorale, "O Haupt voll Blut und Wunden," which has also been appropriated by Bach. The final Quartet and Chorus end with an elaborate and splendidly-written *Fugue*, bringing the hymn to a spirited conclusion. It was capitally sung, the solos been ably sustained by Miss Agnes Wilson, Miss Violet Robinson, Mr. Percy Edmunds, and Mr. B. Mayne. The compositions by students heard for the first time were a cleverly-treated and interesting Romance for orchestra, by E. Cuthbert Nunn ; a Ballade for orchestra, based upon themes of a Scottish character, and very effectively scored, by Learmont Drysdale; and a pleasing *Andante* (from a Symphony in G) by Reginald Steggall. These promising efforts were all warmly applauded. Miss Rose Meyer, Miss Kate Goodson, Miss Ada Tunks, and Mr. W. L. Lamb were heard in various pianoforte compositions; and Miss Emily Squire, Miss Henrietta Mears, Mr. David Hughes, and Mr. Henry Ward gave vocal pieces. Dr. Mackenzie conducted with infinite care and zeal.

On the 6th the Guildhall School students gave a choral Concert, at which they performed Mr. Ebenezer Prout's pretty Cantata for female voices, " Queen Aimée ; or, the Maiden's Crown " (a work composed in 1885), and repeated Mr. Orlando Morgan's Cantata " Zitella."

On the 1st the pupils of the Hyde Park Academy of Music appeared at Steinway Hall, and, as usual, gave an admirable account of themselves. The scheme contained some interesting pieces, among these notably being Hoffman's " Song of the Norns," given with much refinement and intelligence by Mr. H. F. Frost's choir of ladies.

Madame Backer-Gröndahl gave a Pianoforte Recital at Princes' Hall, on the 13th, when she again delighted her audience by her exceedingly clever and refined playing. The Norwegian artist gave a Suite of her own, of which the *Gavotte, Minuet,* and *Finale* found especial favour. The music is skilfully written and delightfully fresh. Some delicate and pleasing songs, also composed by Madame Gröndahl, were interpreted by Miss Louise Phillips. Among other works, Grieg's duet Sonata in C minor (No. 4) was admirably executed by Madame Gröndahl and M. Johannes Wolff.

Mr. Sims Reeves's morning Concert at St. James's Hall, on the 6th, was largely attended. The veteran tenor was in excellent voice, and sang a couple of his familiar songs with all his wonted finish and charm of style. He also joined Mr. Edward Lloyd and

Mr. Ben Davies in an old Italian trio, "Evviva Bacco," written for three tenors; and, rendered by such artists, the quaint old piece proved very interesting. Other well-known artists sang, and Mdlle. Hélène de Duncan, a new pianist from St. Petersburg, played some solos in a manner that elicited emphatic approval and a desire to hear her again.

Fräulein Hermine Spies gave her second Vocal Recital at Princes' Hall on the 2nd. Mr. Waldemar Meyer gave a Chamber Concert at St. James's Hall, on the 4th, assisted by the clever young pianist, Miss Marian Osborn, and other artists.

M. Tivadar Nachèz and Herr Arthur Friedheim gave a Violin and Pianoforte Recital at Princes' Hall, on the 1st. Herr Friedheim exhibited striking mechanical powers in Liszt's B minor Sonata, and M. Nachèz played Max Bruch's Violin Concerto in G minor, with pianoforte accompaniment, the effect of which is by no means satisfactory.

Mr. Johannes Schubert, a pianist hailing from Dresden, made his *début* at a Recital which he gave at Steinway Hall, on the 3rd. He is comparatively young, and has been trained in a good school, his playing being marked by sound *technique*, a clear intellectual style, and, when occasion requires, great brilliancy of execution. Among other Concert and Recital-givers this month were M. de Pachmann, Mr. A. Carli, Mr. Isidore de Lara, Madame Berger-Henderson, Señor Albeniz, Senorita Esmeralda Cervantes, Mrs. Dyke, Madame Liebhart, Miss Agnes Huntington, Mrs. Lynedoch-Moncrieff, and Signor de Piccolellis.

"Marjorie," a three-act comic opera, written by Messrs. Lewis Clifton and J. J. Dilley, and composed by Mr. Walter Slaughter, was produced at a *matinée* performance at the Prince of Wales's Theatre, on the 18th, and favourably received by a large audience. The "book" was by far the weakest feature of this production, neither story nor lyrics being characterised by freshness or inventive resource. The music, however, is bright and pretty, and is remarkably well scored. The solo numbers consist largely of ballads, but the concerted pieces are clever beyond the average, and the choruses tuneful and well written. Miss Wadman, Miss Fanny Brough, Mr. F. Celli, Mr. Tapley, Mr. Monkhouse, and Mr. W. H. Burgon filled the principal parts, and the composer conducted.

OBITUARY.—Francis Romer (composer and teacher of singing), London, 1st; Giovanni Bottesini (contra-bass player and composer), Parma, 7th; Carli Zoeller (bandmaster), London, 13th.

AUGUST.

During the first week or two of August music in London was at an absolute standstill—that is, unless we take into account some performances of English Opera given at the Princess's Theatre by Mr. J. W. Turner's company. The solitary noteworthy achievement in connection with this ill-timed venture was the revival of Macfarren's "Robin Hood," an opera now quite out of date; at any rate, for metropolitan audiences. But even this was so badly staged and indifferently performed that, had it been a masterpiece, it would scarcely have found favour. On the 10th the Promenade Concerts began at Covent Garden, with Signor Arditi as Conductor; and a week later a similar undertaking was started at Her Majesty's, under the direction of Signor Bevignani. The first-named house, perhaps, secured the larger share of patronage, but the excellence of the orchestral work done by a select body of players, under Signor Bevignani, gained very favourable notice, and, towards the end of the season (which lasted ten weeks), the attendance was constantly improving. A prize of fifty guineas for an Orchestral Suite, and another of ten guineas for a Waltz, were offered for competition by the managers of Her Majesty's. A large number of manuscripts were sent in, the prize for the Suite being won by Mr. Ferdinand Dunkley, a student at the Royal College of Music. In course of the Covent Garden season Madame Roger-Miclos, a pianist of considerable talent, made her first appearance in this country.

Obituary. — Robert A. Atkins (Organist of St. Asaph's Cathedral), 3rd; Giacinta Puzzi (vocalist and teacher of singing), London, 18th.

SEPTEMBER.

THE 166th Festival of the Three Choirs, held at Gloucester, on the 3rd, 4th, 5th, and 6th, was, by general consent, admitted to be the most interesting and successful that has ever taken place in that city. It opened on the Tuesday morning with a capital performance of "Elijah," the solos in which were undertaken by Madame Albani, Miss Anna Williams, Miss Hilda Wilson, Miss Mary Morgan, Mr. Edward Lloyd, and Mr. Barrington Foote. The choir acquitted itself exceedingly well. The voices were fresh, bright, and well balanced, the basses giving out an especially fine body of tone; while, in regard to steadiness and precision, little fault was to be found. Mr. C. Lee Williams, who conducted the Festival in virtue of his office as Organist of Gloucester Cathedral, had evidently bestowed vast pains upon the training of his choristers and, what is more, showed that he knew how to get the best possible work out of them. The orchestra—an admirable body of English players, with Mr. J. T. Carrodus as *chef d'attaque*—was handled with like skill and evinced a like confidence in its Conductor's ability. The late Dr. Langdon Colborne (whose death occurred only a few days after the Festival) officiated as organist. He did full justice to his difficult task and to the fine newly-renovated instrument upon which he played.

At the Tuesday evening Concert, in the Shire Hall, the principal work was Dr. Mackenzie's "Dream of Jubal," given under the composer's direction, with Miss Anna Williams, Miss Mary Morgan, Mr. Lloyd, and Mr. Foote as soloists. Mr. Charles Fry again recited Mr. Bennett's noble verse, and the general rendering left nothing to be desired. Two novelties were included in the second part of the programme, one a short Cantata for soprano solo and chorus by Miss Rosalind J. Ellicott, entitled "Elysium," the other a Violin Concerto by Herr Hans Sitt, introduced by Mr. Bernhard Carrodus, son of the eminent player of that name. Miss Ellicott stands in the front rank of amateur lady-composers, and the merit of her previous work, apart from her position as daughter of the Bishop of Gloucester, fully justified the place assigned to this piece in the Festival scheme. It is a very graceful and melodious setting of one of Mrs. Hemans's miscellaneous poems. The poetic idea may not exactly "yearn for musical expression," but the words lend themselves to effective treatment both for solo voice and chorus, and Miss Ellicott has not failed to utilise her opportunities in felicitous fashion. Her music flows on freely and brightly, without break, deriving its chief contrast from the interpolated solo passages (artistically rendered by Miss Anna Williams), and supported by instrumentation which only occasionally, in its exuberant brass and "percussion" effects, betrays the hand of the amateur. The little work was given with admirable smoothness and effect and very warmly received. The new Violin Concerto proved to be a work of decided ability, somewhat involved in structure, but possessing no little melodic interest, and very cleverly written for the solo instrument, the middle and final movements especially. Hans Sitt, a composer hitherto unknown to English amateurs, was born in Prague in 1850, and is now a Professor at the Leipsic Conservatoire and a conductor of one or more musical societies; he has written two Violin Concertos, and the present work (No. 2, in A minor, Op. 21) was produced at Zwickau, in October, 1884. The solo part, which calls for an extensive mastery of technical difficulties, was played by Mr. Bernhard Carrodus with remarkable neatness and dexterity. He had thoroughly mastered his theme, and not even the breaking of a string and a double change of violins could mar the rock-like steadiness of his manipulation. His phrasing was marked by intelligence and distinction, and his intonation was well-nigh irreproachable. Mr. Carrodus was rapturously applauded at the close of the performance.

A large audience assembled to hear Dr. Hubert Parry's "Judith" on the Wednesday morning. As a Gloucester man and the son of the architect whose name is indissolubly connected with the restoration of Gloucester Cathedral, Dr. Hubert Parry must have taken an especial pride in conducting here his Birmingham Oratorio. His music of "Judith" has never sounded more impressive—the grand choruses particularly—than in this sacred edifice, nor could connoisseurs call to mind a better performance. Dr. Parry conducted with unrelaxing energy and never called upon his forces for an effort in vain. Miss Anna Williams and Mr. Edward Lloyd won their old triumphs over again, the other solo parts being adequately filled by Miss Hilda Wilson, Mr. Brereton, Master Jones, and Master Leeson. The Concert concluded with Rossini's "Stabat Mater."

In the evening there was a Concert in the Cathedral, attended by no fewer than 3,500 persons. This "best on record" was variously ascribed to lowered prices, to an increasing taste for good music, to the popularity of the "Creation," and to the interest taken in Mr. Lee Williams's new Church-cantata, "Bethany." The latter work, expressly written for the Festival, commanded the warmest approval. Mr. Joseph Bennett's libretto, an imitation on slightly modified lines of the form exemplified in Bach's Church-cantatas, called for straightforward, unpretentious treatment, and for music which, by its purely devotional character, should at once fit the theme and appeal direct to the hearts of an ordinary assemblage of worshippers. Mr. Williams thoroughly succeeded in supplying what was needful. Of story there is but the barest thread; it is rather, indeed, a picture embodying the scene at Bethany—the supper, the anointing of the feet of Jesus with the precious ointment, the sleep at night—a scene suggested by Mr. Bennett with infinite skill, and accompanied by reflective verses overflowing with religious fervour. The whole of these, excepting a hymn by the Rev. Dr. Neale, are original, the descriptive text being taken from the Scriptures and set forth in recitatives for contralto. Mr. Williams adopts for the most part a distinctly ecclesiastical style, with a slight leaning towards that of Gounod. His choral writing is clear and free from complexity, his orchestration exceedingly refined and well-contrasted. The best points in the Cantata are the soprano air "All that I have is Thine," which Madame Albani sang with intense emotional expression; and the remarkably effective, even dramatic, treatment of the choral passages foreshadowing the sufferings of the Saviour. Here one can perceive the hand of a thoughtful, intelligent, and able musician. The simplicity of "Bethany," apart from its intrinsic merits, should ensure the little work a wide popularity. The performance, which was profoundly impressive, gave entire satisfaction. The choruses were faultlessly sung, and Madame Albani, Miss Wilson, Mr. Lloyd, and Mr. Brereton threw great earnestness into their rendering of the solos.

Thursday's scheme, both morning and evening, contained works from the pen of Sir Arthur Sullivan, and the presence of the composer, apart from the popularity of his music, helped in each instance to secure a large attendance. The long matutinal programme comprised his early oratorio "The Prodigal Son," his "In Memoriam" Overture, Gounod's "Messe Solennelle," and Spohr's "Last Judgment." "The Prodigal Son" came to many as a veritable novelty, for comparatively few remembered its first production at Worcester in 1869, and since that time it has been allowed to suffer undeserved neglect. Why it has so suffered it is hard to understand. The subject is familiar and skilfully treated; the music, despite an occasional use of forms now regarded as old-fashioned, is replete with melodic beauty, and reveals in many a phrase and device the subtle touches which have come to be described as "Sullivanesque." The vocal writing and scoring abound with scholarly interest; and cleverer examples of the composer's skill than the "Revel" chorus, the duet for the father and repentant son, the unaccompanied quartet "The Lord is nigh," and the last two choruses could not easily be found among his latest works. The vocal honours of the performance fell to Miss Hilda Wilson and Mr. Edward Lloyd. The lovely contralto air "Love not the world" was rendered with exquisite taste and feeling; indeed, Miss Wilson's truly artistic use of her superb organ was a subject of general admiration all through the Festival. Madame Albani did justice to the soprano music, and Mr. Barrington Foote essayed the part written for Mr. Santley. The choir sang much better in the evening, when "The Golden Legend" was given in the Shire Hall. To make up for the absence of applause in the Cathedral, an overflowing audience then treated Sir Arthur Sullivan to a series of ovations.

There was a slight falling-off in "The Messiah" attendance on the Friday morning. The whole of the solo vocalists, with the exception of Mr. Lloyd, took part in the performance, Mr. William Nicholl sustaining the tenor music, while Mrs. Ambler-Brereton, in "How beautiful are the feet," met with especial success. This terminated the Festival proper, but in the evening the usual full choral service was held in the Cathedral, Mendelssohn's "Hymn of Praise" being given for the Anthem. The total attendance during the week was 13,496, as against 11,507 at the previous Festival, showing an increase of 1,989. The donations and collections amounted in the aggregate to about £1,200, which was distributed among the charities of the three dioceses. But the total expenditure exceeded the proceeds of the Concerts by £323, and this deficit was met by a call of £1 7s. 6d. upon each steward or guarantor.

OBITUARY.—Grattan Cooke (oboe player), Harting, Sussex, 12th; Langdon Colborne, Mus. Doc. (Organist of Hereford Cathedral), Hereford, 16th; H. B. Farnie (librettist and author), Paris, 22nd; T. Monck Mason (lessee of the King's, now Her Majesty's, Theatre, in 1832), London, 24th; William Winterbottom (bandmaster), Boulogne-sur-Mer, 29th; John V. Bridgeman (musical journalist and translator), London, 30th.

OCTOBER.

The Leeds Triennial Festival, held on Wednesday, the 9th, and the three following days, was the most important musical gathering of the year. This event may truly be said to have possessed a national interest. The proceedings connected with it were followed with the closest attention in every part of the Kingdom, and comments thereupon were by no means confined to our own organs of musical criticism. Germany sent one of her foremost writers to deal with the Festival, and the opinions which he expressed were in every way flattering to the modest pride of this "unmusical country." That the meeting, on the whole, was a brilliant success cannot be gainsaid. On the other hand, to assert that the artistic triumphs of the week were without alloy would be to slightly overstep the bounds of actual truth. There must be a thorn to every rose. Even the sun is not without its "spots."

The vocalists engaged were Madame Albani, Miss Macintyre, Fräulein Fillunger, Madame Valleria, Miss Hilda Wilson, Miss Damian, Messrs. Edward Lloyd, Iver McKay, Henry Piercy, Watkin Mills, Barrington Foote, and W. H. Brereton. The famous Leeds chorus had undergone a careful training at the hands of Mr. A. Broughton, the talented chorus-master, and consisted of 82 sopranos, 56 contraltos, and 18 altos, 77 tenors, and 78 basses; making a total of 311 singers. In the band there are 20 first violins (Mr. J. T. Carrodus leading), 20 second violins, 14 violas, 14 violoncellos, 14 double basses, 4 flutes, 2 piccolos, 4 oboes, 1 cor Anglais, 4 clarinets, 1 bass clarinet, 4 bassoons, 1 contrafagotto, 4 horns, 4 trumpets and cornets, 3 trombones, 1 bass tuba, 2 harps, 3 drums, &c., numbering altogether 120 performers. This magnificent band, made up exclusively of British performers, was probably the finest orchestra that the world could produce. The combined forces met for the first time in the Town Hall, under the direction of Sir Arthur Sullivan, the conductor of the Festival, on the Monday morning. They devoted thirteen hours of that day and eight of the next to the arduous task of going through the whole scheme. A perfect *ensemble* was thus secured; but the heavy continuous labour palpably told upon the chorus, and when judgment upon its merits was challenged at the opening Concert, on the Wednesday morning, in Berlioz's " Faust " (given for the first time at this Festival), the opinions expressed were not in the highest degree favourable. It was thought that the voices were not of such powerful volume as in previous years, and that the attack was not characterised by the same wonderful grip and unanimity. The section that seemed to have suffered most were the tenors. Inferior in quality to the other divisions of the choir, their voices sounded dull and hard and they frequently sang flat, pulling the others down with them. The sopranos were splendid; a purer, finer quality of tone has never perhaps been heard, and the contraltos and basses were also first-rate. But it immediately went forth to the world that the Leeds chorus had again deteriorated, that the glory of the Yorkshire voices had become more than ever a thing of the past. This judgment was soon shown to have been a trifle hasty. More than one experienced critic omitted to make allowance for the overstrain or for the fact that neither Berlioz's " Faust " nor Mr. F. Corder's new cantata " The Sword of Argantyr " was a work calculated to display the capacities of a choir in the most favourable light. Thursday morning told a different tale. Comparative repose for thirty-six hours wrought wonders, and the good, solid choral music contained in such works as Bach's Cantata "God's time is the best," Schubert's Mass in E flat, and Handel's " Acis and Galatea " enabled the Leeds singers to win back their lost laurels to no inconsiderable extent. There were wanting still the phenomenal volume and power, the bold, firm, simultaneous attack, the rock-like steadiness and faultless intonation that had made connoisseurs marvel at bygone Festivals; but, on the other hand, the balance was more even, the quality of the tone was more refined, and the singing, on the whole, was certainly not marked by less expression or less intelligence. In a word, compare the Leeds choir with any but former Leeds choirs and it was still unapproachable.

Mr. F. Corder's "The Sword of Argantyr," a dramatic Cantata in four scenes, specially written for the Festival, was produced at the first evening Concert. The libretto, written by the composer, is founded on a Norse legend, which tells how *Hervor*, a Viking's daughter, passes through a "girdle of ever-burning fire" and obtains possession of the sword Tyrfing, on which was wrought this rune :—

> Draw me not except in fray,
> Drawn I pierce, and piercing, slay.

The shepherd *Hjalmar*, who has passed the fire with her, tries to take it from her, so as to lead her people to battle. She, however, asserts her woman's rights, and refuses to resign her leadership. In the struggle the sword pierces *Hjalmar's* thigh, and he straightway bleeds to death. *Hervor* then returns with her warriors to their wild home in the North, "that all those things might be fulfilled which the spirit of Argantyr had foretold." This stirring story is dramatically told, and in bold, picturesque verse. But the musician was not inspired by his own libretto, nor could he apparently avoid dropping into that odd mixture of styles to which objection has been taken in his previous works. With the exception of a Shepherd's song, an instrumental intermezzo, and two or three of the choruses, Mr. Corder's Cantata contains little calculated to strike the listener or awaken interest. His originality is not of a pleasing kind ; his melodies, when they are tuneful, often lack distinction ; his treatment may be clever, but it is laboured, and the music runs on for bars and bars at a stretch without conveying the least sense of charm, the result being that it wearies and bores long before *King Argantyr's* sword has deprived the warrior-maiden of her new-found lover. Madame Valleria's indisposition on this occasion was a double misfortune. It was unlucky for the lady herself, and it did not improve the chances of "The Sword of Argantyr." Still, it was hardly likely that in her best form this artist could have made acceptable the distinctly ugly music assigned to the heroine. Mr. Henry Piercy made a hit with the Shepherd's air; Mr. Barrington Foote declaimed the legend of the Sword with plenty of energy; and Mr. Arthur F. Ferguson displayed a capital bass voice in the small part of *Argantyr*. Mr. Corder conducted with care, and was warmly recalled. The Concert wound up with a performance of the third act of "Tannhäuser," the solo parts being undertaken by Madame Valleria (*Elizabeth*), Fräulein Fillunger (*Venus*), Mr. Edward Lloyd (who gave a magnificent rendering of *Tannhäuser's* narrative), and Mr. Barrington Foote (*Wolfram*).

Reference has been made above to the work done on the Thursday morning. The rendering of the Schubert Mass was grandly impressive—perhaps the finest ever heard; and that of the Bach Cantata did not come far behind. The lightsome choruses of Handel's Serenade were given with abundant spirit, the well-known "Wretched lovers" producing as much effect as any but a Handel Festival choir could hope to create. The solo parts in these works were sustained by Miss Macintyre, Miss Hilda Wilson, Messrs. Iver McKay, Piercy, and Brereton.

The Organist of the Leeds Parish Church, Dr. William Creser, was the local musician asked to write a composition for the Festival of this year, the outcome being a dramatic Cantata in one scene entitled "The Sacrifice of Freia," brought forward on the Thursday evening. The poem, from the pen of the late Dr. Francis Hueffer, describes in attractive verse the gathering of bands of worshippers in a forest glade on May Day, to sacrifice to *Freia*, the fair deity being praised and appealed to as the goddess in turn of love, beauty, springtide, and war. Dr. Creser's music failed, despite undoubted technical excellence, to make a favourable impression, chiefly owing to an over-elaborate setting of Dr. Hueffer's simple idyll, and an interminable repetition of superfluous *Leitmotives*. At the same time, as a creditable specimen of local talent, Dr. Creser's work was by no means unworthy of a place in the Festival scheme, and unquestionably it fulfilled its purpose in that sense. Loud cheers greeted him after the performance, which he directed with much ability. The choruses were splendidly sung, and Miss Macintyre and Mr. Brereton did their best with the solo portions. The first part of the programme concluded with a magnificent rendering of Spohr's Symphony "The Consecration of Sound." In the second came the sole instrumental novelty of the week, Dr. Mackenzie's "Pibroch," for violin and orchestra. This clever work consists of three movements—viz., a Rhapsody, corresponding to the improvisation with which the bagpipe-player opens his Pibroch; a Caprice, in this case an air with variations founded on the theme of the old Scottish tune "Three guid fellows," and a Dance, the first subject of which is an ancient melody taken from the Skene MSS. Needless to add that a purely Scottish character pervades the entire composition, while the treatment, so far as the solo instrument is concerned, is thoroughly modern in style, and bristles with technical difficulties of the most exacting order. The orchestration is replete with charm and elegance. Altogether, Dr. Mackenzie's "Pibroch," as rendered by Señor Sarasate with the art of a great *virtuoso*, made a very warm impression. The composer conducted, and responded with his accomplished interpreter to an exceptionally hearty recall. A distinct ovation was accorded Mr. Broughton when he came forward to conduct his choir in Mr. Harford Lloyd's Pastoral "The Rosy Dawn." Miss Macintyre gave an artistic delivery of the air from the prison scene in "Mefistofele." Mr. Edward Lloyd sang *Walther's* "Probelieder," and after another solo by Señor Sarasate, the Concert wound up with the Overture to "Mireille."

On the Friday morning a new choral work by that indefatigable musician, Dr. Hubert Parry, was introduced, under his direction, and received with every token of favour. The poem here treated —namely, Pope's "Ode on St. Cecilia's Day"—has furnished Dr. Parry with the groundwork for another of those compositions in which he shows himself such a consummate master of old forms and modern materials. The combination is as subtle as it is curious, and Dr. Parry, as he goes on, proves its scope to be much less limited than might be supposed. It enables him to gratify everybody in turn, from the lover of Bach and Handel down to the ardent Wagnerian. The former perceives his well-beloved models underlying the choral numbers; the latter traces the influence of Bayreuth, here in an orchestral passage, there in a declamatory solo. In "St. Cecilia's Day," as in "Judith," Dr. Parry attains his highest standpoint in the choruses. The opening number, "Descend, ye Nine," is truly magnificent, full of striking contrasts, and clothing Pope's high-flown verse in music of the most expressive and dignified type. The *Finale* for baritone solo and chorus, "Music the fiercest grief can charm," is another piece of spirited and imposing writing, distinguished also by rare contrapuntal skill. The *Arioso* for baritone is not so interesting as the solo in which the soprano describes the unavailing rescue of *Eurydice* and the despair and death of *Orpheus*. This touching piece, plaintive and dramatic by turns, was sung by Miss Macintyre with profound sentiment and admirable vocal art. Mr. Brereton interpreted the baritone solo. The chorus, now in better form than ever, put heart and soul into Dr. Parry's work, sending it forth to the world with an amplitude of sound and grandeur of effect that every choir in the kingdom might be proud to emulate. The composer was twice rapturously recalled by a crowded audience. Señor Sarasate then played the Mendelssohn Violin Concerto—the *cheval de bataille* that ever bears him to triumph — and afterwards came Beethoven's "Choral" Symphony. The latter masterpiece was superbly tendered by orchestra and choir alike, the solos being ably sung by Fräulein Fillunger, Miss Damian, Mr. Iver McKay, and Mr.

Brereton. Opinions may have differed concerning one or two points in Sir Arthur Sullivan's reading, as, for instance, the *tempo* adopted in the *Scherzo*. But, take it as a whole, it was far and away the finest performance of the immortal "Ninth" ever heard at an English Festival.

On the Friday evening another important novelty, expressly written, saw light for the first time. This was Professor Villiers Stanford's Choral Ballad "The Voyage of Maeldune"—a fitting pendant to "The Revenge," which came out at the Leeds Festival of 1886. Like that work it is a setting of one of the Laureate's most stirring narrative poems, the chief difference being that one deals with an historical episode and the other with a legendary story. In the present instance, however, the entire poem is not used; portions are omitted and we find interpolated in the scene describing the Isle of Witches a song from "The Sea-Fairies," which fits in extremely well. Otherwise, alike in its descriptive character and musical treatment, the new Ballad treads upon the same lines as its predecessor. The hero (a tenor) tells the story. He relates how he and his people sail in search of the isle where dwells the man who slew his father; how, blown away from it by "a sudden blast," they are compelled to touch at a number of islands, each under some magic spell that brings them trouble; and how they come to one, the home of an aged saint, who exhorts *Maeldune* to abandon his voyage of vengeance, so that at last, when they again reach the isle where the murderer stands on the shore, they "let him be," and the weary journey ends. All this the solo voice narrates in picturesque declamatory phrases, supported sometimes by other solo voices, but more generally by the chorus. The description of the various islands afforded the composer his richest opportunity, and of this he has availed himself with a graphic power and mastery of resource equal to his finest moments in "The Revenge." The Isle of Shouting, the Silent Isle, and the Isle of Fire are each depicted in distinct appropriate strains; while graceful, sensuous music serves to pourtray both the Isle of Flowers and the Isle of Fruits.

The Undersea Isle has inspired an exquisite bit of "tone-painting"—the gem of the series—assigned to the four solo voices; and the Isle of Witches finds natural expression in a tripping, scherzo-like chorus for female voices with a prominent part for soprano solo. The whole work teems with beauty and poetic charm of a kind not to be resisted; music ever grateful for the singers being enhanced in significance and grace by the most refined and striking orchestration. In its way, therefore, " The Voyage of Maeldune " is a masterpiece, and its success with the Leeds audience was never for an instant in doubt. Rendered *con amore* by all concerned, the performance left absolutely nothing to be desired. The important tenor part had a perfect exponent in Mr. Edward Lloyd; Madame Albani sang the soprano music brilliantly, and Miss Hilda Wilson and Mr. Barrington Foote completed the quartet. Several numbers were loudly applauded, and at the end Dr. Stanford, who conducted, received an enthusiastic double recall. The miscellaneous selection that followed opened with Beethoven's "Leonora" Overture (given with a breadth and *élan* never to be forgotten by those who heard it), and terminated with Mendelssohn's music to " A Midsummer Night's Dream."

A happy juxtaposition on the Saturday morning was that of Brahms's noble " German Requiem " and the familiar but ever-beautiful " Lobgesang " of Mendelssohn. The " German Requiem " was composed by Brahms during his residence at Vienna in the years 1867-8, and was first performed in the Cathedral of Bremen, April 10, 1868. In this country it was first given by the Philharmonic Society in 1873, and later on the " Requiem " was rendered in German by the Bach Choir. To Leeds belongs the honour of first introducing this sublime composition into a Festival scheme—an act of enterprise which the authorities carried out at the preceding Festival in connection with Bach's colossal Mass in B minor. The " Requiem " was finely given, but the interpretation was not free from blemish. Unquestionably affected by the depressing atmosphere caused by fog and rain, the choir sang the earlier numbers with doubtful intonation and a somewhat feeble attack. In the second chorus, "Behold all flesh is as the grass," the tenors particularly sang flat, and later on the wonderful transition on the words "My hope is in Thee" was not at all clearly executed. The succeeding fugue, in which Brahms employs the unusual device of sustaining a tonic pedal throughout, was sung, however, with immense vigour and spirit; and thenceforward the work went magnificently. The orchestra as usual was faultless, making light of a task that was exacting in the extreme. Fräulein Fillunger—replacing Madame Valleria, who was too ill to sing again after her one appearance — did remarkably well in the soprano solo, and Mr. Watkin Mills delivered the passages for bass solo with due dignity and emphasis. It will be taken for granted that a performance which deviated so slightly from the highest level of excellence, and then only for a brief space, left behind no feeling of disappointment. The vast assemblage was evidently very deeply impressed, and bestowed cordial recognition upon Sir Arthur Sullivan, who conducted with even more than his habitual vigilance and tact. In the "Hymn of Praise," which was grandly given, the solos were sustained by Madame Albani, Miss Grace Damian, and Mr. Lloyd.

The Saturday evening Concert—an extra one not included in the regular Festival series—was attended by the largest audience of the week. It opened with a Concert arrangement of Sir Arthur Sullivan's "Macbeth" music. This naturally excluded a great deal of the incidental music composed for the Lyceum revival—in fact, all that would be likely to have no meaning or value apart from the action of the play. The present selection comprised the Overture, the Preludes to the third, fifth, and sixth acts, the chorus of spirits in the air, and the chorus of witches and spirits. It will be readily imagined that Sir Arthur Sullivan's delicate scoring and subtle effects came out in a far truer aspect and with more telling force than in the theatre. The Overture especially made a deep impression, and the two choruses, sung with exquisite delicacy, also evoked hearty admiration. This was followed by a performance of "The Golden Legend," which extraordinarily successful work was first given at Leeds in 1886. If "all's well that end's well," then the singing of the chorus in this Cantata may be said to have reflected a halo of glory upon the proceedings of the whole week. The Epilogue was given with indescribable breadth and grandeur of effect, arousing a depth of emotion shared by no one more acutely than the composer himself, who, it was evident to those around, needed all his self-control to get through the National Anthem that rang down the curtain on the labours of the Festival. How admirably Sir Arthur Sullivan performed his onerous duties; how gloriously the orchestra did its work throughout; how hard and conscientiously the chorus-master, Mr. A. Broughton, and the organist, Mr. A. Benton, laboured in the execution of their important functions; and with what financial and social success the gathering was attended, there can be no need to describe.

The total receipts at the Festival amounted to £10,836, and the total expenditure to £7,694, leaving a balance of £3,142, as against £2,570 at the previous Festival. The committee handed over £2,357 to the medical charities, and the balance was added to the reserve fund, which now amounts to £2,755 10s.

The London Musical Season opened on the 2nd with an Orchestral Concert, given by Otto Hegner, with the assistance of the Royal Amateur Orchestral Society. The audience, a rather scanty one, gave the gifted boy a cordial reception. He looked wonderfully bright and sturdy, had a good natural colour in his cheeks, and had grown considerably since he was last here. His playing astonished as much as ever. In Weber's "Concertstück," which he had not attempted publicly before, the increase of strength in his wrist-power, and the consequent greater fulness of his tone, were clearly noticeable, while his beautifully even touch and brilliant *mécanisme* found plenty of scope in the second section of Weber's composition. He also played Chopin's Berceuse and Polonaise in E flat (Op. 22), besides an encore

OCTOBER.

piece. Mr. Max Heinrich was the only vocalist; Madame Valleria was unable to appear. Mr. George Mount conducted, his band being heard in several well-known pieces. At the Pianoforte Recital, on the 5th, there was a large attendance. Hegner shone to immense advantage in Bach's Italian Concerto, and gave an astoundingly clear, intelligent rendering of Beethoven's Sonata in E minor (Op. 90). He also performed, with rare spirit and *entrain*, a very pretty and graceful Suite in G minor and major, written by himself. At the second Orchestral Concert, on the 9th, Hegner was heard in Chopin's Concerto in E minor; and the programme of his second Recital, on the 12th, included Beethoven's Sonata in D (Op. 10, No. 3). Immediately after these Concerts the youthful prodigy left for America, where, under the management of Mr. Abbey, he entered upon a tour which did not prove successful.

The thirty-fourth annual series of Crystal Palace Saturday Concerts was inaugurated on the 19th. A numerous audience assembled and gave Mr. Manns a warm welcome. The scheme contained several features of general interest, not the least of these being Beethoven's C minor Symphony which, as played by the Crystal Palace Orchestra, is always a treat to listen to. Sterndale Bennett's beautiful Overture, "The Wood-nymph," opened the Concert, and at the end came the ever-popular "Tannhäuser" Overture, appropriately marking the anniversary of the production of Wagner's opera at Dresden in 1845. The novelty of the Concert was a melodious, cleverly scored Interlude from Massenet's latest opera, "Esclarmonde," founded on the nuptial hymn in the second act. Madame Roger-Miclos made a very favourable impression by her artistic rendering of Saint-Saëns's Pianoforte Concerto in G minor (No. 2), the second movement being particularly well played. The lady, a *débutante* at these Concerts, was warmly recalled, and was heard also in a piece called "Inquietude" by Pfeiffer and Chopin's Andante Spianato and Polonaise in E flat. Mr. Lloyd sang in his own inimitable style the prayer from "Rienzi" and a graceful Serenade, "O moon of night" (with orchestral accompaniment), by August Manns. The talented Conductor shared in the applause evoked by the latter, and he directed the entire Concert with characteristic zeal and ability. On the following Saturday a Symphony in B flat (Op. 60), by Dr. Bernhard Scholz, was performed for the first time in this country. The composer, who succeeded Raff as the principal of the Conservatoire of Music at Frankfort, is a man of about fifty-four, and has long enjoyed a reputation among Germans as a theorist, composer, pianist, and Conductor of conspicuous attainments. His rare ability as a contrapuntist stands clearly in evidence in the present work, which was written in 1884, and first performed in that year at Frankfort. It is a Symphony with "so much in it" that to pretend to understand and absorb it all on first hearing would be manifestly absurd. At the same time, it may be doubted whether this polyphonic masterpiece would appeal to amateurs after any number of repetitions through the potent qualities of spontaneity, charm, or genuine inspiration. Dr. Scholz's elaborate work met with ample justice at the hands of Mr. Manns and his orchestra, and was received with cordial approbation. Señor Albeniz made his first appearance at the Crystal Palace and performed the Schumann Pianoforte Concerto, but won more success in his own pieces, which he always plays to perfection. Beethoven's "Coriolanus" and Mendelssohn's "Calm Sea and Prosperous Voyage" were the Overtures that opened and closed the Concert. Mdlle. Gambogi sang and made a marked impression in Gounod's "Ave Maria," which the audience paid her the rare compliment of asking for a second time.

On the 19th, at St. James's Hall, Señor Sarasate began a farewell series of Concerts (Chamber and Orchestral) before his departure for America. Orchestra, or no orchestra, Señor Sarasate has only to announce his appearance and he can safely count upon a full room. His programme on the above date, apart from its consisting exclusively of Chamber music, did not contain one of the works with which the famous *virtuoso* is more particularly associated in the minds of London amateurs, yet was St. James's Hall crowded to repletion. In the opinion of the connoisseurs present, Señor Sarasate has never more thoroughly vindicated his right to be reckoned among the leading interpreters of violin chamber music. Mechanical difficulties, we know, are as nothing to him, but in his rendering of Saint-Saëns's Sonata for pianoforte and violin (Op. 75), and again in Schubert's Fantasie for the same instruments (Op. 159), there was evinced an intellectual refinement and grasp such as only the earnest, deep-thinking artist would be able to exhibit. In Raff's *morceau caractéristique*, "La Fée d'Amour," and in Dvorák's "Danses Slaves," Señor Sarasate was well-nigh unapproachable, as he always is in pieces of this particular *genre*; but his playing throughout the afternoon afforded his listeners equal pleasure and elicited the same warm, spontaneous outbursts of applause. Heard in conjunction with the great Spanish fiddler, and also in one or two solo pieces, was Madame Berthe Marx, a pianist remarkable for her exquisite touch and correct execution, but possessing a frigid, colourless style. At his Orchestral Concert, a week later, Señor Sarasate introduced for the first time to London audiences Dr. Mackenzie's "Pibroch." The clever composition came out on second hearing even better than it did at Leeds, notably the opening movement or Rhapsody, the brilliant yet dreamy character of which was realised by Señor Sarasate with delicious effect. On the part of the gifted soloist it was a magnificent performance, while the accompaniments, under Mr. Cusins, were very creditably played. At the end Señor Sarasate was recalled amid enthusiastic applause, and with him the composer also came forward. Raff's Violin Suite and the Concert-giver's own "Muiñeira" were further included in the programme, besides a so-called "Prelude and Fugue" (with Choral by Abert), attributed to J. S. Bach, and arranged for orchestra. The Prelude was not familiar, and the Fugue was the well-known Organ Fugue in G minor from Book 2. But the combination, overladen with noisy, modern orchestral effects of the most pronounced type, formed at once an insult to the memory of a great master and to the intelligence of a cultivated musical audience. *Wotan's* "Abschied and Feuerzauber," as played by orchestra alone, with the vocal monologue supplied by different instruments in turn, formed another strange feature in the scheme.

The nineteenth season of the Royal Choral Society opened on the 30th with a performance of Berlioz's "Faust." There was a very large attendance, and the popular "dramatic legend" received a splendid interpretation, notably on the part of the choir—perhaps the finest that Mr. Barnby has ever had under his direction. The fine body of tone possessed by the tenors and basses was especially noticed; these being the sections of the choir chiefly reinforced from the ranks of the now-disbanded Novello Choir. Madame Albani, who on this occasion made her final appearance in town previous to her departure for America, imparted her accustomed dramatic significance and vocal charm to the music of *Margaret*. Mr. Henschel's *Mephistopheles* was once more full of grim sardonic humour—in declamation excellent, though in pronunciation not clearly comprehensible. Mr. Iver McKay was the *Faust*, while Brander's song was given by Mr. Ben Grove. The band did its work as well as usual, and Mr. Barnby conducted with the consummate skill of a musician who has a perfect mastery alike of his theme and his forces.

The thirty-second season of the Popular Concerts began at St. James's Hall on the 28th. For the small proportions of the audience the programme had to a certain extent to be held responsible. It did not contain a single work that could be described as a classical masterpiece, the sole item of real importance being the Quartet in E major (Op. 80), by Dvorák, which was introduced to London amateurs in the spring of the year and now given at these Concerts for the first time. The pianist, Madame Haas, was entrusted with nothing of higher interest than a Rhapsody in B minor by Brahms, and Chopin's Nocturne in B major—very neatly played, but at best a poor substitute for the substantial fare which *habitués* would have known so well how to appreciate. The remainder of the scheme was made up of a Violin Sonata by Rüst, exquisitely rendered by Madame Néruda to her sister's accompaniment, and Chopin's Introduction and Polonaise Brillante in C, for piano and violoncello, in which Madame Haas was associated with the gifted veteran, Signor Piatti. These efforts were cordially applauded, and after the Sonata an encore was asked for and granted. Still the material was scarcely of a kind to start the season in brilliant style. The Quartet was superbly executed by Madame Néruda, Messrs. L. Ries, Straus, and Piatti. Miss Liza Lehmann delighted the audience by her unaffected delivery of a graceful old song by James Hook, " Oh, listen to the voice of Love"; and was heard later on in *Lieder* by Emmerich and Meyer-Hellmund, accompanied by Mr. Frantzen.

On the same evening, after an absence of many months, Madame Adelina Patti made her re-appearance in the metropolis at a Concert given in the Albert Hall under the direction of Mr. Kuhe. A vast audience gathered to listen to the illustrious artist. The reception accorded her was of the most enthusiastic character, and each of her solos was encored. Madame Patti was in splendid voice, and her singing was marked by all the incomparable charm of old. Seldom has the distinguished prima donna appeared in better health and spirits ; but it was noticed, not without some astonishment, that since she was last here the *diva's* raven tresses had changed their hue to an auburn tint. Madame Patey, Mr. Edward Lloyd, Madame Néruda, and other artists also appeared, and the orchestra was conducted by Mr. Wilhelm Ganz.

The Royal College students at their orchestral performance on the 31st played under Mr. Holmes's direction the Suite in C, by Bach, Brahms's Symphony in C minor (No. 1), and Mendelssohn's " Hebrides " Overture. Miss Cecile Elieson, a clever young violin scholar, played Saint-Saëns's Introduction and Rondo; and Miss Ethel Webster, Miss S. Pierce, and Mr. H. Beauchamp were the vocalists.

A new romantic Opera, entitled "The Castle of Como," written by the late Charles Searle, and composed by Major George Cockle, Mus. Bac., Oxon., was performed for the first time at the Opera Comique Theatre on the 2nd. The story, taken from "The Lady of Lyons," follows closely upon the lines of Bulwer Lytton's play, the scenes coming in much the same order, while the character of Madame Deschappelles is the only one expunged. No books of the words were issued, consequently it was impossible to form a definite opinion upon Mr. Searle's libretto, but Lytton's text was frequently employed, though in a somewhat mutilated shape. Major Cockle failed to succeed in the task which Mr. Frederic Cowen, in his opera "Pauline," found alike difficult and ungrateful—that of making interesting operatic personages out of Lytton's stilted, artificial characters. His music might be appropriate, and, at times, dramatic, but that was the best that could be said for it. The scene in *Widow Melnotte's* cottage was the best-written and the most interesting; but the *Claude* and *Pauline* were a very tedious couple, and the *Beauseant* was nothing more than a commonplace operatic villain. The *mise en scène* was adequate, and the orchestra, if too loud and large for the theatre, was a particularly good one. Miss Rosina Isidor appeared as *Pauline*, Miss Amy Martin as *Widow Melnotte*, Mr. Cadwaladr as *Claude*, Mr. Leo Stormont as *Beauseant*, Mr. Donnell Balfe as *Colonel Damas*, Miss de Vernet as *Glavis*, and Mr. Henry Pope as *M. Deschappelles*. The Conductor, Signor Coronaro (Faccio's deputy at the Milan Scala), kept his forces together with wonderful tact. In fact, to him was largely due the comparative smoothness of the initial performance and the consequent indulgent reception accorded the opera.

"The Prima Donna," a comic opera in three acts, composed by Signor Tito Mattei, was produced with fair success at the Avenue Theatre on the 16th, and ran for several weeks. The story of an impecunious *Grand Duke's* device for concealing his poverty by making a troupe of French comedians impersonate his ministers and courtiers was rather too thin to be spread over three acts; but it gave rise to some amusing complications. The chief possibilities for creating mirth lay in the part of *Ballard*, the manager of the travelling company referred to, a person whom Mr. Albert Chevalier contrived to make exceedingly diverting. The book of " The Prima Donna " was written some years ago by Messrs. H. B. Farnie and Alfred Murray, and most of Signor Tito Mattei's music had also been composed some time. There was an abundance of bright melody in the score, and altogether the music was decidedly worthy of Signor Mattei's elegant and fluent pen. The chief parts were played by Madame Palma (who made her first appearance in comic opera), Mr. Alec Marsh, Miss Florence Paltzer, and Miss Amelia Grühn, the last-named a *débutante* with a pretty voice and engaging presence.

OBITUARY. — William Michael Watson (song composer), London, 2nd; Adolph von Henselt (pianist and composer), Warmbrunn, Silesia, 12th; O. Métra (dance composer and conductor), Paris, 22nd.

NOVEMBER.

DR. VILLIERS STANFORD'S "Voyage of Maeldune" and Dr. Hubert Parry's " Ode on St. Cecilia's Day" were performed for the first time in London at the Royal Choral Society's Concert on the 13th. The audience for the Albert Hall was not a large one, but it was very demonstrative, and emphatically endorsed the Leeds verdict in each instance. Considering the few rehearsals that had been possible, the performance on the part of the choir was highly meritorious; but, on the other hand, the band was by no means up to the mark, and much of the delicate charm of the orchestration, in the "Voyage of Maeldune" especially, was lost in the big building. Miss Macintyre, Madame Belle Cole, Mr. Edward Lloyd, and Mr. Brereton were the soloists of the evening, and the composers conducted.

The Royal Society of Musicians gave a performance of "Elijah" at St. James's Hall on the 27th. The principal soloists were Miss Anna Williams, Miss Hilda Wilson, Mr. Iver McKay, and Mr. Watkin Mills; and Mr. W. H. Cummings conducted.

Spohr's "Fall of Babylon," written for the Norwich Festival of 1842, and given under the composer's direction at Exeter Hall in 1847, was revived by Mr. Ebenezer Prout at the first Concert of the Hackney Choral Association on the 18th. There are some interesting solos and some magnificent choruses in this Oratorio, but in a dramatic sense Spohr's music does not rise to the level of its theme. The vocalists were Madame Isabel George, Miss Rosa Dafforne, Mr. H. Piercy, Mr. Andrew Black, and Mr. H. Pope, who all acquitted themselves well. The Hackney choir sang with much spirit and with great attention to light and shade. Mr. Prout conducted with his usual skill and intelligence.

The Crystal Palace Concert on the 2nd opened with a new Overture, entitled "Robert Bruce," composed by Mr. F. J. Simpson, a native of Portobello, near Edinburgh, who studied first at Leipsic in 1877, then at the National Training School, and afterwards, in 1885, took the degree of Mus. Bac. at Oxford. The work is intended to depict the career of the Scottish hero, Robert Bruce, and the principal theme employed is the famous tune "Scots wha hae," which, grandiosely treated, forms also the subject of the *Coda*. Mr. Simpson's Overture is boldly scored, and is altogether a work of decided merit and still greater promise. Among other items of the same Concert may be mentioned an extremely good performance by Herr Hans Wessely of Mendelssohn's Violin Concerto, and the expressive singing of Mrs. Hutchinson. The Symphony was Schumann's No. 1 in B flat. On the following Saturday Goetz's masterpiece in F was heard. Madame Anna Falk-Mehlig gave on the latter occasion an exceedingly refined, intelligent rendering of Beethoven's "Emperor" Concerto. The programme further included Berlioz's picturesque Overture to "Benvenuto Cellini" and a Rhapsody for orchestra by Edouard Lalo, heard for the first time in England. The latter work was originally a "Fantaisie Norvégienne" for violin and orchestra, and in that form was played by Señor Sarasate in Paris in 1879. In the same year it was remodelled and a second movement added, and subsequently it met with great favour at the Châtelet Concerts. The Rhapsody is bright, characteristic, and full of variety, and, as is the case with all Lalo's compositions, the orchestration glows with vivid colour. Madame Nordica sang a *scena* from Marschner's opera "Hans Heiling" and the *ballata* "C'era una volta un principe," from Gomes's Opera "Il Guarany." The performance of "St. Paul" on the 16th drew an overflowing crowd. Mr. Manns had taken great pains to secure a satisfactory rendering of Mendelssohn's earlier Oratorio, and was by no means unsuccessful. The choir did its work fairly well, the extra fifty boys' voices telling splendidly in the chorales; and the band was beyond praise. Of the soloists, the chief successes fell to Miss Anna Williams, Madame Marian McKenzie, and Mr. Lloyd. Mr. Brereton, Mr. Robert Grice, and Mr. Henry Bailey also sang, and Mr. Alfred Eyre was at the organ. A week later two works were added to the repertory of the Crystal Palace Concerts—viz., Saint-Saëns's Violin Concertstück in A (Op. 20) and Liszt's Symphonic Poem in C (No. 7), entitled " Festklänge." Neither can be described as a *chef-d'œuvre*, but the art value of the Concertstück may unquestionably be reckoned high above that of Liszt's noisy display of pretentious bombast. M. Saint-Saëns's piece gave Miss Nettie Carpenter an opportunity for a brilliant display of virtuosity on her *début* before a Sydenham audience, and she was received with loud applause. Wagner's "Flying Dutchman" Overture and Beethoven's Seventh Symphony were grandly played under Mr. Manns, and Fräulein Fillunger sang Mendelssohn's "Infelice" and *Lieder* by Brahms and Schubert. On the 30th Sir Arthur Sullivan's picturesque "Macbeth" music was heard here for the first time, and native talent was further represented by Mr. Hamish MacCunn's fine orchestral Ballad "The Ship o' the Fiend." The Symphony was Brahms's No. 2 in D. The Concert opened with a selection from Weber's "Euryanthe," comprising the Overture, Lysiart's *scena* (sung by Mr. Henschel), and the Romance "Glöcklein im Thale," given by Mrs. Henschel. The talented husband and wife were also heard together in Mr. Henschel's charming duet "Gondoliera," which so pleased the audience that it had to be repeated.

A fresh series of London Symphony Concerts was started by Mr. Henschel on the 14th. He again collected an excellent orchestra and he now furnished full analytical programmes at the reasonable price of sixpence. Moreover, in the belief that his Concerts should appeal to the legion of music-lovers who reside near and around London, he lowered his terms of subscription, and again altered the hour for beginning the Concerts from 8.30

to 8 p.m. But despite all this, the attendance at the opening Concert was meagre, and it did not subsequently improve so much as could have been wished. Whether the intended exclusion of novelties this season constituted a wise move is questionable. At any rate, it would not seem to have been so, if a scheme comprising a Suite by Bach, and Overture by Beethoven, and Symphonies by Haydn and Brahms failed at the outset to attract more powerfully. On the other hand, it was scarcely worth while to depart from the said intention in order to bring under notice the youthful efforts of Herr Richard Strauss, present Capellmeister of the Court Theatre at Weimar. Two movements from this young musician's Symphonic Fantasia "Aus Italien" were played at the Second Symphony Concert on the 28th. Herr Strauss (who, by the way, is the son of a celebrated horn-player, and no relation to the still more celebrated Viennese dance-music family) possesses undoubted talent, but it is not yet ripe enough, apparently, to challenge judgment beyond the home circle of modern German art. Whether all Herr Strauss's music is marked by the same diffuse, redundant character, the same pretentious style of treatment, and the same laborious striving after originality, with no better result than a mixed suggestion of Wagner and Brahms, it is impossible to say. Meanwhile, it would not be altogether fair to judge the composer by these isolated movements, with their meandering melodies and fantastic "tone-paintings." Enough that one seeks to depict the Roman Campagna and the other the shore at Sorrento. The same evening's selection also comprised the Overture to "Oberon," Brahms's Variation on a theme by Haydn, Wagner's "Huldigungs Marsch," and Schumann's Symphony in D minor, No. 4.

Sir Charles Hallé's Manchester band made its re-appearance at St. James's Hall, after a ten years' absence from London, on Friday evening, the 22nd, at the first of a series of four Concerts. Again did this admirable body of instrumentalists delight connoisseurs by the perfection of its *ensemble* playing. The advantage of constant working together, for unity of attack and precise observance of light and shade, was shown, for example, in a wonderful rendering of Cherubini's " Anacréon " Overture; but in regard to general excellence the Manchester band could make no claim to be placed upon a higher pedestal than our leading London orchestras, such as the Crystal Palace, the Philharmonic, or the Richter. In addition to the Overture, two of Dvorák's " Legenden " and Berlioz's " Episode de la vie d'un artiste " were played with rare spirit and refinement, while Lady Hallé gave a magnificent rendering of Beethoven's Violin Concerto. The attendance at this Concert was by no means satisfactory; but in point of fact, orchestral music, however excellent its quality, would seem to have little attraction for London amateurs during the winter months.

At the opening Saturday Popular Concerts, on the 2nd, Madame Néruda and Messrs. Ries, Straus, and Piatti gave a perfect interpretation of Cherubini's posthumous Quartet in F (No. 5), heard at these Concerts for the first time. The lovely slow movement was exquisitely played; it made one marvel at the freshness and feeling with which a composer of over 400 works could write at the age of seventy-five. Madame Haas introduced a clever and effective Fugue in E flat minor (Op. 37), by her brother, Alexis Holländer, a Professor resident in Berlin; also a Capriccio by Scarlatti, and, as a encore, a Minuet by Paderewski. All these pieces she played charmingly. Mrs. Henschel received a hearty greeting, and sang, as usual, with irreproachable taste. At the next Monday " Pop " Miss Agnes Zimmermann made her *rentrée* in a couple of pieces by Schumann, which she played with characteristic taste and sentiment. The clever English pianist also accompanied Signor Piatti in his arrangement for violoncello and piano of the third of the " Lessons " written by Ariosti for the viola d'amore—two charming movements, a *Largo* and an *Allemande*, now heard for the first time here. Signor Piatti played them with delightful beauty of tone and phrasing. The Concert opened with Mozart's Quartet in A (No. 5), and concluded with Schubert's Pianoforte Trio in B flat

(Op. 99), rendered in masterly style by Madame Néruda, Miss Zimmermann, and Signor Piatti. A very enjoyable feature of the evening were some duets by Dvorák and Goring Thomas, sung by Miss Lena Little and Mr. Max Heinrich. There was a comparatively meagre attendance both at this and the Saturday Concert of the 9th, when Dvorák's Quartet in E (Op. 80) was repeated. Sir Charles Hallé made his re-appearance amid hearty greetings, and played Beethoven's Sonata in E minor (Op. 90), adding one of Schubert's "Momens Musicales" for an encore. With Lady Hallé he was heard in Schumann's duet Sonata in A minor (Op. 105); and finally the gifted husband and wife, in association with Signor Piatti, executed Beethoven's Variations on "Ich bin der Schneider Kakadu." Miss Liza Lehmann sang songs by Schubert and Villiers Stanford. On Monday, the 11th, Sir Charles Hallé sustained a still heavier part in the proceedings. At the beginning of the Concert he was associated with Madame Néruda (Lady Hallé), Messrs. Ries, Straus, and Piatti in Dvorák's Pianoforte Quintet in A (Op. 81), which was very finely executed. After his solo (Beethoven's Variations in C minor, Op. 36) Sir Charles played two duets with Lady Hallé— viz., Brahms's Sonata in A (Op. 100) and the "Pensées Fugitives" of Heller and Ernst. The vocalist was Miss Marguerite Hall—a pleasing and artistic singer, who had made marked improvement of late. On the succeeding Saturday Sir Charles and Lady Hallé introduced for the first time at these Concerts Brahms's duet Sonata in D minor (Op. 108), which Miss Fanny Davies brought forward at Princes' Hall in the summer. The fine work made a deep impression. In addition Madame Néruda led the Haydn Quartet in D minor (Op. 42), and was associated with Sir Charles Hallé and Signor Piatti in Beethoven's D major Trio (Op. 70). The pianoforte solo was Schubert's Sonata in A minor (Op. 42). Miss Lena Little and Mr. Max Heinrich sang. On Monday, the 18th, Professor Villiers Stanford's new Sonata for pianoforte and violoncello, in D minor (Op. 39) was performed for the first time by the composer and

Signor Piatti. It was written in September, during a visit paid by Dr. Stanford to the "prince of 'cellists" at his villa on the Lake of Como. The opening *Allegretto con moto* is interesting and strongly tinged with romantic feeling; but the middle movement, an *Andante* containing some strongly-contrasted episodes, sounded on first hearing rather fragmentary and diffuse. The *Finale* is an extremely cleverly-written section, wanting neither in animation nor interest. The Sonata was finely played, and applauded with much warmth. Madame Néruda, accompanied by Miss Olga Néruda, was heard in Raff's " Volker," and also in Beethoven's Quintet in C. The Concert ended with Brahms's " Gipsy Songs " for four voices, these being sung by Mrs. Henschel, Miss Lena Little, Mr. Shakespeare, and Mr. Henschel, with Madame Haas at the piano. Miss Fanny Davies made her *rentrée* on the following Saturday, and was warmly welcomed by a large crowd. Her solo was Bach's Chromatic Fantasia, which exacting piece she executed with faultless purity of touch and *mécanisme*, adding for an encore Schumann's Canon in A flat. She also joined Madame Néruda and Signor Piatti in Beethoven's E flat Trio (Op. 70), and accompanied the Brahms "Gipsy Songs," sung by the same vocalists as at the preceding Concert. On the last Monday of the month Signor Piatti brought forward Thirteen Divisions (or Variations) to a ground bass, written by Christopher Sympson for the " Division Viol." This curious example of seventeenth century English music, as now played by Signor Piatti (with Miss Fanny Davies at the piano), made a very pleasing effect and was loudly applauded. Miss Davies also performed Beethoven's Sonata in D minor (Op. 31), and Madame Belle Cole sang. Madame de Pachmann appeared on Saturday, the 30th, and gave a highly finished performance of Schubert's Fantasia Sonata in G (Op. 78). Her sympathetic touch and neat style were manifested with especial effect in the *Finale*, after which the player was thrice recalled. Madame de Pachmann also joined Signor Piatti in Rubinstein's Three Pieces for piano and cello (Op. 11)—a modest item, selected, maybe, in order to commemorate the composer's jubilee, which was celebrated in Russia with much rejoicing on this day. Madame Néruda led Mozart's favourite Quintet in G minor and Madame Bertha Moore sang, Mr. Ernest Ford accompanying.

The students of the Royal Academy of Music gave a Chamber Concert at St. James's Hall on the 4th. Some choral pieces were also included in the programme, these comprising Wesley's anthem " Blessed be God the Father," Brahms's " Ave Maria " for female voices, and Walmisley's part-song " Sweete flowers, ye were too faire." Mendelssohn's Pianoforte Trio in C minor was remarkably well played by Miss Edith Young, Mr. Gerald Walenn, and Mr. C. H. Allen Gill; and Saint-Saëns's Variations for two pianofortes on a theme by Beethoven were capitally executed by Miss Edith Purvis and Miss Christine Taylor. The Principal conducted.

Two Concerts of a second series of four were given by the Musical Guild (on the 12th and 27th), at the Kensington Town Hall. At the first Spohr's Double Quartet in E minor (Op. 87) received a very creditable rendering. The executants were (first quartet) Mr. Arthur Bent, Mr. Wallace Sutcliffe, Mr. Emil Kreuz, and Mr. W. H. Squire, and (second quartet) Mr. Edgar Hopkinson, Miss Zoe Pyne, Mr. H. Hobday, and Mr. J. F. Field. Miss Zoe Pyne and Miss Marian Osborn played Dr. Hubert Parry's " Partita " for violin and pianoforte in D minor; and Brahms's Pianoforte Quartet in A major (Op. 26) received full justice at the hands of Miss Annie Fry, Messrs. Bent, Kreuz, and Squire. The remaining programmes of the series were equally interesting in character, the only items that call for record here being Mr. Henry Holmes's Octet in F, for strings (Op. 56), and a set of National Dances by Mr. Algernon Ashton.

The Wind Instrument Chamber Music Society gave a " Social Evening," on the 15th, at the Royal Academy of Music. The programme contained Reinecke's Trio for oboe, horn, and piano; a Sonata for flute and piano, by Mr. C. E. Stephens; a Quintet for oboe, clarinet, horn, bassoon, and piano, by Mr.

G. A. Osborne; and Spohr's Septet (Op. 147), for piano, wind, and strings. Mr. Stephens and Mr. Osborne—gifted veterans both—took part in the interpretation of their respective works.

The admirably organised Chamber Concerts given annually by the Messrs. Hann began at the Brixton Hall on the 6th. Mr. Hann and his sons supplied the entire executive element, and their refined, intelligent playing afforded pleasure to highly appreciative audiences. Messrs. Hann introduced at their second Concert, on the 27th, a MS. Pianoforte Quintet in C major, by the talented Cambridge musician, Mr. Gerard F. Cobb. This work contains the usual four movements. The *Allegro* opens boldly, and the music generally is interesting. The *Scherzo*, though too short, is distinctly humorous, and the *Trio* contrasts well with it. The slow movement can boast much melodic beauty, though in general effect slightly fragmentary. The *Rondo Finale* is very melodious and graceful. The performance of this clever work by the Messrs. Hann was deserving of the warmest praise. Mrs. Henschel sang.

The London Ballad Concerts began for the season on the 20th, St. James's Hall being full, but not crowded. The programme contained four new songs by popular composers, but none of them made a very palpable success. Madame Antoinette Sterling introduced " Bantry Bay," a rather dismal song by Molloy; Mr. Edward Lloyd sang Hope Temple's "Love and Friendship," which did not suit him; Mr. Piercy was heard in a Ballad by Marzials, called " Stay, darling, stay "; and Madame Belle Cole introduced Stephen Adams's "This work-a-day world." In addition to these artists, there appeared Mrs. Mary Davies, Miss Alice Gomes, Miss Liza Lehmann, Mr. Arthur Oswald, Mr. Plunket Greene, Madame Néruda, and Mr. Eaton Faning's Select Choir. Mr. Sidney Naylor accompanied.

Miss Mathilde Wurm gave an evening Concert at Princes' Hall on the 12th. In her solo pieces the young pianist acquitted herself with distinction, and won the warm approval of her audience. She also joined Mr. Hollander in Brahms's A major

Sonata for pianoforte and violin, and had the assistance of her sister, Miss Alice Wurm, in Saint-Saëns's arrangement for two pianofortes of his " Danse Macabre," both works being extremely well played. Miss Liza Lehmann sang.

Miss Agnes Bartlett, a pupil of Liszt, gave a series of Historical Pianoforte Recitals at the Hampstead Conservatoire Hall, commencing on the 16th. Mr. J. T. Carrodus gave an interesting Chamber Concert in the same Hall, on the 22nd, assisted by three of his sons, Mr. G. F. Geaussent, and other artists.

On the 27th Herr Robert Heckmann and his wife, assisted by Herr Bernhard Thieme (violoncello), gave a Chamber Concert at Steinway Hall. Noteworthy was their admirable interpretation of a Pianoforte Trio in F (Op. 6) by Bargiel, heard once at the " Pops " in 1875.

Herr Schönberger and Mr. Max Heinrich gave conjointly three Concerts at Steinway Hall, the programmes of which were selected from the works of Schubert, Schumann, and Brahms respectively. The first Concert took place on the 28th. It was not very well attended, but the audience derived manifest pleasure from the efforts of these talented artists.

The Musical Artists' Society gave their first Concert of the season at Willis's Rooms, on the 16th, and on the same evening the Popular Concert Union gave an excellent performance of " Judas Maccabæus " at the People's Palace, Mile End.

St. Andrew's Day was celebrated on the 30th with the customary musical honours. Mr. Ambrose Austin gave his annual Scotch Ballad Concert at St. James's Hall, at which the Glasgow Select Choir and some popular soloists appeared. At the Albert Hall Mr. William Carter provided the usual Scotch Festival, and at the Crystal Palace there was a grand evening Promenade Concert, the Saturday orchestra being specially retained.

Madame Patti sang at a second Concert at the Albert Hall on the 4th and made her final appearance on the 18th, when the colossal building was crowded in all parts. Her solo pieces on the last occasion were the air with the flutes from " L'Etoile du

Nord" and the waltz from "Roméo"; and with Mr. Edward Lloyd she sang the so-called madrigal duet from the latter opera. These pieces were all encored, and after the waltz there was a double encore. The other artists who appeared were Miss Alice Gomes, Madame Antoinette Sterling, Mr. Max Heinrich, Miss Kuhe, and Misses Marianne and Clara Eissler. Mr. Randegger conducted in the place of Mr. Ganz, who was suffering from a domestic bereavement.

"The Red Hussar," a comic opera in three acts, libretto by Mr. P. Stephens, music by Mr. Edward Solomon, was brought out at the Lyric Theatre on the 23rd, and received with a tolerable amount of favour. The story is full of improbabilities and complications, while the dialogue is largely devoted to stale quips and cranks, instead of helping to make the action clearer. Mr. Stephens's lyrics are, happily, superior to his jokes, although showing an equal lack of inventiveness. Mr. Edward Solomon's music goes a long way towards atoning for his collaborator's shortcomings, but it does not go far enough. Its interest and power drop off just when both are most needed—that is to say, in the second act amid the feeble and ridiculous incidents occurring in the English camp near Bruges. The *Red Hussar* is a female English ballad-singer in disguise. She follows her lover to the wars when, a penniless gentleman, he enlists under Marlborough and goes over to fight in Flanders. How she becomes one of Prince Eugene's Hussars it would be difficult to say; but in addition to this, she contrives, by some feat of gallantry, at once to save her lover's life and get raised to the rank of sergeant. When the scene shifts back to England, the *Red Hussar* re-appears in the strangest way as a fine lady decked in silks, satins, and jewels, and brought on in a sedan chair. Ultimately it is discovered that she is the heiress to a rich estate, and in the course of an exceedingly clumsy *dénouement* she succeeds in marrying herself to the man of her choice. The whole of the first act and the tenor song and the duet in the second comprise the very best work that Mr. Solomon has yet put into a comic opera. There is a distinction and a symmetry in his melodies that they could not boast in his early days of composition. The choruses are unimportant, but Mr. Solomon's orchestration is as rich in ingenuity and device as ever. The entire opera was admirably interpreted under M. Ivan Caryll's guidance. Miss Marie Tempest and Mr. Ben Davies carried off the chief honours of the performance, while Mr. Hayden Coffin, Mr. Arthur Williams, and Miss Florence Dysart were also in the cast.

OBITUARY.—Frederic Clay (composer), Great Marlow, 27th.

DECEMBER.

M. PETER BENOIT'S Oratorio "Lucifer" was vouchsafed its second hearing at the Albert Hall on the 4th. It again made the impression of being a work of considerable imaginative power and no slight originality, but, on the whole, did not prove more interesting than when given here for the first time in April. Mr. Barnby conducted a remarkably smooth and efficient performance, the choir again acquitting itself of its difficult task with conspicuous ability. The solos were now in entirely different hands. Miss Macintyre and Madame Belle Cole jointly sustained the *rôle* of *Fire;* Mr. Iver McKay sang very well indeed the tenor solo allotted to *Water;* and, in the absence of M. Blauwaert (who was too ill to come over and repeat his fine impersonation of *Lucifer*), Mr. Watkin Mills "doubled" the parts of the *Fiend* and *Earth*, declaiming his music with rare vigour and force. The composer was once more among the audience—not a very large one, by the way.

At the Crystal Palace Concert on the 7th the principal work in the scheme was Mr. Frederic Cliffe's clever Symphony in C minor (Op. 1), now given here for the second time. It was warmly applauded, and the composer was called to the platform. Miss Marian Osborn, until recently a student at the Royal College, made her *début* with marked success, giving an extremely neat rendering of Beethoven's G major Pianoforte Concerto and Mendelssohn's Prelude and Fugue in E minor. Goldmark's picturesque Overture "Sákuntalà" was the novelty of the afternoon, and Madame Louise Pyk sang in place of M. Blauwaert. On the 14th, at the last Saturday Concert of the year, Mr. F. H. Cowen's Old English Idyll "St. John's Eve" was performed for the first time. Written for the express purpose of fitting the limited executive resources of our minor choral societies, this Cantata can be given either with a small or a large orchestra, and at no point is the music of such a nature as to make exigent demands upon its interpreters. The poem is in Mr. Joseph Bennett's happiest vein. His flowing lyrics are, as usual, full of varied expression, and the story embodies a genuine village idyll of bygone days. The characters are four in number—viz., *Nancy*, a village maiden (soprano); *Robert*, a young villager (baritone); *Margaret*, an ancient dame (contralto); and *The Young Squire* (tenor). In three scenes we are shown how *Nancy*, advised by old *Margaret*, gathers a rose at midnight on St. John's Eve to keep until Christmas, when, if she find it unfaded, she is to wear it, and the man who plucks it from her bosom will be her husband. In due time Christmas Day comes round and the maiden displays an unfaded rose. But the man who takes it is the uncouth *Robert*, whom *Nancy* forthwith rejects, whereupon *The Young Squire* steps forward and claims *Nancy* as his bride. It was he who had sent a new bloom to replace the faded rose, and he now offers the village beauty his hand and heart. The simplicity of this poetic idea finds its counterpart in Mr. Cowen's charming music, which breathes an Old English spirit, and teems with melody of the most graceful kind. The choruses and instrumental preludes and dances are among the most attractive features of the work, while of the solos, the tenor Serenade "O Zephyr, stirring 'midst the leaves," is unquestionably the gem. The performance, which was directed by the composer, may not have been free from blemish, but it did the new work justice. Miss Macintyre, Miss Hilda Wilson, Mr. Edward Lloyd, and Mr. Plunket Greene comprised the solo quartet. The choir was excellent, and the band beyond reproach. Mr. Cowen had to respond to an enthusiastic ovation, and his composition met with high approval on every hand. Grieg's "Landkjending," for baritone solo, chorus, orchestra, and organ (Op. 31), was performed for the first time in England at the same Concert. It is a characteristic setting of a short poem by

Björnsen, describing the discovery of a new land and the founding of a kingdom by the Scandinavian hero, Olaf Trygvason. The music is full of dignity, expression, and colour, especially beautiful being the religious melody for the solo voice (sung by Mr. Albert Fairbairn), which, repeated by the chorus, concludes the piece with fine effect.

At Sir Charles Hallé's second Orchestral Concert, on the 6th, the audience did not attain to such proportions as it should have, looking at the nature of the programme and the excellence of the performance. The works given were Dvorák's Third Symphony in F, Beethoven's Pianoforte Concerto in G (the solo part played by Sir Charles Hallé himself), Gadé's "Hamlet" Overture, the *Entr'acte* in B flat and ballet air from Schubert's "Rosamunde" music, and two movements from Handel's "Concerto Grosso" in B minor.

Mozart's "Notturno-Serenade" in D, for four orchestras, was introduced at the London Symphony Concert on the 12th. The exact date of this composition is unknown, but is supposed to be 1777, and in any case the work may be regarded as a youthful *jeu d'esprit*, interesting on account of its curious form rather than attributes of a higher order. Each orchestra consists of first and second violins, viola, violoncello, and two horns. The purpose of the division is to secure echo effects, these being produced by a repetition of the concluding phrase of a passage. Thus, the first orchestra, which is also the largest, gives out the subject *forte*, and the last few bars are taken up by the remaining three orchestras in turn, each repeating it more softly than the other. The movements are three in number — viz., an *Andante*, an *Allegretto*, and a *Menuetto*, and all are unmistakably Mozartian in their melodiousness and grace. In addition to the novelty, which was neatly interpreted, the programme contained Beethoven's Symphony in B flat (No. 4), the love scene from Berlioz's "Romeo and Juliet" Symphony, and the "Trauermarsch" and "Walkürenritt" of Wagner. Mr. Henschel conducted with plenty of spirit, and was the recipient of abundant applause.

Included in the Popular Concert programme on Monday, the 2nd, were Mendelssohn's String Quintet in B flat (Op. 87) and Schumann's favourite Pianoforte Quintet in E flat (Op. 44). The executants were Madame Néruda, Miss Fanny Davies, Messrs. Ries, Straus, Gibson, and Piatti. After an excellent rendering of Beethoven's Sonata in D (Op. 10), Miss Davies played as an encore one of Mendelssohn's Characteristic Pieces. Miss Marguerite Hall sang songs by Schubert and Brahms, accompanied by Miss Carmichael. The same week Professor Stanford played his new Sonata in D minor, with Signor Piatti, for the first time to a Saturday audience, and Brahms's "Gipsy Songs." were repeated with the same quartet as before, save that Miss Marguerite Hall replaced Miss Lena Little. Madame Néruda "led" Beethoven's Quartet in F (Op. 18), and was encored in the same composer's Romance in G. Madame Haas was the pianist at this Concert, and again on Monday, the 9th, when she played Beethoven's Sonata in A flat (Op. 110), the rest of the programme being entirely familiar. The admirable singing of Mr. Plunket Greene, in pieces by Brahms and Hubert Parry, calls for mention. On the following Saturday and Monday, Miss Fanny Davies was the pianist, giving Schumann's "Carnival" at one Concert and five or six numbers of his "Kreisleriana" at the other. The concerted works were again selected from among the most familiar in the repertory, while the vocalists on these respective occasions were Mdlle. Agnes Janson and Miss Liza Lehmann. At the afternoon Concert of the 21st a Beethoven programme was performed, including such favourites as the "Waldstein" and "Kreutzer" Sonatas, and the "Rasoumowski" Quartet in F. Sir Charles Hallé took part in the Sonatas, and Miss Marguerite Hall sang. The series of Concerts before Christmas terminated on the 23rd, when Mozart's Clarinet Quintet (with Mr. Lazarus at his usual post), Beethoven's Trio in C minor (Op. 1, No. 3), Chopin's Barcarolle (played by Mdlle. Janotha), and portions of Raff's "Cyklische Tondichtung" (executed by Madame Néruda), with songs for Fräulein Fillunger, made up an attractive programme. The average attendance during the month was large, more especially, of course, on the Saturday afternoons.

The only Christmas performance of " The Messiah " in central London was that given at St. James's Hall, on the 20th, by the South London Choral Association, under Mr. L. C. Venables, the able Conductor of this institution. The Oratorio went fairly well, the solos being undertaken by Mrs. Hutchinson, Miss Hilda Wilson, Mr. Henry Piercy, and Mr. Andrew Black.

Another Choral Concert on the same evening was that given at Alexandra House by pupils of the Royal College of Music, the work essayed here being Berlioz's Sacred Trilogy " L'Enfance du Christ," first introduced to Londoners by Sir Charles Hallé in 1880. The work, however, has never reaped the benefit of that introduction. It is treated with an indifference which its musical beauties certainly do not warrant, and which the popularity of the same composer's secular masterpiece, "La Damnation de Faust," makes it difficult to explain. Hence were thanks due to the authorities of the Royal College for performing " L'Enfance du Christ " at the College Concert that marked the close of the term. The religious charm and subdued grandeur of Berlioz's music were fully recognised and appreciated by all who heard it, and it received adequate justice at the hands of the students, under the painstaking guidance of Professor Stanford. The solos were sustained by Miss Richardson (*Mary*), Mr. J. Sandbrook (*Joseph*), Mr. E. G. Branscombe (*Narrator*), Mr. S. P. Musson (*Herod*), and Mr. Chas. J. Magrath (*Father of the Family*).

The Royal Academy students took part in a Choral and Orchestral Concert at St. James's Hall on the 11th, the programme opening with a " Christmas Carol " (MS.), by Miss Mary Toulmin, a pupil of Mr. Corder's. The Carol, set to words by Miss Julia Goddard, was neatly put together, and the composer had to respond to a deserved recall. Of the pianists Miss Amy Horrocks, Miss Maude Wilson, and Miss Mabel Lyons most distinguished themselves; while three Australian pupils of Mr. Randegger (Mrs. Florence Bethell, Mr. C. Edwards, and Mr. F.

H. Morton) displayed capital voices and good style in the dungeon trio from "Fidelio." Dr. Mackenzie, the Principal, conducted.

At an Orchestral Concert given at the Guildhall on the 7th, by students of the Guildhall School of Music, the Lord Mayor (Sir Henry Isaacs) attended in state, and was duly honoured with Mr. Weist Hill's "Civic Anthem." A selection from Berlioz's "Faust"—musical and instrumental excerpts only—gave great satisfaction. A Nocturne for violin and orchestra, by Mr. Joseph Speaight, a student, was played, Mr. John Saunders executing the solo. The first movement of a Symphony in G minor, by Miss Edith Swepstone, another talented student, was also introduced with marked success. The Concert was admirably conducted by the Principal.

Mr. and Mrs. Henschel sang before crowded audiences at their Vocal Recitals, at Princes' Hall, on the 4th and 11th. The programmes were well chosen and of exceptional interest, several compositions by Mr. Henschel being included.

The fiftieth birthday of Mr. J. H. Bonawitz was celebrated at the Portman Rooms on the 3rd by a Concert of his vocal and orchestral works. Included in the programme were selections from Mr. Bonawitz's operas "Ostrolenka," "Irma," and "The Bride of Messina"; excerpts from his "Requiem" and "Stabat Mater"; the serenade from his Symphony in C minor; and a new Introduction and Scherzo for piano and orchestra, played for the first time by the composer himself.

At their opening Concert of the season, on the 4th, the Westminster Orchestral Society provided an interesting scheme, in which, among other things, Miss Josephine Lawrence played Weber's "Concertstück," and Mr. F. Griffiths played a Flute Concerto by F. Langer for the first time. Miss Annie Marriott and Mr. Musgrove Tufnail were the vocalists.

Miss Emma Barnett's Pianoforte Recital at St. James's (Banqueting) Hall, on the 10th, derived special interest from the first performance of a Sonata in A minor, by Mr. J. F. Barnett, wherein the talents of the brother as a composer and the sister as an executant were advantageously exhibited. The new work is in three movements, and of these the *Finale* (a Saltarello) pleased most on first hearing. The Sonata as a whole earned hearty admiration. Miss Barnett also played Schumann's Fantasia (Op. 17) and a number of smaller pieces by modern masters.

Mrs. Francis Ralph gave a Chamber Concert at Princes' Hall on the 11th, at which she introduced (with Mr. Gerald Walenn) a Romance for violin and piano and an Air with variations for piano, both clever and pleasing compositions, from her own pen. Madame Mary Davies and Mr. Bridson sang, and Mr. Charles Fry gave a couple of recitations.

The Stock Exchange Orchestral Society gave its first Concert of the season at St. James's Hall on the 10th. The Male Voice Choir, an organisation not less excellent and efficient in its way than the band which Mr. George Kitchin conducts so admirably, also took part in the Concert. Among the instrumental items were Mendelssohn's "Italian" Symphony, Sterndale Bennett's "Parisian" Overture, Massenet's "Scènes Alsaciennes," and the Overture to Ambroise Thomas's "Raymond," which were all given with a degree of refinement and spirit above the level of ordinary amateur playing. Mr. Arthur Payne was successful in his violin solos, and Fräulein Fillunger sang.

At the Hyde Park Academy Students' Concert at Steinway Hall, on the 12th, Mr. H. Frost officiated for the last time as Conductor at this institution. He concluded his labours with quite a *tour de force*, for his young ladies came off easy victors in a struggle with the exacting chorus of Sea-Fairies, from Stanford's "Voyage of Maeldune."

After a run of fourteen months "The Yeomen of the Guard" at the Savoy gave place, on the 7th, to a new comic opera by Mr. W. S. Gilbert and Sir Arthur Sullivan, entitled "The Gondoliers; or, the King of Barataria." Mr. Gilbert's share in the new work is worthy of his reputation. Discarding the travesty of "Ruddigore" and the serious interest of "The Yeomen of the

Guard," he returns to his old love, "topsy-turveydom," and revels once more in paradox and incongruity. The lyrics are in Mr. Gilbert's happiest vein, and the dialogue, though there is less of it than usual, contains quite the customary proportion of quaint conceits and merry quips and cranks. The plot deals with the confusion of interests and identities arising out of the search for the lost heir to the throne of Barataria. The individual in question is supposed to be one of two Venetian gondoliers, who are invested with the joint sovereignty of the country, and who carry on the government on strictly Republican lines until the rightful king turns up in another person. From this motive springs a chain of extremely amusing incidents, treated by Mr. Gilbert in his customary skilful and humorous fashion, the interest being well sustained to the last. It has been generally conceded that "The Gondoliers" is the equal of "The Mikado" for freshness, brightness, and animation. The "local colour" may not be so completely novel, but it is very nearly as delightful and quite as truthful. The first act is redolent of gay, sunny Italy—that Italy which we read about and see in pictures. The stage represents a beautiful tableau of the Piazzetta and the Grand Canal at Venice, as that famous place might have looked 150 years ago when crowded with pretty *contadine* and gaily-clad gondoliers. What Mr. Craven's brush and Mr. Percy Anderson's pencil do here for the eye, Sir Arthur Sullivan's music does for the ear. The gifted composer has fairly ransacked the store of Italian forms and rhythms to provide music that shall suggest as well as please. The dashing Neapolitan song for *Antonio*, with chorus; the jolly Barcarolle for the two gondoliers; the familiar Abruzzi "drone" in the bridal chorus; the delicious imitation of the Rossinian style in the greeting (to real Italian words) between the gondoliers and the *contadine;* and the spirited Saltarello movement that comes in the *Finale*—these are all delightful in themselves and perfect in their illustrative colour. In the second act, which takes place in Barataria, there enters a Spanish element, and this the composer duly reflects in his stately gavotte-quintet (quaintly

K

sung and quaintly danced), and his genuinely Spanish Cachucha, the execution of which by Miss Geraldine Ulmar, Miss Jessie Bond, Mr. Curtice Pounds, and Mr. Rutland Barrington is a triumph of its kind. But "local colour" is all very well in its way; there must not be too much of it. An opera by Sir Arthur Sullivan without the purely Sullivanesque would be an anomaly, and that mistake has happily not been committed in "The Gondoliers." The Grand Inquisitor's songs, more than one sentimental ballad, and much of the delicious concerted music—above all, that wonderfully clever and comic quartet with the combined themes in the second act—bear the stamp of the composer's individuality in its clearest aspect, while the instrumentation simply teems with characteristic touches of delicate fancy and humour. The performance was full of life and "go," and showed old favourites and new-comers alike in the most favourable light. The quartet of artists above-named were truly admirable as the gondoliers and their wives. A youthful *débutante*, Miss Decima Moore, won emphatic favour; while the absence of Mr. Grossmith was more than atoned for by the co-operation of two talented comedians like Mr. Frank Wyatt and Mr. Denny. Miss Rosina Brandram and Mr. Brownlow were also in the cast. The success of "The Gondoliers" was pronounced in unmistakable fashion on all sides, the cheers that greeted author, composer, and manager on the first night foreshadowing a long and prosperous run.

OBITUARY.—Charles H. Marriott (dance music composer and conductor), Hastings, 3rd; Madame Moscheles (pianist, widow of Moscheles), Detmold, Germany, 13th; Carl Formes (bass singer), New York, 16th.

BIRMINGHAM.

THE pause in local musical affairs, consequent upon the Christmas holidays, extended to February 4, when Messrs. Harrison resumed the popular Subscription Concerts in the Town Hall. The interest on this occasion was centred in little Otto Hegner, who appeared here for the first time, and greatly charmed the audience by his expressive performance of pieces by Chopin and Schumann, and perfectly astounded them by his wonderful execution in Liszt's second Rhapsodie Hongroise. Miss Marianne Eissler introduced Dr. A. C. Mackenzie's "Benedictus," for violin, the beauties of which were cordially recognised. The vocalists were Madame Nordica, Madame Patey, Mr. Orlando Harley, and Signor Foli, Mr. Wilhelm Ganz officiating as pianist. On the 15th the same *entrepreneurs* gave a further opportunity of judging of the capabilities of young Hegner, who, under their auspices, gave a Pianoforte Recital in the Town Hall. He played in masterly style Bach's Suite Anglaise (No. 2) and Beethoven's Sonata in E flat (Op. 31, No. 3), and in smaller pieces by Chopin, Hans Huber, Paderewski, and others exhibited remarkable finish and taste. At their fourth Concert, March 4, Messrs. Harrison once more brought Hallé's celebrated orchestra here. This is always the greatest musical treat of the year. A novelty in the programme was Bizet's Suite "Roma," which charmed all hearers. Beethoven's Overture in C (Op. 124), seldom heard here, was given in grand style, and Lady Hallé played two movements of the E major Concerto of Vieuxtemps, and Sir Charles Hallé gave two of the three pieces by Grieg, known as "Aus dem Volksleben" (Op. 19). The vocalists were Miss Hope Glenn and Mr. Henry Piercy. From May to October is an interregnum, musically speaking, the only breaks in which are those of comic opera; and the first herald of the approaching season is nearly always the new series of Popular Concerts given by Messrs. Harrison. On October 14 Madame Patti, with a host of lesser stars, gratified a large and fashionable audience, Mdlle. Janotha making her first appearance here. At the second Concert, November 25, the vocalists were Madame Nordica, Miss Macintyre, Miss Hope Glenn, and Signor Foli, with two eminent violinists, Messrs. Tivadar Nachèz and Johannes Wolff, and another *débutant*, Mr. Luigi Arditi.

Mr. Stockley's Orchestral Concerts were resumed on February 7, but the programme was made up of items more or less familiar. We had, however, the pleasure of hearing Mackenzie's "Benedictus" as scored for orchestra, which was admirably performed, the whole of the first and second violins (numbering nearly thirty) playing the melody with remarkable unity and effect. Mdlle. Antoinette Trebelli and Mr. Edward Lloyd were the vocalists. On March 14 Mr. Stockley brought forward a novelty, a Suite de Ballet in E flat, by A. Goring Thomas, originally written for the Cambridge University Musical Society. This, though musicianly in every way, seemed to us somewhat heavy. The two melodies for string orchestra, by Grieg, met with universal acceptance, and were played with much refinement. The vocalists were Miss Fanny Moody and Mr. Charles Manners, who appeared for the first time in Birmingham on the Concert platform. At the Concert of May 2, Dr. Hubert Parry conducted his "Suite Moderne," composed for the Gloucester Festival of 1886, and the "Danse Macabre" of Saint-Saëns was heard here for the first time in its proper orchestral form. The first work was heard with pleasure and admiration; the other excited a kind of wonder, but little beyond. Miss Nettie Carpenter played in admirable style Max Bruch's Violin Concerto in G minor, and Madame Nordica and Mr. Charles Banks gave some operatic pieces. Mr. Stockley entered upon his seventeenth series of Orchestral Concerts on November 7, when Mr. Frederic Cliffe's Symphony in C minor was produced. The work made a deep impression here, the skilful handling of the orchestra in the first and final movements being very conspicuous, and the melodic wealth of the *Ballade*—albeit resembling in its initial theme *Senta's* ballad in "The Flying Dutchman"—striking the attention of all. Mr. Cliffe, who proved himself an able Conductor, met with a most enthusiastic reception. The "Graceful Dance" from Sullivan's incidental music to "Henry VIII.," and Wagner's study, "Träume," as arranged for violin solo and orchestra, were also novelties here. Mr. F. Ward played the solo admirably. Madame Nordica and Mr. Ben Davies sang.

The third Concert of the Festival Choral Society was given in the Town Hall on February 21. The programme was miscellaneous, and comprised part-songs, sung with extraordinary delicacy and finish, but with a certain dragging of the time, apparently inevitable with a chorus of 400 voices. Meyerbeer's 91st Psalm, Mr. A. R. Gaul's Anthem, "O praise God in His holiness," and part of Leonardo's "Dixit Dominus" were performed. Madame Georgina Burns, Madame Marian Mackenzie, Mr. Iver McKay, and Mr. Leslie Crotty contributed vocal solos. Mr. Stockley conducted. The Society gave Mendelssohn's "Elijah," on March 28, with Madame Nordica, Miss Hilda Wilson, Mr. Edward Lloyd, and Mr. Watkin Mills as vocal principals. On October 24 this Society commenced its thirtieth series of Subscription Concerts with a performance of Handel's "Samson," when Miss Macintyre made her *début* here in oratorio. As most of the music allotted to *Delilah* was cut out, the lady had not much to do, but her singing of "Let the bright seraphim" was brilliant and effective. The other soloists were Miss Damian, Mr. Charles Banks, Mr. Brereton, and a local bass, Mr. H. A. Sims, who, as *Manoah*, was fairly good. The second Concert took place on December 2, the programme being made up with Gounod's "Messe Solennelle" (St. Cecilia), Stanford's "Revenge," and Mendelssohn's "Walpurgis Night." The performance was a good one, particularly of Mendelssohn's work. The principal vocalists were Madame Clara Samuell, Mrs. Payton, Mr. Iver McKay, and Mr. Watkin Mills. The organ, which had been closed for the last six months for re-construction, was employed again for the first time, Mr. C. W. Perkins officiating with his usual skill. Mr. Stockley conducted. The annual performance of Handel's "Messiah" was given on December 26. The vocal principals were Madame Clara Samuell, Miss Lizzie Neal, Mr. C. Banks, and Mr. Grice. Miss Neal is a native of Birmingham, and on this occasion made her *début* here in oratorio. Before studying at the R.A.M. she was a pupil of Mr. Charles Lunn.

Chamber Concerts do not pay in Birmingham, as local musicians have found out to their cost. Madame Agnes Miller, a non-resident pianoforte teacher with an influential connection here, has for some seasons past given one or more Concerts of this kind, however, and on February 28 brought a short series to a close. She was supported by the Shinner Quartet. On November 28 Madame Miller began a new series of four Concerts. In conjunction with Mr. Ludwig Straus, a fairly interesting programme was gone through, the principal item being the Sonata in D minor (Op. 108) of Brahms, now heard here for the first time: The comparative simplicity and clearness of outline of this work appealed directly to the audience, and the Sonata was very favourably received. Mr. Straus played a Sonata in G, by Tartini, not familiar here, and Madame Miller gave well-known pieces by Mendelssohn and Schumann.

Coming to other than serial Concerts, the first important event of the year was the appearance of Mr. Max Pauer, who gave a Pianoforte Recital, before a small audience, in the Masonic Hall, on February 9. He sustained a varied and exacting programme with marvellous technique and power, excelling in Schumann's "Etudes Symphoniques" and Liszt's twelfth Rhapsodie. He also played, for the first time in Birmingham, Chopin's Allegro de Concert in A (Op. 46), but the work did not create a great impression. On the 12th a Concert was given at the Midland Institute, with Mr. Carrodus as the principal performer. Miss Fanny Davies, whom Birmingham people are proud to claim as one of themselves, gave a Recital on behalf of a local charity. The programme included Schumann's "Faschingsschwank aus Wien" (Op. 26), Beethoven's Variations and Fugue in E flat (Op. 35), and a novelty in the shape of a Valse Impromptu (in A flat, Op. 1, No. 2), by Nicolai von Wilm, of Wiesbaden. This last was very attractive, although too much in the style of Chopin to be credited with much originality. At this Recital Miss Hope Glenn sang Schubert's "Erl-King." At a second Recital, on the 26th, Miss Davies was assisted by Signor Piatti, who had not been heard here in chamber music for some time. Miss Davies played Bach's great Fugue in A minor, and the concerted pieces were Mendelssohn's Sonata in D (Op. 58) and Rubinstein's Sonata in D (Op. 18), for pianoforte and violoncello. Signor Piatti gave his well-known "Bergamasca" and an Impromptu on an air from Purcell's "Indian Queen."

The Edgbaston Amateur Musical Union, founded some five-and-twenty years ago by Mr. J. B. Duchenim, has done good work in its time, and keeps up its reputation as an efficient amateur orchestra. Under the conductorship of Mr. W. Astley Langston a Concert was given in the Vestry Hall, Edgbaston, on April 11, when Spohr's first Symphony in E flat was performed. This work had probably never been previously heard in Birmingham.

On Good Friday the Midland Musical Society, conducted by Mr. H. M. Stephenson, an amateur, gave a performance of Gounod's "Redemption" in the Town Hall. This Society, appealing to the artisan classes, gives performances at nominal charges, and always secures an overflowing attendance. On November 16 "Samson" was performed by this Society, when an incident occurred too good to pass unrecorded. Some persons, attracted by the title of the oratorio on the posters, went to the Town Hall expecting to witness the feats of the "Strongest

Man in the World!" When they found out the nature of the performance they indignantly demanded their money back.

At the Concert of the Clef Club, on May 9, the programme included Heinrich Hoffmann's fine Serenade for flute and strings (Op. 65), performed, it was thought, for the first time in England. Mr. Piddock was the flautist, local artists supplying the strings. Another item of interest was a clever Prelude and Fugue for two Pianofortes by Mr. Battison Haynes, played by the composer and Mr. C. W. Perkins. Dr. Herbert Wareing likewise conducted a selection from his Cantata "New Year's Eve."

On November 18 a Concert was given in the Masonic Hall by a local baritone, Mr. A. Mancus, who proved himself the possessor of meritorious vocal and dramatic powers, and his *début* was successful. On the 21st Mr. Oscar Pollack and Madame Pollack gave their annual Concert. The programme included Gounod's new "Ave Maria" on Bach's second Prelude, the solo being well sung by our talented contralto. Mr. Rechab Tandy, the American tenor, made a successful first appearance here at this Concert. On the 28th the Glasgow Select Choir paid its second visit to this city, and delighted the large audience, which filled the Town Hall, with some refined part-singing. On December 9 a complimentary Concert was given to Dr. C. S. Heap, when his Cantata "The Maid of Astolat" was performed here for the first time. The vocal principals were Mrs. Hutchinson, Miss Emilie Lloyd, Mr. Orlando Harley, Mr. D. Harrison, and Mr. W. Evans. There was an excellent band, and a chorus of remarkable quality, numbering 400 voices. Dr. Heap conducted a performance which admirably brought out the merits of his composition. It is a reflection upon Birmingham that this able work has had to wait so long for a hearing in its composer's birthplace; but it is no use ignoring the fact that musical matters are neither in a flourishing nor satisfactory condition here.

Master Isidore Pavia, a pianist of about fifteen years of age, played at the Madrigal Concert at the Midland Institute, December 16, and gave a Recital the following afternoon. The young artist, without being a phenomenon, displayed great talent as an executant. Among local events of interest was the production at Walsall, March 13, of Prout's "Red Cross Knight," under the direction of Dr. Heap.

The cheap Saturday Night Concerts in the Town Hall—admission from threepence to a shilling—attract large audiences; and in addition to those given by the Musical Association and others, the Birmingham and Midland Musical Guild has entered the arena, and by high-class miscellaneous programmes, executed by the best local artists, hopes to do something to raise the taste of the people at large. So far their efforts have been successful, judging from the demeanour of the large audiences attending the two Concerts already given on October 19 and November 30.

We had no visit from the Carl Rosa Company this year, and it was not to be wondered at; for very often their admirable performances have been given to empty houses, the public behaving in a capricious manner beyond understanding. On February 11 Mr. J. W. Turner's Company began a three weeks' season at the Grand Theatre, reviving Macfarren's "Robin Hood."

A Lecture on "Beethoven" was given by the present writer at the Handsworth Free Library, on January 24, when several pieces from the recently published volume (Breitkopf & Härtel) of the master's posthumous works were performed for the first time in England, including the *Allegretto* in C minor. On November 18 Sir John Stainer gave a highly interesting Lecture on "Hymn Tunes" to the members of the Midland Institute, illustrated by the Madrigal Choir, under the direction of Mr. Stockley.

STEPHEN S. STRATTON.

BRISTOL.

The Madrigal Society's Concert on January 17 attracted its votaries in large numbers. There were two interesting items in the programme—viz., Dr. W. A. Barrett's eight-part Madrigal, "On a mossy bank," which received its first public rendering, and Mr. Santley's "T'other day as I was twining." Mr. D. W. Rootham conducted. On the 28th a new venture was started by Mr. W. F. Trimnell, the chief music-master of Clifton College, in the shape of a series of Orchestral and Vocal Concerts. Musically, except for a little roughness, the Concert was successful, but the attendance was very poor. A band of fifty, led by Mr. Theo. Carrington, played items familiar to Bristolians, with one exception—namely, Dr. A. C. Mackenzie's "Benedictus," which was performed for the first time in the Western city, and at once won the favour of the audience. Miss Emily Spada was the vocalist.

Mrs. Viner-Pomeroy's third Classical Chamber Concert of the season was given on February 4. The artists were Mrs. Roeckel (piano), Mr. Ludwig (violin), Mr. E. Woodward (viola), and Mr. A. Waite (violoncello).

The second Orchestral and Vocal Concert, at the Victoria Rooms, on the 11th, drew a scanty audience. Haydn's "Clock" Symphony was the most important work performed. At Miss Lock's third Popular Chamber Concert, on the 13th, among other works Mozart's Piano Quartet in E flat (No. 3) was well played by Miss Lock, Mr. Hudson, Mr. F. S. Gardener, and Mr. E. Pavey.

Miss Florence Eyre, a young Clifton lady, and pupil at the Leipsic Conservatoire of Carl Reinecke, gave a Concert at the

Victoria Rooms, on the 18th, and displayed much talent. Professor Brodsky, a finished violinist, here made his first appearance in Clifton. Mr. Augustus Simmons gave a Concert on the 18th.

On February 22 and 23 Sir George Edwards gave a couple of Concerts on the lines of the Triennial Festival, at the Colston Hall. For the purpose a special choir was brought together by Mr. D. W. Rootham to study Haydn's "Creation," Félicien David's "The Desert," Mendelssohn's "Hear my prayer," and other works, and Sir Charles Hallé and his Manchester band were engaged. The choir, directed by Mr. D. W. Rootham, sang "The deep repose of night" and "The lark's song" of Mendelssohn, with beauty of tone, clearness of enunciation, and correct phrasing. Mr. J. L. Roeckel's "Christian's Armour" Cantata was given in Redcliff Church on the 25th, under the direction of the composer.

At the third Orchestral and Vocal Concert, on the 25th, Mr. Theo. Carrington was the solo violinist. The "Ladies' Night" of the Orpheus Glee Society, a fine association of male voices, fell on the 28th, when a large auditory assembled in Colston Hall. The soloists were Messrs. Jones, Harper Kearton, J. F. Nash, W. Thomas, and H. J. Dyer. Mr. Riseley conducted, and furnished the novelties—viz., "The old church bells," a bass solo and four parts; and "Where'er my footsteps stray," a tenor solo and five parts, both compositions being favourably received. The perfect way in which everything is sung by the Orpheus Glee Society makes their annual Concert one of the musical treats of the year. Mr. George Riseley was the Conductor.

Mozart's Motet "Glory, honour," was the principal work performed by the Bristol Musical Society at the Saturday Popular Concert, on March 2. The vocalists were Mrs. Clare Wright, Mr. Dyved Lewys, and Mr. John Jones. Organ solos by Mr. G. Riseley, cornet solos by Mr. Covielo, and selections by the band were also given.

The fourth Classical Chamber Concert took place on March 4.

The executants were Mrs. Roeckel, Messrs. Ludwig, J. O. Brooke, M. Rice, E. Woodward, and J. Pomeroy.

On March 5 St. Mary's Choral Society (Tyndall's Park) gave a performance of Spohr's "God, Thou art great," at the Alexandra Hall. Miss Florence Cromey, Miss Blinkhorn, Mr. S. W. Pullen, and Mr. W. H. Wickes were the solo vocalists. Mr. F. Rootham conducted.

St. Barnabas' Choral Society performed G. Fox's "The Jackdaw of Rheims," with orchestral accompaniment, on March 4.

At the Saturday Popular Concert, on March 23, a new composition, entitled "The Sailor's Good-night," written by Mr. George Riseley, was sung in public for the first time by Mr. Lawford Huxtable, the composer accompanying. The choir sang part-songs, under Mr. Geo. Gordon.

Sir Chas. Hallé and Lady Hallé gave a Recital at the Victoria Rooms, on the 26th. Mr. Lieblich gave a Concert on the 30th.

At the Popular Chamber Concert, on April 2, Miss Lock, Messrs. Hudson, Gardner, and Pavey were the executants, and Miss Amy Carter sang. A large audience attended the annual Concert given on the 29th by Mr. John Barrett's Choir. Beethoven's "Praise of Music," and two sections, "Spring" and "Winter," from Haydn's "Seasons," were admirably performed. The soloists were Madame Pennington, Miss Marie Gane, Miss Florence Cromey, Miss A. Maby, Mr. E. T. Morgan, and Mr. J. F. Nash. Mrs. Brockbank Young was the pianist, and Mr. Barrett conducted.

St. John's (Redland) Choral Society gave Bridge's "Boadicea" at their annual Concert, on April 15. The soloists were Miss Gertrude Eyre, Miss F. C. Jones, Messrs. Morgan, Albery, J. Lomas, W. H. Wickes, Dr. C. Harles, Messrs. Wilcox and Macgregor. Mr. A. E. Hill was the Conductor. Macfarren's "May Day" was performed by St. Saviour's (Redland) Choral Society, on the 16th. The principal vocalists were Mrs. C. Bigg, Mrs. J. Dole, Miss F. Cromey, Mr. Ford, and Mr. Trowbridge. Mr. Vaughan Tittle conducted.

The Bristol Society of Instrumentalists, formed in the autumn of last year, and now numbering 120 amateur performers, gave their first "Ladies' Night" at the Colston Hall, on the 21st, and surprised everyone by their excellent playing. Mr. Carrington, the leader, contributed a violin solo. Vocal pieces were given by Mrs. Nixon and Mr. O. J. Thomas. Mr. Geo. Riseley was the Conductor.

Hutchinson's "The Story of Elaine" and Locke's "Music to Macbeth" were performed by the Bristol Operatic Society on June 4.

The Bristol Choral Society met in October for rehearsal, under the direction of Mr. G. Riseley. The membership of the new Society exceeded 500 within a month of the first meeting. The Bristol Society of Instrumentalists, which had increased in membership to 100, also met to study under the same Conductor.

During the two first weeks of October the Carl Rosa Opera Company visited the Prince's Theatre. The new operas (to Bristol) presented were Meyerbeer's "Star of the North" and Wallace's "Lurline."

On October 19 the first of a series of Chamber Concerts was given by Messrs. Theo. Carrington, F. Gardner, Andrew Waite, and F. Huxtable. Miss Maggie Davies and Mr. Lawford Huxtable were the vocalists. At the second Concert interest centred chiefly in a couple of new pieces written by Miss Ellicott—viz., a pleasing Romance and Polonaise for violin, admirably played by Mr. Carrington, the composer accompanying.

Miss Lock's first Popular Chamber Concert of the fifth season took place on October 22, the executants being Miss Locke, Messrs. A. Hudson, Gardener, and Pavey. The concerted works included a Trio in D, for piano, violin, and violoncello, a pleasing composition written by Mr. J. W. Hudson, the brother of the violinist.

Señor Sarasate gave a Recital at the Victoria Rooms on the 23rd to a crowded and delighted audience.

The Annual Gathering of the South Midland Section National

Society of Professional Musicians took place on the 23rd, Mr. C. E. Stephens being the invited guest.

On October 22 the first meeting of the newly-formed Bristol South Choral Society was held, and that of the Bristol East Choral Society took place on the 25th.

Two "Intermediate" Concerts were given by the Bristol Musical Festival Society, on November 1 and 2. On the first day Mendelssohn's music to "A Midsummer Night's Dream" received an admirable rendering, Miss Marie Gane and Mrs. Probert-Goodwin excellently singing the solos. Leslie's suave "Lullaby of Life" was deliciously sung by the Festival Choir, Mr. D. W. Rootham, the Chorusmaster, conducting. Miss Macintyre, Miss Damian, Mr. Maldwyn Humphreys, and Mr. Henschel were the vocalists. Gounod's "Death and Life" ("Mors et Vita") was performed in English on the 2nd. Mesdames Nordica and Enriquez, Messrs. Iver McKay and G. Henschel sang the solos, and Sir Chas. Hallé's band co-operated. The work received an interpretation worthy of the Society, and evidently made a deep impression on the vast audience assembled from Bristol and districts around.

The Montpelier Choral Society, a new body, met for the first time on November 18, and on the same day Mr. Sims Reeves bade farewell to the Bristol musical public.

Mr. Frederick Lamond, the clever young Scotch pianist, was the chief attraction at Mrs. Viner-Pomeroy's Chamber Concert on the same date. The concerted works included a Trio in B minor (Op. 2), for piano, violin, and violoncello, written by Mr. Lamond, and now introduced to frequenters of these gatherings.

Mozart's Mass in C (No. 1) was performed at the Saturday Popular Concert on November 23. The performances, on the same occasion, of Messrs. F. Goddard, H. Bell, R. Englemann, and W. H. Hannan, a quartet of trombone players, created much interest.

St. Barnabas' Choral Society gave their annual Concert on November 27. The chief vocalists were Mesdames J. Jones,

Matthews, Escott; Messrs. T. H. Gore, E. Tapp, and T. H. Blandford. Mr. Matthews was the Conductor. Mr. C. Lee Williams directed the first performance here of his work "The Last Night at Bethany," in Redcliff Church, on the 27th. Van Bree's "Cecilia's Day" was rendered by the St. Mary's (Tyndall's Park) Choral Society, also on the 27th, under Mr. F. Rootham's direction.

On December 1 the first part of a new Sacred Cantata, "The Second Advent of the Redeemer," written by Mr. W. Fear Dyer, was rendered in St. Nicholas Church, of which the composer is organist. Two works specially written were included in the scheme for the Gleemen's "Ladies' Night," on the 5th. They were a choral scena, "Enceladus," written to Longfellow's words by Dr. C. W. Pearce; and a part-song, "Shine out, stars," composed by Miss Ellicott. The former, which is a really fine composition, was effectively sung under Dr. Pearce's direction, and was well received.

The second Classical Chamber Concert of the thirteenth season took place on the 9th. A Quartet in B flat, for two violins, viola, and violoncello, by Miss Ellicott (already played in London), headed the programme, and was skilfully interpreted by Messrs. Ludwig, E. Halfpenny, V. Marriot, and J. Pomeroy. The last-named artist played a recently-written Rêverie for violoncello, also from the pen of Miss Ellicott, who accompanied it.

At the second Popular Chamber Concert of the fifth season, which fell on December 10, Prout's Quartet in F (Op. 18), for piano, violin, viola, and violoncello, received an excellent interpretation at the hands of Miss Lock, Messrs. A. Hudson, Gardner, and A. Waite. The only other noteworthy piece was an Idyll for violin, viola, and piano, written by the violinist of the evening.

The newly-formed Social and Musical Society in connection with the University College, Bristol, held their first meeting on the 12th.

At the Saturday Popular Concert, on December 14, Miss Alice Gomes and Mr. Maldwyn Humphreys were the vocalists. The choir sang a number of choruses and part-songs with greater precision, better tone, and more intelligence than ever before perhaps. Mr. Riseley played organ solos, and the band performed selections, Mr. Gordon conducting.

The most interesting item in the programme of the third Musical Matinée of Messrs. Carrington, Huxtable, Gardner, and Waite, on December 14, was a new Trio in G, for piano, violin, and violoncello, written by Miss Rosalind Ellicott. The work, which is graceful, pleasing, and one of the most scholarly that has come from the pen of the talented lady, was well interpreted by the composer, Mr. Barrington, and Mr. A. Waite.

The Bristol Sullivan Society gave an admirable performance of "Princess Ida" on December 18, under the direction of Mr. Leonard M. Day. In the second part of the programme was a new humorous Cantata, entitled "The Ghost," words by the late Hugh Conway, music by A. H. Behrend, which made a very favourable impression. Mrs. Leveritt, Messrs. Abbott and Dyer were the soloists. Miss Pauline Day's services as pianist deserve to be recognised.

The new Sacred Cantata, "The Second Advent of the Redeemer," was sung in its entirety for the first time at St. Nicholas Church on the 22nd. The work may be said to have added to the reputation of Mr. Dyer, who had already won success as a composer. He presided at the organ, and the solos were taken by Mrs. Probert-Goodwin, Mrs. C. White, Messrs. Grey, Farebrother, Frederick Dyer, and Liscombe.

A highly commendable performance of "The Messiah"—the only one given here during the Christmas season—was given in the Church of St. Agnes by Mr. John Barrett's choir on the 27th. The soloists were Madame Pennington, Miss Cromey, Mrs. White, Miss Maby, Madame Rosa Bailey, Miss Aldersley, Mr. E. T. Morgan, and Mr. J. F. Nash. Mrs. Brockbank Young presided at the organ, and Mr. John Barrett conducted.

EDMUND J. SHELLARD.

CAMBRIDGE.

The chief musical interest of the year has as usual centred in the University Musical Society, of which the newly-elected Provost of King's is President and Professor Stanford the Conductor. The performances in connection with this Society have been—

(1) *In the Lent Term*—Four Concerts of the series known as the " Wednesday Popular Concerts " for Chamber Music on the four Wednesdays in February. The chief executants were the usual string quartet, Messrs. Gompertz, Inwards, Kreuz, and Ould, with Professor Stanford (and on one occasion Miss Fanny Davies) at the pianoforte, and the vocalists, Madame Sophie Löwe and Messrs. Plunket Greene, W. F. Blandford, and Beaumont. The programmes contained, amongst other works, Dr. Hubert Parry's Pianoforte Trio in B minor, Professor Stanford's Pianoforte Quintet in D minor (Op. 25), and a very ably-written String Quartet (MS.), by Mr. Charles Wood, formerly Composition Scholar at the Royal College of Music and now Organist Scholar of Caius College. In addition to these Concerts the Society, by the kind permission of the Provost and Fellows of King's College, gave, on March 7, a performance of Mozart's " Requiem " and Handel's Sixth " Chandos " Anthem in their magnificent Chapel, the extraordinary acoustic properties of which can only be realised by those who have had the good fortune to be present in the Chapel on such an occasion. The performance was in all respects most admirable, although it would have been far better to have done the " Requiem" only; the temperature of the Chapel in February being such as to debar many from attending any

L

performance exceeding a very moderate length. Messrs. Burnett and Gompertz led the orchestra, and Professor Stanford conducted. The soloists were Miss Liza Lehmann, Miss Lena Little, Mr. Holberry Hagyard, and Mr. Plunket Greene. On March 15 the Society gave a Chamber Concert, with the valuable co-operation of Dr. Joachim, assisted by Messrs. Gompertz, Ludwig, Hausmann, and Professor Stanford. The programme contained Beethoven's Quartet in E minor (Op. 59, No. 2) and Brahms's C minor Trio (Op. 101). Mr. Plunket Greene, whose singing completely took Cambridge by storm, sang songs by Brahms, Schubert, and Joachim, as well as some of those rare old Irish melodies so exquisitely arranged by Dr. Stanford. March, 1889, it will be remembered, was the Jubilee of Dr. Joachim's career as a public artist, and his visit to Cambridge was made the occasion of a banquet in his honour (held, by kind permission of the Master and Fellows, in the Hall of Caius College), which was well attended by many past members of the University Musical Society, as well as those now in residence. Some very excellent speeches were made, but none so good as that of the great musician himself.

(2) *In the Easter Term* the usual two Concerts were given—viz., a Chamber Concert, on Wednesday, May 15, which included Beethoven's Septet, Goetz's Pianoforte Quintet (Op. 16), and David's Concertino for bassoon (Op. 12). The executants were Messrs. Gompertz, Kreuz, Ould, White, Egerton, Borsdorf, Wotton, and Professor Stanford. Mrs. Hutchinson sang songs by Scarlatti and Brahms. The Orchestral Concert, on Tuesday June 11, consisted of an admirable performance of Dr. Parry's "Judith," the vocalists being Miss Anna Williams, Miss Lena Little, Mr. Ben Davies, and Mr. Plunket Greene.

During the summer vacation the Society is practically non-existent, but this year the vacation has been notable as a period of preparation for a new departure which claims special notice. For anything like adequate performances of Choral and Orchestral Music, Cambridge has of late years been exclusively dependent

CAMBRIDGE.

upon University effort, the old Town Society having gradually died of inanition some eight or ten years since. It occurred to Professor Stanford that there was room for the establishment of a definite series of Concerts to be supported by Town and University alike, independently of any actual Society. A committee was accordingly formed, consisting of representative men of all sections of local musical activity, and mainly owing to the great personal influence and exertions of Dr. Stanford himself a Guarantee Fund was formed, and the new series is now a *fait accompli*. The scheme is for a set of eight Concerts, to be given in the Guildhall during the two Winter Terms, two in each Term being Orchestral and two Chamber. The subscription for the whole set of eight is only £1 1s., and provision is made for a considerable number of unreserved seats at a shilling a Concert. Not only is the bait of popular prices held out, but the programmes are scrupulously restricted in length, and the discomfort and risks of evening dress at the winter time of the year are strenuously protested against. It is gratifying to be able to state that the attendance at the first four Concerts given in November was such as to prove the wisdom of these provisions. At the same time, it is obvious that the limited capacity of the Concert Room and the low prices will necessitate the utmost economy if the Concerts are to be self-supporting. It is satisfactory to note, not only on this account, but still more on educational grounds, that the pick of the local amateur orchestras, both University and Town, have been admitted to take a share in the work. Another noteworthy feature in connection with these Concerts is that Professor Stanford has, with the consent of the University Board of Musical Studies, so far combined his posts of Professor and Conductor as to utilise these Concerts for the work of the Professorial Chair, by lecturing on the history, construction, and instrumentation of the chief orchestral works contained in the programmes, and the University, regarding these performances as "illustrations" of their Professor's Lectures, have contributed a substantial sum from the University chest to the Concert fund. It is obvious, therefore, that in this new departure we have the elements of a movement which, if permanent, must contribute most materially to local musical culture and development. It remains to be seen whether its usefulness will not have to be discounted to some slight extent by a diminution in the work, the opportunities, and possibly the financial position of the University Musical Society itself. It is, for instance, understood that these Concerts are to take the place of the old established "Wednesday Popular Concerts" hitherto given by the Society, and the last Michaelmas Term was perhaps the first in the history of the Society since its institution in which it has given no sign of its existence by Concert or public performance of any kind. At the first of these new Concerts, on November 6, the programme contained Beethoven's "Leonora" Overture (No. 1), "Emperor" Concerto (played by Mr. Dannreuther), and Mozart's G minor Symphony; and at the fourth, on November 27, Mendelssohn's "Hebrides" Overture, the "Eroica" Symphony, and Piatti's Violoncello Concerto (Op. 26), played by the composer. The vocalists were the Hon. Mrs. Robert Lyttelton (November 6) and Miss Emily Davies (November 27). Mr. Burnett led the band, and Professor Stanford conducted. At the two Chamber Concerts, on November 13 and 20, the programmes contained Beethoven's Trio in B flat (Op. 97) and String Quartet in C major (Op. 59), Schubert's Quartet in A minor (Op. 29), and Dvorák's lovely Pianoforte Quintet in A major (Op. 81). A new set of "Liebesbilder" by Mr. Kreuz (of the Royal College of Music) for viola and pianoforte, and songs by Franz, Goetz, Jensen, Rubinstein, and Charles Wood completed the programmes. The executants were Messrs. Gompertz, Inwards, Kreuz, and Ould, with Miss Fletcher (R.C.M.) and Mr. Charles Wood at the pianoforte, and the vocalists were Miss Anna Russell and Mr. Branscombe.

Another incident of the musical year in Cambridge has been the establishment of the University Musical Club. This, though under the management of a separate committee, and intended to be self-supporting, is to a certain extent in affiliation with the University Musical Society, which has advanced the money for its "outfit." It is worked on much the same principles as the corresponding Club at the Sister University, and Club Concerts are given in the rooms every Saturday night.

Cambridge, like Oxford, is noted for its Choral Services, which are undoubtedly a very important factor in the musical attractions and influences of the place. In this connection the year just ended will be principally known as the "organ-restoration" year, the three most important organs, those of King's, Trinity, and St. John's, having all been in the hands of Messrs. Hill & Son for the introduction of "tubular pneumatics" and other improvements and additions. The additions to King's organ have been considerable, involving a fourth manual (solo), as well as other extensions. The prevailing opinion seems to be that the "fluework" has been somewhat overweighted with reeds, an excess which the peculiar acoustic properties of the building tend to emphasise rather than conceal. The principal additions at Trinity consist of a set of open thirty-twos on the pedal in the place of some stopped sixteens—a third diapason and a bourdon on the great organ; and an enlargement of the choir organ, which is now divided—some of it being transferred to the portion of the case (the "chaire" organ) at the back of the player. This portion has been projected into the chapel to the great improvement of the appearance of the case, as well as to the advantage of the solo singers, who thus have the accompanying portion of the organ brought nearer to them. The prolonged silence of these organs has been in one respect of great service to the choirs in question, as it has developed that accuracy and refinement of vocalisation which is so essential in good unaccompanied singing. The organ at Trinity has not yet been re-opened, but that at King's has been in use again for some time. Bennett's "Woman of Samaria" was sung at the opening service.

As regards other musical efforts, there is not much to chronicle. That most worthy of mention is a performance, in King's College

Chapel (on June 12), of "Israel in Egypt," under the conductorship of Dr. Mann, who deserves great credit for his untiring and enthusiastic efforts to get together the material for such performances in a place and at a time where all available hands are so pre-occupied in other directions.

The Cambridge Choral Union—an attempt to revive associated musical effort in the Town as distinct from the University which deserves every encouragement — gave Handel's "Acis and Galatea" on May 2, under the conductorship of Mr. W. C. Dewberry (R.A.M.); and his brother, Mr. F. Dewberry, who is the Borough organist, played Handel's B flat Organ Concerto with orchestra at the same Concert.

There were the usual number of "College" Concerts and of "Penny" Concerts for the people, as well as Organ Recitals at the Guildhall and in Trinity and other College Chapels.

The number of Concerts given by those not locally connected with the place was not large. In fact, it seems to be at last pretty well understood among Concert-givers generally that Cambridge is the reverse of a "happy hunting-ground" in this respect, though it has taken years of disappointment and financial reverse to get them to take this lesson adequately to heart. Sir Charles and Lady Hallé are always sure of a hearty welcome in their annual visit here, and the very natural curiosity to hear the veteran Sims Reeves drew a large audience a few weeks back.

There was no "Greek Play" at Cambridge last year, but matters are in train for one in November, 1890, and the incidental music will be written by Dr. Hubert Parry. There is also some talk of getting up a performance of Glück's "Iphigenia" sometime in May, but the arrangements for it are still *in embryo*.

X.

EDINBURGH.

THE most striking feature in the programmes presented to our audiences during the last year is the ever-increasing number of items by Scottish composers. We do not repudiate the Imperial "English School," but we are proud of that important section which represents national talent, and which looks so often for inspiration to national themes.

Mention should first be made of the Orchestral Concerts given under Sir Charles Hallé's *bâton* at the Reid Festival—the one service for which we have to thank the memory of that far-seeing amateur, General Reid, who left his money to the cause of music in Scotland. The administration of the funds in connection with the bequest has long been a sore subject. There is a Professor with no students; a chair and no power to examine for degrees; a library not available to musicians in Edinburgh save by the courtesy of the Professor. It is with regret we read the announcement that Sir Charles Hallé's band is next February to make its last appearance in Edinburgh. Some money will thus be left free to be applied in another way. "What will they do with it?" is the question. A beautiful performance of the "Pastoral" Symphony was the feature of the "Reid" programme (February 14), which also included the Schumann Concerto, Mackenzie's "La Belle Dame," and the "Academic" (Brahms) and "Athalie" Overtures. The two Concerts given, as usual, in connection with this annual memorial of General Reid were an Orchestral (February 13) and a Chamber Concert (11). At the former the Overtures were "Egmont" and "Meistersinger"; the Symphony was the "Italian," and Lady

Hallé roused the enthusiasm of her Edinburgh audience by her rendering of Vieuxtemps's Concerto in E major.

When diminishing receipts and repeated calls on the guarantors made it advisable for the Edinburgh Choral Union to rest on its oars, Messrs. Paterson and Son stepped in and engaged the orchestra on which the Choral Union had depended, and although fewer Concerts were given, and the subscriptions were somewhat higher, we were saved from the disgrace of having no winter Orchestral Concerts in a capital which prides itself on its culture, musical and artistic. Among the Symphonies were Villiers Stanford's "Irish" (a novelty here), Schumann's in B flat, and Schubert's in C major. The Overtures comprised Grieg's beautiful "Im Herbst," and Mr. Hamish MacCunn's "Dowie Dens o' Yarrow." Our young countryman's Orchestral Ballad "The Ship o' the Fiend" was also given, and on the night of the "Dowie Dens" he conducted his Cantata "Bonnie Kilmeny," the choral part of which was most successfully sustained by Mr. Kirkhope's choir. Mr. MacCunn was afterwards entertained with Mr. Manns by the Edinburgh Society of Musicians.

An Edinburgh artist, Madame Helen Hopekirk, played the "Emperor" Concerto on her re-appearance here (January 15), and won a decided success. M. Johannes Wolff was introduced to Edinburgh (January 19), making his appearance in Godard's A minor Concerto, and at once found himself a favourite. The other soloist (January 8) was M. Gillet (violoncello). The pecuniary and artistic success of these Concerts has justified Messrs. Paterson in again submitting a similar scheme to the public and the subscriptions are fully taken up. At the second Concert, on December 16, was heard the first performance of Dr. A. C. Mackenzie's "Cotter's Saturday Night."

This work was enthusiastically received on first hearing, and a closer study reveals new elements of beauty in Dr. Mackenzie's picturesque instrumentation and themes more graceful and spontaneous than he sometimes gives us. The poem is not eminently suited for a musical setting, and Dr. Mackenzie has erred in dwelling too minutely on some minor details which, passed over so lightly in the poem, make there a broad and homely effect, whereas in the more ideal language of music they only disturb the picture. A delightfully national flavour runs through the work in characteristic rhythms and intervals, and the composer rises to a great height of passion in his setting of the verse beginning "O tender love," a lovely little bit of writing. His patriotic peroration, "O Scotia, my dear, my native soil," had the ring of earnestness and sincerity about it, which produced its due effect on the audience. Dr. Mackenzie was heartily applauded at the close of the work.

It is a pity that the Wagner "boycott" is still kept up. The "Meistersinger" and "Lohengrin" Preludes can hardly be said to fairly represent the Bayreuth master. Fortunately Mr. Henschel chose "Wotan's Abschied" as one of his solos, but we ought not to have to depend on fortuitous influences for the inclusion in our programmes of music which other towns and countries have so many opportunities of hearing.

The Edinburgh Amateur Orchestral is a very healthy association, and its performances amply justify the large public support it always commands. Under Mr. Carl D. Hamilton it gives most satisfactory renderings of such works as Haydn's and Mozart's Symphonies, and even Mendelssohn's Overtures and his "Italian" Symphony. Other amateur societies—the St. Andrew's, conducted by Mr. Geo. W. Lingard, Mus. Bac., and the Orpheus, by Mr. John Greig, Mus. Doc., Oxon.—testify to the growing taste for and interest in the greatest of all instruments, the orchestra.

The Edinburgh Choral Union is manfully fighting its uphil battle. Its prestige suffered sadly when it was forced to abandon the orchestral part of its annual scheme, and even the great improvement in the chorus under strict regulations and Mr. Collinson's skilful training has not restored to it its former share of public favour. The junction with Messrs. Paterson's enterprise, wherein they assisted Mr. Manns's orchestra in the "Cotter's

Saturday Night," and with next year's Reid Festival, where they are to be accompanied by Hallé's orchestra in the "Hymn of Praise," will perhaps waken the Choral Union and the Edinburgh public to a sense of mutual responsibility.

An Association which has made rapid strides, thanks to its Conductor and many extraneous and obvious advantages, is Mr. Kirkhope's choir. It attains now nearly to the perfection of choral singing, and has left the smaller halls where its former successes have been gained. The Music Hall is not now too large for its audiences, and an increase in its numbers is rendered practicable. Whatever difference of opinion there may be about the terms of admission to the choir, nothing but praise can be given to the enterprise that undertook and the patience which so triumphantly overcame the difficulties of the Brahms "Requiem" (April 16). The work was brilliantly rendered. At the same Concert were performed Gounod's "Gallia" and Mendelssohn's 98th Psalm; also a Quartet by Brahms. The winter Concert was given on December 9, when Mendelssohn's "Walpurgis Night" and Rheinberger's "Christophorus" were performed.

Mr. Waddel's choir, now under the leadership of Mr. Millar Craig, made several successful appearances with a selection of madrigals, as illustrations to a Lecture delivered by M. Kunz at the Philosophical Institution and in the Synod Hall, and as part of their summer Concert programme (June 5). The choice of Macfarren's "Outward Bound" as the choral work was disastrous. The vessel is unseaworthy, and no mermaids were needed to prophesy its fate. The choir is now engaged in the rehearsal of a much more important and interesting work, Astorga's "Stabat Mater."

Mr. J. A. Moonie's Choir is a most enterprising association, and well deserves the large measure of success it has commanded. Last March it attacked Dr. Stanford's "Revenge," and also gave us the first opportunity of hearing Mr. MacCunn's "Lord Ullin's Daughter." Mr. Moonie's Male Voice Choir, as well as Mr.

Millar Craig's Male Glee Club, and the old established Harmonist Society, show how general is the taste for this delightful branch of choral music. It is impossible to mention in detail all the minor choral associations, which take their names from nearly every district of the city, and find a centre in nearly every church choir.

In our world of Chamber music, the Edinburgh Classical Chamber Concerts hold the most important place in virtue of their regularity and earnestness of purpose. Messrs. W. Townsend and Paul Della Torre are the best local pianoforte players and their efforts are ably seconded by Mr. Colin Mackenzie (violin) and Mr. Grant McNeill (violoncello). At two Concerts, in January and February, they presented Trios by Schubert, in B flat; Mendelssohn, in D minor; and Beethoven, in B flat (Op. 97). At their first Concert of the present winter season (December 4), by engaging the services of Mr. Conrad Laubach (viola), they were able to undertake Schumann's Quartet in E flat and Mendelssohn's Trio in C minor. The solo work of Messrs. Townsend, Mackenzie, and McNeill showed in every instance marked advance—a Sonata by Dvorák in D minor, for pianoforte and violin, and a brilliant rendering of Liszt's D flat Concert Study, being the most notable items.

The Chamber Concerts organised by Herr Alfred Gallrein are rather irregular in date and design. There is no doubt that what is gained in opportunity is lost in homogeneity. Still, good work is done, and we are indebted to Herr Gallrein for the opportunity (March 1) of hearing an interesting Sonata by Spohr, for the violin and harp (Mdlles. Marianne and Clara Eissler), besides some clever harp solos, and also (February 1) Sonatas by Goltermann and Corelli for the violoncello. *Entrepreneurs* of Chamber Concerts, in a town where these are not very common, have large responsibilities, which Herr Gallrein will do well to recognise. Support will not be wanting.

Other Chamber Concerts were given by Herr Heckmann, in Queen Street Hall (November 8), and Madame Drechsler

Hamilton (December 17). On March 20 the Philosophical Institution provided the annual treat which is regarded as the close of our regular musical season. Additional interest was given to last season's Concert by the Joachim Jubilee, to which Sheriff Mackay referred in a graceful speech, Dr. Joachim replying in a very few words. He was afterwards entertained by the Society of Musicians.

Madame Helen Hopekirk gave a Recital at the Literary Institute (January 18), in course of which she played Beethoven's "Appassionata," Chopin's B minor Scherzo, and Liszt's Twelfth Rhapsody in splendid style. She received quite an ovation. At the first of two Lectures by Mr. Franklin Peterson on Beethoven, Madame Hopekirk played Sonatas in illustration of the master's first and second "periods."

Mr. Paul Della Torre, who is undoubtedly the best of our younger pianists, as far as technique goes, undertook a Beethoven Recital in the Freemasons' Hall, on March 23. The performances were uniformly good, and the intention was excellent; but the selection of works was not calculated to carry out the evident attempt to illustrate the development of the Sonata form in Beethoven's hands.

On October 14 Señor Sarasate presented Dr. Mackenzie's "Pibroch," which he had just played at the Leeds Festival. Madame Berthe Marx made a most favourable impression on her first appearance in Edinburgh.

Otto Hegner gave a Recital, on February 25, at which he delighted and astonished his audience.

Sir Charles Hallé's annual Recital was given on October 19, when he was assisted as usual by Lady Hallé.

The opera season in Edinburgh is very short, and presents very inadequate fare. Meyerbeer's "Star of the North" was the novelty this year, and a careful study and splendid mounting at once established it as a favourite.

Madame Patti paid us a visit on October 29; and on November 16 Madame Valleria and other artists gave a

Concert, at which the two *virtuosi*, MM. Wolff and Nachèz, gave a magnificent rendering of Bach's Concerto in D minor, for two violins. M. Wolff also played at the annual Blind Asylum Concert, in the Synod Hall (April 6), where he was heard in a duet Sonata, by Rubinstein, with Miss Clara Lichtenstein. Miss Macintyre sang and Miss Detchon recited.

The Edinburgh Society of Musicians has steered safely through its initial shallows and is now fairly established. Besides ordinary meetings, they entertained last year Sir Charles Hallé, Dr. A. C. Mackenzie, Mr. Hamish MacCunn, Mr. Manns, and Dr. Joachim, in celebration of his jubilee. On the last occasion Miss Fanny Davies was also among the guests. Lectures, papers, or Chamber music forms the ordinary programme at the Society's weekly meetings. A Benevolent Fund and a library have been constituted in connection with the Society.

Public Lectures on Music were delivered at the Philosophical Institution by M. Jules Kunz, on Madrigals (to which Mr. Waddel's choir supplied the examples), and by Mr. Franklin Peterson on "Parsifal," illustrated by music and limelight views.

FRANKLIN PETERSON.

GLASGOW.

IN most things that concern the higher interests of the musical art the Glasgow Choral Union takes the lead on the banks of the Clyde. This organisation has experienced many vicissitudes in a career dating back to 1843, when it had its origin in "The Society for Performing the Oratorio of 'The Messiah.'" The band of enthusiasts sang, as may be imagined, from MS. In those days they could hardly have dreamed of a shilling copy of Handel's "eloquent sermon." The reminiscence is not inappropriate, inasmuch as our record of 1889 begins with the time-honoured New Year's Day performance of "The Messiah" by the Choral Union. It was the fourth Concert of the choral and orchestral subscription series, 1888-9, directed by the Society, and here it may be convenient to state that the choir—so well trained by Mr. Joseph Bradley—averages a numerical strength of 350 voices; also that the band engaged for the season consisted of seventy-five performers, selected from the best orchestras in the country, with Mr. August Manns as conductor —a post which he has held with signal credit to himself for many years. The programmes were, as usual, drawn up by the Sydenham Conductor, and the material will speak for itself. At the fifth Concert we had, amongst other good things, the Introduction to "Tristan und Isolde," Beethoven's Violin Concerto (for Mr. M. Sons, the able leader of the orchestra), Dvorák's " Scherzo Capriccioso," Haydn's Symphony in B flat (No. 4 of the Salomon set), and songs from Madame Belle Cole. On the evening of the 8th Raff's Concerto for violoncello and orchestra (Op. 193), and Praeger's Prelude to Byron's " Manfred " were heard for the first time at these Concerts; the Symphony was Beethoven's No. 2, and Liszt's first Hungarian Rhapsody concluded a remarkably well-sustained programme. The violoncello soloist was M. Gillet, a player of very considerable attainments. At the seventh Concert Dr. Villiers Stanford's "Irish" Symphony had the place of honour. Madame Helen Hopekirk was heard in Beethoven's Fifth Pianoforte Concerto, and Mdlle. Elvira Gambogi sang. Herr George Müller, the *ripieno* violin of the band, essayed Max Bruch's Concerto in G minor at the eighth Concert, the programme of which also included Schumann's Symphony (No. 1) in B flat, and Mr. Hamish MacCunn's Ballad for orchestra, "The Ship o' the Fiend." M. Johannes Wolff made his first appearance here on the evening of the 29th, when he played with entire acceptance in Godard's "Concerto Romantique" for violin and orchestra, and there was an altogether delightful performance of Schubert's Symphony in C, the so-called "No. 10." The tenth Concert was entirely choral, when the Union won very frank approval in Mendelssohn's "First Walpurgis Night" and in Sullivan's popular Cantata "The Golden Legend." Popular Concerts in connection with the scheme just briefly reviewed took place, as usual, on the Saturday evenings. The programmes included several standard Symphonies and Overtures, as also miscellaneous selections of hardly less interest than those submitted at the classical series.

The records for February comprised little of consequence, saving that on the 8th the Hillhead Chamber Music Association gave its second Concert of the season. The artists were Sir Charles and Lady Hallé and M. Vieuxtemps, who gave a singularly fine performance of Beethoven's Trio in D (Op. 70). The programme also included an almost perfect rendering of Brahms's Pianoforte and Violin Sonata in A major, and Schubert's Trio in B flat (Op. 99). On the 21st little Otto Hegner came to St. Andrew's Hall and met with a distinct success.

March was, as usual, a busy month with the smaller Choral Societies in Glasgow. The inexorable laws of space can only, however, permit us to say that several of these choirs made highly creditable appearances in works of a more or less familiar type. On the 1st the Hillhead Association just-named gave its third and last Concert of the season, when Miss Fanny Davies and Miss Marie Soldat supported a programme of sterling worth. Its leading features were Schumann's Sonata in A minor (Op. 105), Bach's Preludio, Ménuet, and Gavotte (E major Suite), and Chopin's Andante Spianato and Polonaise. The young Birmingham pianist had her customary warm greeting, and the reception accorded Miss Soldat must have been exceedingly gratifying to the fair Austrian, who made her first appearance here. Her pure and massive tone, brilliant *technique*, and artistic perception will not soon be forgotten. The Promenades at the Fine Art Institute call for record, if only on account of the agreeable programmes always submitted by Mr. W. H. Cole. A Symphony invariably attracted large numbers of amateurs on the Saturday afternoons.

On April 4 the eleventh and concluding Concert of the Glasgow Choral Union series took place. The close of the season was postponed to this date in order that the services of Dr. Joachim and party might be secured. A programme of Chamber music was quite a new feature in the history of the Society. It was not superlatively strong, but Mozart's Quartet in C major (No. 6), the *Andante* with Variations from the "Kreutzer" Sonata, and Schumann's Quintet in E flat (Op. 44), supported by the great Hungarian violinist, Messrs. Piatti, Ries, A. Gibson, and Miss Fanny Davies, gave the crowded audience unmixed satisfaction. On the 9th Dr. Bridge's fine Cantata "Callirhoë" was performed by the Bridgeton Choral Society, under the direction of Mr. George Taggart, a local amateur of skill, and at the annual Concert of the Kyrle Choir a new Choral Ballad sought and obtained favour. This was Mr. C. Hall Woolnoth's setting of Longfellow's "The Skeleton in Armour," remarkable for its clever pianoforte accompaniment, as also melodic invention of no mean order.

Early in May—the 6th—the Carl Rosa Opera Company entered upon a week's engagement at the Theatre Royal, when "The Star of the North" was played no fewer than four times. The work was wonderfully well staged, and Madame Georgina Burns and her coadjutors secured large favour. From the opera week onwards to September, our records were almost a blank; there is, indeed, little "tuning up" during the summer and early autumn —the "doon the water" season—but at the gatherings of the Glasgow Society of Musicians the interests of the harmonic art are not by any means forgotten. This organisation includes both the professional and the amateur element, it is true to its original aims, and specially remarkable for its hospitality to artists visiting the city of St. Mungo. In August Dr. Joachim came to Glasgow to receive the degree of LL.D. from its ancient University, and ere September had been well ushered in coming events were casting their proverbial shadows before them. Our leading Musical Society, for example, was in the field with a preliminary prospectus, and the City Hall Concerts (Saturday and Monday evenings) were in operation, schemes chiefly on "ballad" lines, but noticeable for the array of leading artists often to be found on the East-end Concert platform.

The Glasgow Choral Union season, 1889-90, opened on October 15, when Chamber Music was again submitted. The artists were Señor Sarasate and Madame Bertha Marx, and Miss Ella Russell charmed her large St. Andrew's Hall audience with operatic arias. At this Concert the accomplished Spanish violinist played with electric effect Dr. A. C. Mackenzie's stimulating "Pibroch," and the new comer, Madame Marx, gave ample evidence of her remarkable ability as a pianist. A couple of nights later Sir Charles and Lady Hallé were heard at the Queen's Rooms in a budget of good things, which included the latest Sonatas for violin and pianoforte from the pens of Brahms and Grieg; and on the 28th a short-lived series of Promenade Concerts commenced in St. Andrew's Hall. The work accomplished by Mr. Cole and his orchestra of forty capable players deserved, it is not too much to say, the highest encouragement. Once more it falls to be noted that the Concert, on the 31st, headed by Madame Adelina Patti, carried everything before it.

Mr. Edwin Wareham's Concert, on November 5, introduced to a Glasgow audience Miss Ethel and Master Harold Bauer, in Grieg's Pianoforte and Violin Sonata in C minor. Madame Clara Samuell and Mr. Andrew Black sang with their wonted favour, the Glasgow baritone giving evidence of a development in style which his numerous friends were hardly prepared for. The miscellaneous Concerts of the month were, it may be feared, in excess of the demand. Mr. Edward Lloyd drew, to be sure, a crowded audience to the Monday "Pop," at which he was engaged, and Mrs. Alice Shaw speedily whistled herself into the good graces of a large St. Andrew's Hall gathering; but Madame Valleria's appeal, on the 18th, was strangely overlooked by her many admirers hereabouts. Possibly the Carl Rosa Company proved a formidable counter-attraction. It was a "Faust" night at the opera, and with Mdlle. de Lussan as *Marguerite*. In this character, and in the title-*rôle* of "Carmen," essayed on another occasion, the fair American achieved, it is no exaggeration to say, a success quite out of the common order. The opera season extended to fourteen representations.

At the bi-weekly meeting of the Society of Musicians, on November 9, the results of a prize competition were announced. Mr. Allan Macbeth came first with his sacred Cantata "The Land of Glory," a work which does him infinite credit. Mr. W. T. Hoeck was awarded second prize for a pianoforte and violin piece, and Mr. T. S. Drummond was third for a song. The adjudicators were Dr. A. C. Mackenzie and Dr. W. A. Barrett. It may be of interest to note that on fine Sunday evenings Concerts took place at the Gaiety Theatre of Varieties, and at the Star Music Hall, for a benevolent object; the programmes were mainly drawn from the domain of sacred music, but a dash of the secular element slipped in, and there was at least one very good orchestral performance, that of the Overture to "William Tell."

On December 5, the Bridgeton Choral Society gave Mr. F. H. Cowen's popular Cantata "The Rose Maiden," and on the same evening Mr. Alexander Lucy, a young Glasgow pianist, who has lately studied abroad, essayed a Recital. It was an earnest endeavour, but Mr. Lucy's powers are as yet immature.

On the 12th the first Orchestral Concert of the Glasgow Choral Union series was given, and in the presence of an audience which nearly filled St. Andrew's Hall. Mr. August Manns had a very cordial welcome. The orchestra was in wonderful trim, and gave remarkably good performances of Dr. A. C. Mackenzie's "Twelfth Night" Overture, a selection from Grieg's interesting "Peer Gynt" Suite, the "Lohengrin" Prelude, and Mozart's ever-fresh G minor Symphony. Lady Hallé gave a superb performance of the Beethoven Violin Concerto. On the 14th the first Saturday Popular Concert of the series took place. The programme included Beethoven's second Symphony, and M. E. Gillett, the principal cello of the orchestra, was heard in a Concerto, from the pen of Lalo, remarkable for its poverty of invention and pretentiousness. Fräulein Marie Fillunger made her first appearance before a Scotch audience and had a deservedly enthusiastic welcome. What will in all likelihood be regarded as the leading event of the season came off on Tuesday, the 17th, the performance for the first time in Scotland of Beethoven's Mass in D. The Glasgow Choral Union sang their exacting music with surprising vigour, staying power, and accuracy, showing, amongst other things, the care bestowed upon the rehearsals by Mr. Bradley, who conducted, and who must be felicitated on a performance of singular merit. The band was also worthy the occasion, and the leader, Mr. Sons, played the beautiful violin solo in the "Benedictus" with fine musical feeling. The soloists were Mesdames Fillunger and Belle Cole, Mr. Harper Kearton and Mr. Brereton.

On the 21st Raff's "Lenore" Symphony had the place of honour in the programme, and Mr. F. J. Simpson's Overture, "Robert Bruce," attracted no small measure of interest by reason of the composer's nationality, and his faculty for saying something good in musical commemoration of the hero of Bannockburn. Mr. Iver McKay sang Mr. Manns's elegant Serenade, "O moon of night." At the Subscription Concert, on the 23rd, another Scotch musician was to the fore, in Mr. Frederick Lamond, whose Symphony in A (MS.) now received its initial performance. The work was originally laid out on the lines of a Serenade, "but in the course of elaboration each movement grew into one of symphonic form and proportion." That the Symphony is brimful of promise cannot be doubted. Mr. Lamond, while a disciple of Brahms, can think for himself, his utterances are melodious and graceful—instance the fine slow movement—and if his orchestration does not always enrich the fabric in the highest degree, yet the young Glasgow composer's knowledge of the resources of his art is of first importance. After the performance Mr. Lamond also appeared as the soloist in St. Saëns's characteristic Pianoforte Concerto in C minor (No. 4). On the 28th Mr. Philip Halstead was the attraction at the third Popular Concert. This young pianist has studied in Leipsic, much had been heard concerning his abilities, and in Mendelssohn's second Concerto he was fully equally to the demands of the music. Later on the fluency, elegance, and clearness of his style in a "Ballade" of Reinecke's, earned for him a perfect storm of applause. Other items in the programme included Dr. Mackenzie's ever-welcome "Benedictus," and a couple of choruses from Mendelssohn's "Antigone" and "Œdipus at Colonos," well sung by the male voices of the Choral Union, under the direction of Mr. Bradley. The programme for the Concert on the 30th was selected by *plébiscite*. It comprised the Overture to the "Magic Flute"; Minuet for Strings (Boccherini); Overture, "Tannhäuser"; Symphony (No. 8) in B minor (Unfinished), Schubert; Spring Song and Spinning Song (arranged for orchestra), Mendelssohn; Selection from Ballet Music in "Faust" (Gounod). The solo pianist of the evening was Mr. Franz Rummel, who played in Beethoven's Fifth Concerto. F.

LIVERPOOL.

THE celebration of a jubilee does not fall to the lot of every musical organisation, and, if only for the reason that the Liverpool Philharmonic Society, during 1889, completed its fiftieth season, would the year be a notable one in the annals of art in the second city of the empire. It was therefore amid no inconsiderable commotion, and with no little expectation, that January dawned upon us, for the " Dream of Jubal " had been commissioned by Mr. Walton Clark, the chairman of the premier provincial Society, and query and comment was rife as to what Dr. Mackenzie's jubilee composition would be like. This will be alluded to in its proper place; but it undeniably finds an important position in the annals of the year.

In course of the operatic season, given at the Court Theatre by the Carl Rosa Company, Halévy's opera " The Jewess " was first produced here in its English garb, this being followed later on by Meyerbeer's " Star of the North."

The Philharmonic Concerts occurring in January were two in number. At that on the 8th Schubert's comparatively unfamiliar E minor Overture, and Mendelssohn's " Melusine," together with Berlioz's " Fantastic " Symphony, formed the leading orchestral features. Madame Nordica was the only vocalist.

On the 28th the " Lustspiel " Overture of Smetana was played for the first time here, the other Overtures being Wagner's " Meistersinger " and Berlioz's " Francs Juges." Another first hearing was that of Bizet's " Roma " Suite. Brahms's " Gipsy Songs " were also introduced by Miss Fillunger, Miss Lena Little, Mr. Shakespeare, and Mr. Thorndike; but they made no great impression. At this Concert Mr. Willy Hess, the new leader, made his *début* as a soloist, and played Ernst's difficult Concerto in F sharp minor, with remarkable fluency and facility.

On the 9th the third Concert of the Birkenhead Subscription Series was given, Sir Charles and Lady Hallé being the chief attractions; and the second of the Bootle Orchestral Concerts fell on the 29th. The Birkenhead Concerts have been established too many years to count, and date almost out of the memory of the oldest inhabitant of the "city of the future," as Disraeli called the place. Their history is, however, a worthy one. Bootle, on the other hand, only floated an initial scheme late in 1888; but it has, under the direction of Dr. Sanders, the secretary, and Mr. A. E. Workman, the Conductor, become a recognised and well managed institution. The Xaverian Society, under Mr. J. Ross, gave "Elijah" on the 16th, then ending a not very lengthy career; and there were during the month performances of "The Messiah," under Mr. Arvon Parry and Mr. McCulloch, at Wavertree and Walton respectively, "Judas" being given at Waterloo. The Glasgow Select Choir, under Mr. J. M. Craig, visited the city on the 25th, and again gave some delightful part-music. The Recitals at Dreaper's Rooms were during the month resumed, with Miss G. Holme at the pianoforte.

On February 5 was produced at the Philharmonic Hall Dr. Mackenzie's "Dream of Jubal." It will not be out of place here to state that the Liverpool Philharmonic Society was founded in 1840, but owing to alterations effected in the arrangement of the seasons, that of 1888-9 became the fiftieth. The chairman of the period, Mr. Walter C. Clark, very happily conceived the idea of celebrating the occasion by commissioning a special work, and the result was the production of "The Dream of Jubal," by Mr. Joseph Bennett and Dr. Mackenzie. The whole cost was defrayed by Mr. Clark, and his period of office proved a memorable one from several points of view. The utmost enthusiasm prevailed at the Jubilee Concert, the principals engaged for the performance being Miss Macintyre, Miss Janet Russell, Mr. Edward Lloyd, and Mr. J. R. Alsop, the contralto and bass being good local vocalists. The following Concert, on the 19th, was unimportant, except that Brahms's double Concerto for violin and violoncello was given for the first time here.

The fourth Concert of the Birkenhead Subscription series fell on the 6th, with Mr. Schiever's Quartet as the chief performers, the latter being a decidedly clever party of chamber performers. Later on Mr. Max Pauer gave a Pianoforte Recital, and so also did a good local pianist, Miss Webster. Gounod's " Philemon and Baucis" was re-produced on the 23rd. It had been twice given in 1888, by Mr. and Mrs. Louis, with amateur assistance. On the 28th Miss Freda Fedderis gave a popular Concert, and on the 29th " Elijah " was given by the choir of the Liverpool Institute of Music (Tonic Sol-fa) with creditable results, under Mr. S. Hardcastle. The People's Orchestral Society, of sixty-five amateur players, illustrated a Lecture given for the Sunday Society, by Mr. A. E. Radewald (now the local representative of the R.A.M. and R.C.M. examination scheme). Mr. Jude commenced a series of Ballad evenings; and there were several performances of " The Messiah " in the locality, notably one at Widnes, by the Birkenhead Cambrian Choral Society, a veteran organisation, under Mr. D. O. Parry. Mr. W. T. Best had during the month to suspend his regular Organ Recitals on account of ill-health, but fortunately the attack of his old enemy proved a light one.

Sullivan's " Prodigal Son " formed the chief item of the first Lenten Concert of the Philharmonic Society, and was given on March 12. A notable event was the first performance, on March 5, of " Ritter Olaf," a Cantata by Charles Braun, in which Heine's weird poem was treated with such skill and effect as to lead to the expectation of great things from the pen of the youthful composer. The Cymric Vocal Union revived Mendelssohn's " Festgesang," for male voices, on the 20th, but it proved a somewhat dull affair. The last Bootle Subscription Concert came off on the 25th with Haydn's "Farewell" Symphony.

Bottesini's "Garden of Olivet" was the Lenten Oratorio at the Cathedral, being given under Mr. F. H. Burstall, and with Mr. Collins as organist; and elsewhere there were numerous performances, at this time, of Stainer's "Crucifixion." Mr. Stavenhagen gave a Recital on the 30th, and gained golden opinions. During the same month Mr. J. Ross directed an Orchestral Concert for the Sunday Society, and Mr. Swift's West Kirby Society gave Barnby's "Rebekah."

Cowen's "Ruth," conducted by its composer, ended the Philharmonic season on April 2, and again was evidence given of the excellent material of which the local chorus is constituted. On April 16 the singing members of the Society were treated to a supper by the directorate, such an event being hitherto almost unheard of in the in some respects peculiar annals of the Philharmonic Society.

The directors of music at the two schools for the blind, Messrs. W. D. Hall and Mr. J. T. Brown, produced at their respective institutions Schubert's delightful "Song of Miriam" and Fox's "Jackdaw of Rheims" within a week or so of each other. On Good Friday Mr. W. I. Argent (Mr. H. Hudson being at the organ) directed the annual Corporation Concert, at which "The Messiah" was given, in St. George's Hall.

In Birkenhead Mr. Appleyard's St. Cecilia Society gave Astorga's "Stabat Mater." Bennett's "May Queen" was also given, after many years' rest, by the St. Paul's Choir, on the 29th, and the following evening it was produced at Runcorn. Aptommas, the Welsh harpist, gave some Recitals, commencing on May 9, but the audiences were not large. Dvorák's "Spectre's Bride" was produced by the Rock Ferry Society, under Mr. W. R. Pemberton.

The Eisteddfod held in Brecon in August did not create the usual local stir, the distance to the scene of the gathering being so far removed from this city. The singing of the natives of the principality, which gained royal commendation on the occasion of the Queen's visit to Llangollen and Dala, is entitled to mention. Early in the autumn the Liverpool Opera Society gave a series of capital performances at the Shakespeare Theatre, under Mr. J. O. Shepherd. Not only do the members of this organisation render invaluable help in the chorus of the regular Carl Rosa Company during the season in this city, but they prove competent to give operas by themselves, recruiting principals from their own ranks.

Once past Michaelmas and our regular season may be said to have again begun, the first Concert of the Philharmonic Society falling on October 8, with Grieg's "Peer Gynt" Suite, of which a capital performance, under Sir Charles Hallé, was given. On the 22nd Mr. Hamish MacCunn conducted his "Lay of the Last Minstrel" amid a scene of enthusiasm unequalled in the memory of those present. A north country quartet, consisting of Miss Macintyre, Madame McKenzie, Mr. Iver McKay, and Mr. A. Black were engaged as principals. Among the various local institutions again getting into harness must be noted the Societa Armonica and the People's Orchestral Society, probably the largest amateur band in the kingdom. Mr. Lee Williams's "Last Night at Bethany" was given at St. Francis Xavier's Church under Mr. Ross during the month. Mr. Ross inaugurated choral and orchestral societies in the Cheshire suburb of Liscard.

The distribution of the local awards granted by T.C.L. and the R.A.M. took place at St. George's Hall on the 19th and 26th respectively, Mrs. Gladstone officiating at the latter, during which a testimonial was presented to Mr. Argent, the retiring representative of the R.A.M., by over fifty of his fellow professors. On October 27 the newly-formed orchestra of the Liverpool Sunday Society made its first appearance with marked success at the Rotunda Hall.

Concerts were given by the Philharmonic Society on November 5 and 19. The programmes contained no novelty. Neither were the performances of equal merit, and in musical circles these facts gave rise to much comment. With November the local Recital and Chamber Music season may be said to have fairly begun. Among the pianists who thus appeared may be named Mr. A. S. Dale, a highly promising musician, who played at Dreaper's on the 2nd; Mr. W. Faulkes, a well-known local artist, who followed at the same place on the 16th; Mr. Falcke, a Parisian medalist and showy performer, who appeared at the Art Club on the 16th; and Mr. S. Welsing, one of our foremost resident musicians, who played at St. George's Hall on the 30th. Mr. Willy Hess's "Manchester" Quartet played at the first Conversazione of the Art Club, managed by Mr. H. E. Rensberg, on the 4th. On the 13th Messrs. Theodore Lawson and Haigh Kinsey gave a Chamber Concert at St. George's Hall, at which a rather promising Trio for pianoforte, violin, and violoncello, by the last-named musician, was produced. November also found the People's Orchestral Society at work on a Wagner programme at the City Hall, and at one of the Sunday Society meetings.

. On the 30th the Musical Club entered permanent premises in Lord Street. There was a performance of Chamber Music on the occasion, and a large muster of professional and lay members. The Club was founded in 1884, with Sir George Macfarren as President, and has flourished ever since. The present President is Mr. F. H. Cowen, the resident Vice-President, Mr. W. D. Hall, and the Hon. Secretary, Mr. Carl Heinecke.

The second Concert of the Birkenhead Subscription series, given on December 4, was of the ballad order. A day later, Spohr's "Last Judgment" formed the annual Advent Oratorio at the Pro-Cathedral, Mr. Burstall being at the organ and Mr. Argent conducting. The second of Mr. Schiever's Chamber Concerts, and Miss Margaret Webster's farewell Recital, fell on the 14th, and both were well attended. The first public performance of the Mallarey Society, under Mr. Ross, took place on the 19th, with Hamish MacCunn's "Bonnie Kilmeny."

Mr. Best's Recitals at St. George's Hall happily went on throughout the year with hardly a break, and the Corporation organist is to be congratulated upon his present excellent state of health.

At Chester the Musical Society gave, on March 5, J. F. Bridge's "Callirhoë," and Sullivan's "Kenilworth" music; on October 28, a Miscellaneous Concert, and on December 16, "The Messiah." In addition to these public performances there was a private one given at Eaton Hall, on the occasion of the visit of the Duke and Duchess of Teck. Dr. J. C. Bridge, the Organist of the Cathedral, conducted these Concerts, for each of which an orchestra was specially engaged. On August 1, one thousand voices took part in a Choral Festival at the Cathedral. On November 23, the Rev. C. H. Stewart was presented with a gold watch and £440 on vacating the office of Precentor of the Cathedral; Chamber Concerts were given by Mr. Bauerkeller; the local Orchestral Society also kept to the front; and the Glee Club did some work. The year ended with an Eisteddfod, participated in by the large number of Welsh residents in Chester, which was once a Welsh city.

The Concerts at the Southport Winter Gardens continued under Mr. Wright, the programmes being as good as could be expected. Mr. H. Hudson, the Conductor of the Birkdale Amateur Musical Society, gave, in April, Prout's "Red Cross Knight" and Stanford's "Revenge," and on December 1 Rossini's "Stabat" and MacCunn's "Bonnie Kilmeny." Under the same direction, in April, Handel's "Acis and Galatea" and Mendelssohn's "Athalie," and in December Handel's "Messiah" were given by the Southport Musical Guild. For all these performances an orchestra was engaged. Mr. Clarke's Society, among other works, gave Mendelssohn's "St. Paul," and Mr. A. E. Bartle was successful with a series of classical evenings.

W. I. ARGENT.

MANCHESTER.

FOREMOST among the musical doings of this city, and indeed of this district, stand the Subscription Concerts—now in their thirty-second season—of Sir Charles Hallé. Not only do they afford the happiest opportunities for hearing orchestral music adequately interpreted, and offer to our younger students facilities very far beyond those available a few years ago for becoming acquainted with the wonderful modern development of art; but they make Manchester a centre from which, during the winter months, increasing mission-work is undertaken, spreading and advancing all around a love of the best works of the great masters. With a splendid subscription list, and encouraged by the confidence and liberal support of the public, Sir Charles Hallé is placed above all danger of financial mishap, and is able unreservedly to follow his own taste and to carry out freely his designs. During five months of each year the band plays almost every day under his direction, so that he is able to secure a unity of purpose and a general finish of execution which, in spite of some weakness among the strings, and a good deal of unrestrained exuberance among the brass, could scarcely be surpassed. During the year we have enjoyed opportunities of re-studying the wonderful Third and Seventh Symphonies of Beethoven, and Mendelssohn's ever fresh "Italian"; and have grown more familiar with Brahms's elaborate Fourth Symphony in E minor, and with Dvorák's No. 3 in F. Of Berlioz's "Symphonie Fantastique" we have had more than enough; its sixth performance leaves us without desire to hear any more of it for some years. Our further intimacy with such efforts may be deferred until we have gained a knowledge of the many English works which still await a hearing here. It may be that the very favourable reception of Hamish MacCunn's Ballad "The Ship o' the Fiend," given under the composer's direction, will open the door wider to the large compositions of many of our native writers, and enable us to keep pace more promptly with modern ideas of the scope and capabilities of orchestral music. Herr and Madame Grieg were very warmly received; and the little sketches for strings and works for the band generally were very delicately interpreted. Especially have we delighted in the *con amore* rendering of Beethoven's Violin Concerto, by Lady Hallé, and of the G major Pianoforte Concerto, by Sir Charles. Nor was the devotion of the artists to the unfolding of the author's meaning unnoticed when Lady Hallé and Signor Piatti joined in elucidating the mysteries of Brahms's dual Concerto. Señor Sarasate attended the first Concert, playing Raff's "La Fée d'Amour," and his own "La Muiñeira"; and Herr Joachim introduced Stanford's Suite for the violin. At the miscellaneous Concerts the vocal element is always strictly subordinate. Nevertheless, during the year we have opportunities of hearing many of the chief singers of the day.

Of the six Choral Concerts, one evening is always devoted to "The Messiah," one to Berlioz's "Faust," and one to either "Elijah" or "St. Paul," so that not much room is left for novelty. As a matter of fact, Mackenzie's "Rose of Sharon" blossomed here only in the spring of 1889, rather long after its merits had been weighed in many smaller places. After it we had Rubinstein's "Paradise Lost"—scarcely such a work as we may delight in, greatly as we love oratorios. Since the commencement, in October, of the present season there have been a revival of Handel's "Theodora" and a third performance of Sullivan's "Golden Legend," under the direction of its composer. "Theodora," in spite of several powerful choruses, and a somewhat enhanced freedom of style in several of its movements, proved decidedly wearisome. The choir evinced the great care bestowed upon it by its new trainer, Mr. R. H. Wilson.

The Concerts of Mr. de Jong next claim attention. Mr. de Jong is very liberal in supplying vocalists of reputation, and is perseveringly working up his band to a higher capacity. This winter he has enjoyed the help of Mr. G. W. Lane's Philharmonic Choir, so that upon occasion he has under his command nearly 400 performers. After the Patti Concert, with which the season commenced, we had the Valleria party in a selection from "Tannhäuser" and other excerpts; and, still advancing in completeness, a full recital of Gounod's "Faust," with a band and choir so much more powerful than we ever have in our theatres that the whole performance went with a swing and fulness of tone giving a clearer idea than usual of the strictly musical merit of the opera. We warmly welcomed a young local *Marguerite*—Miss Mabel Berrey—gifted with a voice of beautiful quality, with considerable musical sensibility, and with general qualifications that should compel her to subject all to a course of study more exacting than she has yet undergone.

Among the crowd of Saturday evening entertainments may be specified Mr. Barrett's at the enormous St. James's Hall and Mr. Cross's at the Young Men's Christian Association. It would be well could our caterers for the public arrange so as not to interfere with each other's success by crowding all our lighter music into one night of each week.

The importance of that diligent culture of music which is maintained on all sides by the smaller Choral Societies prevailing in and around Manchester could not be over-rated. The enthusiastic amateurs may not be able to grapple with the expense of an orchestra sufficing for the production of the full effect of the works practised, but they exhibit eagerness to become acquainted with new compositions by week after week meeting for the practice of music not undertaken elsewhere in this city. Among them are the Vocal Society of Dr. Henry Watson; the more purely amateur Athenæum Musical Society, under Dr. Hiles; the Broughton Musical Society, conducted by Mr. R. H. Wilson; the Pendleton Choral Society, directed by Mr.

F. W. Blacow, and the Philharmonic Choir of Mr. Lane. During the year the Vocal Society has extended its lines from Tallis's Forty-part Motet to Gounod's "Gallia"; at the Athenæum Bridge's "Callirhoë," Cowen's "Song of Thanksgiving," Hubert Parry's "St. Cecilia's Day" (also produced by the Vocal Society) have been given; and Mr. Wilson's Choir has given "Callirhoë" and Hiles's Cantata "The Crusaders"—the latter work selected for performance at the great American Conference of Musicians as representative of modern English composition. It will be a happy thing for Manchester when some means have been devised of uniting all the musical resources of the city under one head. Since October, at the Concert Hall, two Orchestral Concerts have been given, including Mendelssohn's "Midsummer Night's Dream," Schumann's "Spring" Symphony (Op. 38), Mozart's Symphony in D (No. 1), and smaller works; but the interest there lies chiefly in the Chamber Concerts which are occasionally given and in the Afternoon Recitals, which Sir Charles Hallé liberally continues, and to which this season somewhat of an historic character is imparted by the arrangement of the programmes.

In conjunction with Signor Risegari and other coadjutors, Herr Sachs ventured upon a Chamber Concert in the spring of the year; but, as at the Recitals of Herren Stavenhagen and Schönberger, the encouragement was not adequate to the merits of the performance. At the Town Hall Mr. Kendrick Pyne continued to draw audiences probably larger than those attracted by Organ Recitals in any other town, and the half-yearly visits of M. Guilmant had undiminished interest for the lovers of the serious music suitable for the noblest of instruments.

H. HILES.

OXFORD.

THE year has been marked by a great deal of musical activity in various directions. It is indeed astonishing, considering that the City of Oxford is neither large nor wealthy, to find how many performances of one sort or other have taken place. In the range of Oratorio Concerts, however, only two require notice. On March 12 the Choral Society gave Beethoven's "Sinfonia Eroica" and Dvorák's "Stabat Mater," and the performance was one of the finest ever heard in Oxford. The Society, which has just closed its seventieth season, has, perhaps, never put a better chorus on the orchestra than on this occasion, and the difficult music of the Bohemian composer was excellently rendered. The soloists were all singers of established reputation, with the exception of Mr. A. F. Ferguson, an academical clerk in Magdalen College Choir. The manner in which this young singer rendered the bass part was really admirable, and caused many prophecies of future successes in store for him. Some of these prophecies have been already more or less fulfilled by Mr. Ferguson's singing in "The Sword of Argantyr" at the last Leeds Festival.

On June 24 the Philharmonic Society gave a performance of Dr. Bridge's "Callirhoë," Mr. Harford Lloyd's "Song of Balder," and Mozart's G minor Symphony. Dr. Bridge conducted his own work, and met with a warm reception both from his numerous friends in Oxford and also from the general public. The bright and pleasing music of the Cantata proved much to the taste of a "Commemoration" audience.

Chamber Music makes very few appearances in public, though it is cultivated in the University with remarkable enthusiasm, and possesses two distinct institutions devoted to it. A Concert was given in aid of the funds of the University Musical Club on March 8, at which Dr. Joachim played the "Kreutzer" Sonata, besides leading Haydn's "Kaiser" and Schumann's A major Quartets.

The University Musical Union gave two Invitation Concerts during the year. At the first, on February 21, in Keble College Hall, Herr Ludwig and his quartet played. For the second, on November 25, in Christ Church Hall, the Heckmann Quartet was engaged, but at the last moment the viola player fell ill and broke up the quartet, much to the disappointment of people of Oxford, with whom they have been established favourites. However, the Concert proved a peculiarly pleasing one. In Madame Heckmann the audience found a pianist of the very highest order, and it is scarcely possible to imagine a finer performance of Schubert's Trio in B flat major (Op. 99) than was given on this occasion. A feature of special interest in Concerts was the performance for the first time of Professor Stanford's new Pianoforte Trio in E flat major, the composer himself playing the pianoforte. The second and third movements pleased best at first hearing; but the whole work was full of charm. Professor Stanford has written much of late, and written much well; but, perhaps, this Trio will prove to have even more permanent elements of popularity than some of the music on a larger scale that has been recently heard.

Two Concerts were given by the Orchestral Association. On February 16 the scheme included Beethoven's "Pastoral" Symphony and Violin Concerto (first movement) and Cherubini's "Anacréon" Overture. On November 23 their chief efforts were Beethoven's "Fidelio" Overture, Mendelssohn's "Scotch" Symphony, Beethoven's Romance for violin and orchestra in F major, and Mozart's "Zauberflöte" Overture. The February Concert was practically the first public appearance of the Association, and regarded in this light it reflected great credit on them; but the improvement manifested in the November Concert was really remarkable, and warrants great expectations of the future of this hard-working body. There were still far too many "passengers" amongst the strings, but as they had the good sense to do no mischief, the general effect of the performance was good.

It is now time to turn to what is one of the most distinctive features of Oxford music—viz., the College Concerts. Of late years considerable rivalry has been exhibited in this direction, with the result of raising to a very high level the standard of the performances. The series of College Concerts that takes place in the "Eights" week almost rises to the dignity of a Musical Festival. The first two days of this week of Concerts were occupied by Balliol College, where Farmer's "Cinderella" was given on May 25, and a Haydn Symphony, with other works, on May 26. Next day there was a miscellaneous Concert at Trinity College, and on May 28 the Rev. Wellesley Batson's music to "The Faithful Shepherdess" was performed at Exeter College Concert, under the composer's direction. The second part of the programme included a very pleasing Minuet and Trio by Mr. F. C. Woods, the Organist of the College. On May 29 Worcester College took its turn in the series with a programme including Brahms's "Rinaldo," Lloyd's "Longbeard's Saga," and Beethoven's "Kreutzer" Sonata for violin and pianoforte. The main features of Merton College Concert, which took place on May 30, were Mozart's E flat major (clarinet) Symphony and J. F. Barnett's "Building of the Ship," conducted by the composer. Lastly, at Queen's College Concert, on May 31, Grieg's "Landkjending" was heard for the first time in this country, and a new Cantata by Prout, called "Damon and Phintias," composed for the occasion, was produced, under the composer's *bâton*. This was, of course, the principal musical event of the year in Oxford. The old Greek story was cleverly arranged by the librettist in two scenes of great dramatic interest, and Mr. Prout had furnished them with most dramatic music. The interest of the work rose throughout, and it was closed with a most admirable *Finale*, "O love, thou breath of heaven." Though each scene is written continuously, the work is divided into numbers in the usual way, and of these, *Damon's* air, "O'er lawn and lea," and the beautiful chorus, "Just a tear-drop," possessed especial charm. There seems to be an increasing demand in England for Cantatas for men's voices, and "Damon and Phintias" is a most important and valuable addition to the *répertoire*. Nothing has been said of the merits of the various performances. In almost every case good renderings were secured, and at Merton and Queen's both band and chorus were really admirable. Looking back over such a week of music, it must be pronounced infinitely creditable to the enthusiasm and skill of the Oxford undergraduate.

Besides this important week of Concerts, a number of other College Concerts on a slighter scale were given during the year. On June 19, Jesus College, the Welsh College, gave a Concert, largely consisting of national music; and, on June 20, both Keble and Pembroke Colleges gave Concerts of more or less interest. On November 24 Mr. Farmer celebrated his hundredth weekly Concert at Balliol, with a programme in which figured Mozart's Pianoforte Concerto in D minor; and, on December 3, Merton College gave Handel's "Ode on St. Cecilia's Day." Of smaller College Concerts the name is legion, and with that remark they must be allowed to pass.

An interesting feature that marked the close of the year was the visit to Oxford of M. Alex. Guilmant, the well-known organist of La Trinité, at Paris. With that graceful courtesy so distinctive of our neighbours across the Channel, he offered to give two Organ Recitals in Oxford, in aid of the Ouseley Memorial Fund. The offer having been gladly accepted, he gave a Recital in Balliol College Hall, on the evening of December 3, and in the Sheldonian Theatre on the afternoon of December 4. It is hardly necessary to say that the celebrated composer for the organ received a hearty welcome in Oxford, or that his admirable playing enchanted all listeners. In every style he seemed equally at home, and his improvisations, one of them on a theme supplied by the Magdalen College chimes, were masterly in the highest degree.

The occasion of M. Guilmant's visit leads naturally to some notice of what is in many ways the most important event of the musical year in Oxford—viz., the change in the Professorship of Music. Early in April the late Professor, the Rev. Sir F. A. Gore Ouseley, passed suddenly away. The vacant post was filled at the beginning of June by the appointment of Sir John Stainer, and without even suggesting the least reflection on his predecessor, it is certain that music in Oxford has been a great gainer by having a resident Professor. Sir John Stainer at once proceeded to remedy a serious defect in the position of music at the University, by establishing a teaching staff. Taking advantage of the great strength available, he almost at once appointed deputy-professors to teach most of the important subjects. Musical "form" was assigned to Mr. Hadow, of Worcester College; composition to Mr. Lloyd, of Christ Church; counterpoint, to the Rev. Dr. Mee, of Merton; harmony, to Dr. Roberts, of Magdalen; acoustics, to the Rev. F. J. Smith, of Trinity; pianoforte playing, to Mr. Taylor, of New College; and the organ, to Mr. Woods, of Exeter College. As the Professor's object was to establish the study of music as a genuine part of the University curriculum, every student was obliged to bring leave from his tutor to pursue the study of music. The results of the first term's work have gone to prove the existence of a number of serious students, and there seems every reason to believe that the scheme will result in shortly bringing about a genuine Oxford School of music. When it is remembered how the effects of University teaching reach out into every corner of the country, as successive generations of students disperse, it seems hardly possible to predict how great may be the influence of this new scheme on the state of music throughout the country at large. Nor has Sir John Stainer been content with this achievement. For about a quarter of a century there have been two large Choral Societies in Oxford—the Choral Society and the Philharmonic Society. The new Professor has found means to induce these Societies to amalgamate their forces, so as to form one large Society; and he has also persuaded the Madrigal Society to dissolve itself, with a view of combining in one great body all the choral resources of the place. The new Society was to commence operations with the New Year, and it may be confidently anticipated that it will be able to challenge comparison with any in the country.

J. H. MEE.

YORKSHIRE.

APART from the Leeds Festival, 1889 has been distinguished by a great number of Concerts of high merit, more particularly those which took place at the beginning of the year. One of the earliest events in Leeds was a Concert given on January 22, when Herr Dittmar was associated with Mr. E. Misdale, of Bradford, in Grieg's Sonata in C and in other classical selections. Miss Jessie Beavers, a Leeds soprano, was the vocalist, and made a very favourable impression. At Mr. Haddock's sixth musical evening, on January 29, Mdlle. Jeanne Douste made her first appearance in Leeds and won golden opinions. Mr. W. Cooke, a native of Leeds, gave a Pianoforte Recital on February 4, before a large and appreciative audience. The Concert-giver was associated with Mr. E. Haddock in his Sonata in D minor for pianoforte and violin, which gave evidence of earnest aim and much melodic beauty. The Leeds Temperance Choral Society gave a performance of Haydn's "Creation" in the Town Hall on February 5, the principals being Madame Larkcom, Mr. Holberry Hagyard (first appearance), and Mr. Dan Billington. The band and chorus numbered 250, all total abstainers. Mr. J. Thompson was the Conductor, Mr. J. W. Acomb the leader of the band, and Mr. A. F. Briggs presided at the organ.

Mr. F. Dawson, a well-known and talented local musician, gave a Pianoforte Recital at the Philosophical Hall, on February 6. The principal piece was Grieg's Sonata in C, in which the pianist was joined by Herr Dittmar. On February 9 the

Leeds Amateur Orchestral Society gave their first Concert of the season at the Church Institute, which was fairly successful.

The fifth Leeds Subscription Concert took place at the Coliseum on February 21. Schubert's Symphony in C major (given for the second time in Leeds), Mendelssohn's "Hebrides" Overture, Sullivan's "In Memoriam" Overture, and Gounod's Overture to "Mireille" were the principal pieces in a diversified programme. Mr. Willy Hess was the violinist, and Dr. Creser took his place at the organ. Miss Emily Spada made a successful first appearance here as vocalist.

On March 11, Mr. E. Haddock's ninth Musical evening introduced another pianist for the first time to a Leeds audience in the person of Miss Mathilde Wurm. The chief works rendered were Brahms's Sonata in A, and a Sonata in G minor, by F. Kilvington Hattersley, who appeared both as composer and pianist.

The Chamber Concert given on March 13 was the last of the Subscription series. Dr. Joachim "led" Schubert's Quintet (Op. 163), having as coadjutors Mr. H. Smith and Herr Hausmann (violoncellos), Mr. Gibson (viola), and Mdlle. Marie Soldat (second violin). Miss Fanny Davis and Fräulein Fillunger were the other artists engaged.

The Leeds Philharmonic Society gave an excellent performance of Dvorák's "Stabat Mater," on March 20, at the Coliseum. Madame Nordica made her first appearance in Leeds at this Concert, Mr. Edward Lloyd and Mrs. Alfred Broughton being the other vocalists. The chorus was especially commendable. The second part of the programme included Hamish MacCunn's "Lord Ullin's Daughter" and Hubert Parry's "Blest pair of Sirens."

Mr. E. Haddock's tenth and last Musical evening took place on March 25, Mdlle. Jeanne Douste being the pianist. The programme included a tender melody for the muted violin, by Mr. Percy Haddock, which was performed for the first time.

Dr. Spark issued invitations for a rehearsal of his new

Oratorio "Immanuel," at the Town Hall, on April 4. The Oratorio, though melodious, has the fault of at times being too light and showy to be in perfect keeping with the subject. The orchestra was represented by a pianoforte and the organ—instruments which were somewhat inadequate, though judiciously used. Miss Annie Hoyle (soprano), Miss Chadwick (contralto), Mr. A. F. Briggs and Mr. Gilbert Jackson (tenors), and Mr. J. Browning and Mr. H. Kemp (basses) rendered the principal parts with credit, and the choruses were sung by a small but well-selected choir. In compiling the book of words, Dr. Spark acknowledged his indebtedness to the Rev. Dr. Conder.

The Leeds Musical season may be said to have re-commenced in earnest with the Subscription Concert of November 6. Fräulein Fillunger was the vocalist, and Mr. Willy Hess solo violinist. Hallé's band gave a polished rendering of Weber's "Euryanthe" Overture and the "Scotch" Symphony. The novelty was Grieg's Suite "Peer Gynt." The second Subscription Concert took place on December 11, when Schubert's Octet was given for the first time here, under the leadership of Mr. Carrodus. At the first Philharmonic Concert of the season, on November 20, "St. Paul" was given, with Madame Nordica, Miss Beatrice Wrigley (of Wolverhampton), Messrs. Ben Davies and Watkin Mills as principal vocalists. A word of praise is due to Messrs. Wood, Higgins, and Haigh, members of the Society, for very useful aid.

For the 1889-90 season Mr. Edgar Haddock reduced the number of his Concerts to six. He commenced on November 19 with a programme fully up to the expected standard of excellence. Mdlle. Douste was again the pianist. Mdlle. Antoinette Trebelli sang.

The Leeds Church School Choral Festival took place in the Victoria Hall on November 19. The chorus numbered 700, half being children and half adults. The programme consisted of anthems, carols, and choruses. Mr. Alfred Beulon contributed a couple of solos on the organ with his customary skill and judgment. Mr. W. H. Harrison, at the Conductor's desk, kept his forces under excellent control.

A Scottish Concert was given at the Coliseum on November 25 by the Glasgow Select Choir, under the conductorship of Mr. J. Millar Craig.

The Christmas production of the Philharmonic Society was "The Messiah" at the Victoria Hall, December 18, the principals engaged being Miss Macintyre, Madame Belle Cole, Mr. Barton McGuckin, and Mr. Brereton. In reviewing the musical events of the year in Leeds, mention must not be omitted of Dr. Spark's weekly Organ Recitals at the Town Hall, which fully maintained their popularity.

The musical season of 1889 in Bradford was brimful of variety, and generally of great interest, whilst in the immediate district many old-established vocal societies showed increased vitality and progress. A few new Societies have also sprung into existence, with every prospect of success and usefulness. The Subscription Concerts, of course, held the place of honour in local musical estimation. The series was resumed on January 18 with a Ballad Concert, at which Mr. Henschel appeared in the threefold capacity of composer, vocalist, and pianist. The Concert also served to introduce a violinist new to Bradford, Miss Nettie Carpenter, while Mr. Orlando Harley and Mdlle. Janotha were also retained.

At the Subscription Concert on February 15 Bizet's "Roma" Suite was presented for the first time. Mdlle. Marie Soldat and Herr Hausmann played, and Miss Alice Whitacre was the vocalist.

An admirable performance of "Elijah" was a worthy climax to a series of Concerts marked by excellence all along the line. Save Mr. Santley—the "only true Prophet"—none of the leading quartet, including Madame Nordica, Madame Belle Cole, and Mr. Piercy, had been heard in that work in Bradford. Local amateurs in the persons of Miss Clara Marshall, Madame Ashcroft-Clarke, Mr. Wm. Coates, and Mr. H. Connelly also rendered efficient aid. Sir Charles Hallé, as usual, commanded his highly-trained forces, and Mr. J. H. Clough took his accustomed place at the organ.

At the commencement of the twenty-fifth season in October the Subscription Concerts Committee found themselves in such an agreeable financial position as to be able to promise an extra Concert free to subscribers—a series of seven, therefore, instead of six being announced. The first Concert took place on October 25. The principal items were the Overtures to "Der Fliegende Holländer" and Spohr's Dramatic Concerto, with Madame Néruda as solo violinist. Novelty was represented by Grieg's Suite "Peer Gynt" and a couple of Dvořák's "Légendes." Miss Macintyre was the vocalist. At the Ballad Concert on November 22 Madame Valleria and her troupe appeared.

A Choral Concert took place on December 13, when Benoit's "Lucifer" was performed, with Miss Annie Marriott, Madame Patey, Mr. Iver McKay, M. Blauwaert, and Mr. Bantock Pierpoint in the solo parts. The composer was present. Parry's "Blest pair of Sirens" was given at the same Concert for the first time in Bradford.

The 1889 musical season in Bradford was rich in Chamber Concerts, given by Mr. E. Misdale at the Mechanics' Institute, by Mr. S. Midgley at the Church Institute, and by other well-known local musicians. Mr. E. Misdale's Concert on February 5 was something more than a Chamber Concert, the services of the Bradford Glee Union being retained. Their rendering of part-songs by Mendelssohn lent agreeable variety to an excellent programme. Miss Emilie Young was the vocalist, and Herr Dittmar, of Leeds, the violinist. Mr. Misdale also gave a couple of high class Concerts in the latter part of the year. Mr. Midgley's Concert on March 15 was chiefly noticeable for the appearance of Mdlle. Soldat. Mr. Percy Cooke, a local amateur, by his rendering of a grand Polonaise, by Popper, on the violoncello, showed himself an adept, giving great promise for the future. Madame and Miss Tomlinson sang duets by Brahms,

Mendelssohn, and Vincent with much finish. After the summer interval Mr. Midgley again broke silence on October 15. His present coadjutors were Signor Risegari, Mr. Farnow, and Miss Brigg, of Kildwick Hall—the latter an amateur vocalist bearing an honoured local name.

The Bradford Festival Choral Society lost nothing of its old vitality and energy, a fact amply proved both by the attendance of members at the many rehearsals, and by the actual amount of arduous work accomplished. In addition to performing the heavy choral work in connection with the Subscription Concerts, it showed an admirable example of enterprise and courage by introducing Dr. Parry's "Judith" for the first time to a Bradford audience on April 12. Mr. Sewell's band executed its share in the work with conspicuous merit. Miss Clara Leighton in the title-*rôle* sang commendably. Considering the difficulty of the work, the chorus came through with flying colours. The performance of Mr. Ebenezer Prout's "Hereward" on November 15, however, was not equal in merit to that of "Judith." Among local societies the Bradford Musical Union (Conductor, Mr. B. Watson) and the Bradford Glee Union (Conductor, Mr. C. Anderson) have pursued a steady and prosperous course. The former Society gave a Concert at St. George's Hall on December 20 for the benefit of the Infirmary, the principal vocalists being Miss Emilie Norton, Mrs. Ashcroft Clark, Mr. W. Knight, and Mr. W. Thornton.

The Bradford Glee Union gave their annual Concert at the Mechanics' Institute on March 13, performing, among other things, Caldicott's "Queen of the Valley." The principal vocalists were clever amateurs—Miss A. Saville, Madame Armitage, Mr. C. Blagbro, and Mr. Alfred Barnes. Master P. Cathie, a juvenile violinist of exceptional ability, also appeared. This Society gave an entertainment on December 9, the programme being entirely selected from the works of Sir H. Bishop.

The Bradford Amateur Orchestral Society gave their second Concert on March 22 under the conductorship of Mr. E. Haddock.

Haydn's Seventh Symphony in D and the Overtures to "Masaniello" and "La Dame Blanche" were performed with precision.

Amongst minor events Mr. J. St. Hense's Concert on March 4 should not be passed over. Mr. C. Heinrich gave an agreeable musical evening at the Church Institute on April 5. Mr. J. H. Clough was instrumental in producing Sullivan's Cantata "On Shore and Sea" at the Kirkgate Chapel (May 9). On December 3 the Bradford Kyrle Society gave Gaul's "Holy City." On December 6 the children of the Bradford Board Schools presented, for the first time, in St. George's Hall, a Cantata entitled "Flora's Garden Party," by Mr. A. C. Cowley, the Musical Inspector of the School Board. The work showed taste and skill in choral writing, and met with a distinct success.

The Keighley Musical Union has made rapid strides, manifesting ability to grapple with choral works of considerable magnitude. The Cleckheaton Philharmonic Society, for several winters organised and trained by Mr. S. Midgley, of Bradford (a position from which he has now retired), acquitted themselves creditably both in choral and orchestral work. The Lightcliffe Choral Society, under the conductorship of Mr. Rooks, have shown steady improvement and ability to successfully tackle such works as Mendelssohn's "Athalie" and Cowen's "Rose Maiden." The Shipley Amateur Musical Society were not inactive during the year, and showed decided advancement. The Pudsey Choral Union made successful progress under the conductorship of Mr. H. Robertshaw, giving their annual couple of Concerts in a most commendable manner. The Calverley Choral Society, under the conductorship of Mr. James Hall, proved themselves a body of singers capable of presenting choral works with freshness, spirit, and precision; as have also the members of the Geadont District Harmonic Society. During the year the Manningham Musical Union was formed.

At the Huddersfield Subscription Concert on January 15 Sir Charles Hallé, Madame Néruda, Madame Bertha Moore, and

Mr. Paersch were engaged. At the next subscription Concert Madame Minnie Hauk and her Concert party appeared. Berlioz's "Faust" was given on March 24 by the Huddersfield Choral Society. The principals were Madame Mary Davies, Mr. Chas. Banks, Mr. W. Barton, and Mr. Watkin Mills, Sir Charles Hallé's band assisting both on this occasion and at the miscellaneous Orchestral Concert of December 10.

J. TATHAM.